RELIGION IN AMERICAN POLITICS

RELIGION IN AMERICAN POLITICS

Charles W. Dunn, editor
Clemson University

A Division of Congressional Quarterly Inc.
1414 22nd Street N.W., Washington, D.C. 20037

Library of Congress Cataloging-in-Publication Data

Religion in American politics / [edited by] Charles W. Dunn.
    p.   cm.
  ISBN 0-87187-486-5
  1. Religion and politics--United States--History--20th century.
  2. United States--Religion--1960-   I. Dunn, Charles W.
  BL2525.R468   1989
  322'.1'0973--dc19   88-22285
                                                                        CIP

To Carol, Charlie, Josh,
Teresa, and Maria

CONTENTS

PREFACE

The relationship of religion and politics in the United States is characterized by a number of tensions. What role, if any, should religious interests play in politics? Of what value is religion to politics when it does play a part in the making of public policy? Tension also exists within religious interests. Can there be agreement, even within the ranks of a particular denomination, about which "political" issues to advance? Members of the clergy who run for office or take partisan stands reveal the tension between their political and religious roles.

In *Religion in American Politics* seventeen scholars examine the dynamics of tension in four crucial areas. Part I explores the heart of most disputes about religion and politics: the Constitution, particularly the origins and intentions of the "free exercise" and "establishment" clauses of the First Amendment. Part II reviews the wide-ranging contributions that arise out of religious participation in today's secular American society, including a greater sense of community and commitment. Part III analyzes specific ways Americans express their religious beliefs in the political arena—voting and interest group activity. Part IV looks at evangelical protestants—typified by personalities like Pat Robertson and Jerry Falwell and their organizations, the Christian Broadcasting Network and the Moral Majority—that have been at the center of controversy on issues of religion and politics.

The diverse points of view represented here should provide the reader with a well-rounded introduction to this increasingly important field of study. Several of the essays in the collection first appeared in the *Journal of Political Science* (Spring 1988). The chapters by Robert Booth Fowler, Clarke E. Cochran, Neal Riemer, and Paul J. Weber were selected for inclusion in that special issue devoted to religion in American politics.

Many people have contributed to the success of this endeavor. I am particularly grateful to Joanne Daniels, director of CQ Press, and Nancy Lammers, managing editor of the book department of Congressional Quarterly. Nola Healy Lynch provided invaluable assistance in editing the manuscript. As always, my colleagues at Clemson University have been supportive of my work.

Charles W. Dunn

THE DYNAMICS OF DEMOCRATIC TENSION: RELIGION IN AMERICAN POLITICS

Charles W. Dunn

From the courthouse to the campaign trail, religion in American politics looms large on the landscape of legal controversy and political discourse. The sounds of sharp legal clashes from keenly contested religion and politics cases echo through courtroom corridors. Should creation be taught alongside evolution? Should a moment of silence be allowed at the beginning of the school day? Should abortion be allowed? Should the nativity scene be displayed on public property?

Since 1976, the presidential campaign trail has produced Jimmy Carter and Ronald Reagan, who profess to be "born again"; Walter Mondale, the son of a Methodist minister; Geraldine Ferraro, who incurred the stinging rebuke of Cardinal O'Connor for her pro-abortion position; Jesse Jackson, who proudly bears the label *reverend;* Pat Robertson, who though shedding that label earnestly sought the support of religious conservatives; and George Bush, who modified his positions on abortion and other issues to win the hearts of religious conservatives in the Republican party. Republicans, seeking to woo discontented Democrats, have offered platform planks in the 1980s calling for the abolition of abortion, the return of school prayer, and aid to parochial schools. From 1960 to 1984, Democratic national platforms did not mention deity, while those of the Republicans made frequent references to God.

The issues are real. The emotions are intense. The solutions are problematic. In the courtroom and on the campaign trail, religious interests are playing for high stakes. They are influencing American politics, but in the process they are also being moved as pawns on the political chessboard. From any perspective, religion is not playing its intended role in American politics.

Religion in American Politics

American society today is faced with divisions that no one in the past could have predicted. Most of the framers of the Constitution were steeped in the various forms of Protestantism of their time; the prohibition of state religion and the principle of separation of church and state must be understood to lie in the context of the framers' common Christianity, as will be discussed later in this introduction. They would not be likely to understand civil libertarians' call to divorce anything resembling religious values from public life in all its manifestations.

Yet the founders of the United States could not have anticipated the effects of industrialization and immigration in the nineteenth century. Many social scientists, including Marx, attempted to formulate theories to account for the changes they saw taking place, and they predicted the demise of religion in industrial society. Proponents of modernization theories contended that the forces of education, industrialization, and urbanization would make religion obsolete. As people became better educated and moved from farm to city, they would no longer need the crutch of religion, but rather would recognize that their problems could be solved by higher education and advances in science. Marxian analysis declared that religion, the opiate of the masses, would become obsolete as people rose up to throw off the shackles of the elitist economic tyranny perpetrated by religious dogma about acceptance of their servant status.

Yet religion continues to be a major influence around the world. In the United States, most people hold traditional religious beliefs and identify with a local church, synagogue, or other religious organization. Superficially at least, religion has become *more* important in the lives of Americans as religious issues have entered the political arena in unprecedented fashion. Religious concerns range from the issues of war and peace to poverty and personal morality.

To influence the realm of power politics with their religious concerns, Americans have organized many interest groups, conservative and liberal, to fight for their beliefs. Conservative religious interest groups include the Moral Majority (renamed the Liberty Federation), the Religious Roundtable, Concerned Women for America, and Eagle Forum; liberal religious groups include the National Council of Churches and the lobbying arms of most of the mainline Protestant churches. Even People for the American Way, organized to fight against the interests of the Moral Majority, would die on the vine were it not for the prominent liberal religious leaders on its board. On both sides, groups call on the beginning of the First Amendment to the Constitution, "Congress shall make no law respecting an establishment of religion, or prohibiting the free exercise thereof," and on the role of religion in American political history.

How far does religion, and Christianity in particular, penetrate American democracy? Almost a century ago, the U.S. Supreme Court in what would today be an unthinkable decision unanimously declared in *Church of the Holy Trinity v. U.S.* (143 U.S. 471) that "we find everywhere a clear recognition of the same truth ... that this is a Christian nation." After reviewing the background and language of the colonial charters, the Declaration of Independence, the U.S. Constitution, the state constitutions, and other sources, the Court emphatically stated:

> There is no dissonance in these declarations. There is a universal language pervading them all, having one meaning: they affirm and reaffirm that this is a religious nation. These are not individual sayings, declarations of private persons: they are organic utterances; they speak the voice of the entire people. While because of a general recognition of this truth the question has seldom been presented to the courts, yet we find that ... "Christianity, general Christianity, is, and always has been a part of the common law."

Today some Americans still faithfully believe that America should be a Christian nation and prayerfully hope for reclamation of that claim. They would like for one of today's Supreme Court justices to speak in the way Justice David J. Brewer did at Harvard College in 1905: "This Republic is classified among the Christian nations of the world. It was so formally declared by the Supreme Court of the United States ... in the case of Holy Trinity Church v. United States." [1] In today's secular society, that is wishful thinking.

Until recently scholars have avoided examining religion and politics, although religion has greatly influenced American politics and society through such movements as abolition and prohibition, civil rights and equal rights, and many others. Their failure to study and to discuss religion and politics has created a major vacuum in our understanding of American democracy. Why this oversight?

One reason, according to scholars like Seymour Martin Lipset and Peter L. Benson, is that there is simply a reluctance to study a subject with the stigma of religion and politics.[2] Other issues and problems have been considered more important and appealing to scholars, and religion and politics has somehow been considered outside the pale of legitimate scholarship. Another reason, according to Peter L. Berger and Richard John Neuhaus, is that "there is a profoundly antidemocratic prejudice in public policy discourse that ignores the role of religious institutions in the lives of most Americans." [3] Further, as Michael Novak argues, "There is a hidden religious power base in American culture, which our secular biases prevent many of us from noticing." [4]

For whatever reason, though, the walls of reservation and opposition to the study of religion in American politics are crumbling.

Since 1983 a number of works devoted to the subject have been published, and the body of specialized research has grown rapidly.[5]

Where does all of this leave us? Americans are a religious people in a political system that has apparently abandoned religion. The churches disagree on what to do about the situation. Scholars have just begun to try to clarify the issues. Thus begin the tensions of the debate on the role of religion in American politics.

Pluralism and the Origins of Tension

America has always been heterogeneous to some extent, accommodating different ethnic groups, races, classes, and religions. The concept of pluralism allows the competing interests fostered by such differences to coexist in a single political entity. But does that mean that the mixture is devoid of values and a sense of direction? We can look back into American history for some sense of what pluralism has meant from the beginning until now.

The Early American Era

In the colonies Protestant Christianity dominated. French Roman Catholic writer Alexis de Tocqueville wrote: "The greatest part of British America was peopled by men who, after having shaken off the authority of the Pope, acknowledged no other religious supremacy: They brought with them into the New World a form of Christianity which I cannot better describe than by styling it a democratic and republican religion."[6] According to Harvard University historian Samuel Eliot Morison:

> Puritanism was a cutting edge which hewed liberty, democracy, humanitarianism, and universal education out of the black forest of feudal Europe and the American wilderness.
>
> Puritan doctrine taught each person to consider himself a significant if sinful unit to whom God had given a particular place and duty, and that he must help his fellow men.
>
> Puritanism is an American heritage to be grateful for and not to be sneered at because it required everyone to attend divine worship and maintained a strict code of moral ethics.[7]

Both early colonial and college charters bore the marks of Protestant, and particularly Puritan, Christianity. For example, the Fundamental Orders of Connecticut (1638-39) said that its purpose was "to maintain and pursue the libery and purity of the gospel of our Lord Jesus which we now profess, as also the discipline of the Churches, which according to the truth of the said gospel is now practised amongst us."[8] The Harvard College charter at its founding in 1636 declared, "Everyone shall consider the main end of his life and studies to know God and Jesus Christ, which is eternal life." [9]

Elsewhere in the colonies, established churches were common, with Puritan or Congregational churches in the North and Anglican churches in the South. Seven of the thirteen colonies—Connecticut, Georgia, Maryland, Massachusetts, New Hampshire, South Carolina, and Virginia—had established churches, while Delaware, New Jersey, New York, North Carolina, Pennsylvania, and Rhode Island did not. It was also common for the colonial charters and early state constitutions to require religious tests for holding office. Even in pluralistically tolerant Pennsylvania in 1776, members of the legislature had to take this oath: "I do believe in one God, the creator and governor of the universe, the rewarder of the good and the punisher of the wicked. And I do acknowledge the Scriptures of the Old and New Testament to be given by Divine inspiration." In Delaware, the Constitution required the following pledge in 1776: "I do profess faith in God the Father, and in Jesus Christ His only Son, and in the Holy Ghost, one God, blessed for evermore; and I do acknowledge the holy scriptures of the Old and New Testament to be given by divine inspiration." [10]

Although church membership in the colonies was low, requirements for membership were stringent. Church attendance was far higher than church membership. And religious influence was pervasive. Jewish and Roman Catholic numbers were minute. But in spite of its predominance, Protestant Christianity was far from monolithic. Pluralism, not unity, characterized Protestant Christianity. Among the colonists were Baptists and Moravians, Quakers and Presbyterians, Mennonites and Congregationalists, Anglicans and Methodists, and more. Add to that the deism of Thomas Jefferson and Benjamin Franklin. Although it had relatively few adherents, deism had influence beyond its numbers due to the power and prestige of some followers who were well educated and well placed politically. Deists and Protestants disagreed on many doctrines, such as the divine inspiration of the Bible and the deity and virgin birth of Jesus, but they did agree on separation of church and state and the importance of individual liberty. Most important, they were able to agree on the principal issues confronting the founding of American government.

The Early Nineteenth Century

From the founding to the Civil War, the broad picture changed little. Church membership went up as membership standards were lowered and religious divisions increased. Religious diversity in America increased since the Revolution, as Unitarianism, which denied the deity of Christ and other cardinal Protestant doctrines; Transcendentalism, which taught that everyone has the spark of divinity and no one is born into sin; and utopian religions, which wanted to establish perfect communities, came on the scene. Also the nineteenth-century immigration of Jews, particularly from Germany, and Roman Catholics, especially from Ireland, began to create the potential for even greater challenges to the dominance of Protestant Christianity.

Protestant Christianity exercised very cautious activism during the period from the founding to the Civil War, on the whole leaving politics to politicians. Those few Protestants who were activists stood against slavery in the North, advocated prohibition, called for Sunday blue laws, and espoused reform of prisons and mental institutions. Alexis de Tocqueville best expressed the general mood: "In the United States religion exercises little influence upon the laws and upon the details of public opinion; but it directs the customs of the community, and by regulating domestic life, it regulates the state." [11] In short, Protestant Christianity had little challenge to its dominance and hence did not need to assert itself in the political realm. The tensions, however, that were to blossom fully more than a century later were discernible during this era, as many conservative Protestants felt the shift of civic life toward a secularism they could not countenance. Yale University President Timothy Dwight, speaking in 1801, solemnly declared:

> You must take your side. There can be no halting between two opinions.... Between them and you there is, there can be, no natural, real, or lasting harmony.... Will you imbibe their principles? Will you copy their practices? Will you teach your children, that death is an eternal sleep; that the end sanctifies the means? that moral obligation is a dream? Religion a farce? ... Will you burn your Bibles? Will you crucify anew your Redeemer? Will you deny your God? [12]

The Civil War to World War II

From the Civil War to World War II, the forces that ultimately would challenge Protestant dominance gained momentum. These included the immigration between 1900 and 1914 of thirteen million Roman Catholics and Jews, the sharp theological divisions within Protestantism, and the further advance of pluralism. Catholics and Jews, still a distinct minority, did not challenge Protestant dominance, but Protestants began to feel their presence. Protestants responded by trying to end or to slow immigration, by strengthening an emphasis upon Bible reading in the public schools, and by engaging in great citywide revival meetings with an emphasis upon personal salvation and social reform through such endeavors as prohibition.

Protestantism saw its strength further erode through internal divisions. Conservative Protestants divided into more denominations with the new holiness and pentecostal movements. Ascendant liberal Protestantism began to divide from the historically dominant conservative Protestantism and to capture control of mainline Protestant denominations, colleges, and seminaries. Two of the most widely publicized battles were over control of Princeton Seminary and the northern Presbyterian denomination; liberal Protestants won both. New theological ideas like the social gospel and neo-orthodoxy encouraged liberal Protestants to increase their political activism, with the goal of bringing about the kingdom of God on earth through the lever of governmental social action (the Methodist Social Creed of 1908 was an early statement of this liberal social gospel theology). Neo-orthodox theology attempted to retain traditional conservative Protestant theological terms like sin, heaven, hell, righteousness, and salvation, but to redefine and modernize their meanings. Conservative Protestants fought back, but they lost most of the battles for control of the denominational and educational machinery.

Post-World War II Era

From World War II to the present, the influence of historically dominant Protestantism dramatically declined. Prohibition was lifted, Sunday closing laws were abolished, Bible reading and prayer in the schools were terminated, abortion was legalized, nativity scenes on public property were challenged, sermons by clergy at baccalaureate services were ended, prayer before athletic events was disputed, and homosexuality gained legal recognition. The list of challenges and changes could go on.

Roman Catholics used their enlarged and better educated numbers to help elect the first Roman Catholic president in 1960 and to gain financial aid for parochial schools in the 1965 Elementary and Secondary Education Act. With an aversion to the dictates of Protestant culture on such matters as alcohol consumption and Sunday sabbath laws, Roman Catholics, along with Jews, provided further impetus for the decline of conservative Protestant culture.

For liberal Protestants and Jews, the 1960s were a great time of bringing their religious convictions to bear on American society with dramatic efforts on behalf of the civil rights movement and its best-known leader, the black Baptist preacher Martin Luther King, Jr. The American Civil Liberties Union, with many liberal Protestant and Jewish members, successfully challenged the tenets and traditions of America's conservative Protestant culture on many fronts, but particularly in the courts on such issues as prayer and Bible reading in the schools.

Within Protestantism, however, conservatives gained new vigor.

During the late 1970s, leaders and interest groups organized on a massive scale to challenge liberal Protestantism and the demise of America's once dominant conservative Protestant culture. Besides organizing interest groups and using television to promote their causes, they started Protestant parochial schools in large numbers to combat the secularizing influences of the public school system.

By the late 1970s, conservative Roman Catholics felt the challenge to their own culture and convictions on matters such as abortion and homosexuality. During President Ronald Reagan's administration, conservative Protestants and Catholics increasingly joined to fight for common interests, which strengthened the role of Catholics in the Republican party. Conservative religious groups began to make their presence felt on the national scene as liberal groups had previously.

Protestant resurgence has been largely the product of fundamental, charismatic, pentecostal, and evangelical denominations and organizations. The fastest growing churches during the 1970s and 1980s have been independent, fundamental Baptists; charismatic churches; pentecostal denominations, such as the Assemblies of God; and the Mormons. The candidacy for the Republican presidential nomination of Pat Robertson reflected the rapid growth of conservative Protestantism, especially among the charismatics and pentecostals.

The Roman Catholic Church, divided by the changes of Vatican II during the 1960s, grew less rapidly than before. The charismatic movement also made significant penetrations into the Roman Catholic community. From the 1960s to the present, Jews have seen their conservative branches grow—the orthodox and conservative congregations—as more Jews began to take historical Judaism seriously. Also, Jews found new allies among fundamental and evangelical Protestants whose biblical views incline them to support Israel. Despite some Republican overtures, however, Jews have generally remained in the Democratic party. Those overtures might have been more successful had Republicans not so openly cultivated conservative Protestants and Roman Catholics.

Blacks, overwhelmingly Protestant, shifted their allegiance from the Republican party of Abraham Lincoln to the Democratic party of Franklin D. Roosevelt during the 1930s, and they have remained there in overwhelming numbers; normally over 90 percent of blacks vote for Democratic presidential candidates. Black allegiance to the Democratic party was further strengthened by the passage of the Civil Rights and Voting Rights Acts of 1964 and 1965 and by Jesse Jackson's presidential candidacies in 1984 and 1988. Jesse Jackson's close ties with Arab and Muslim leaders, however, made many Jews who had previously been strong supporters of the civil rights movement reluctant to support him.

For much of its history, the black civil rights movement had depended greatly on Jewish financial, intellectual, and political support.

The origins of tension on religion and politics issues lie in pluralism. First, immigration contributed to pluralism and tension as Catholics, Jews, and other immigrant groups challenged Protestantism's dominance. Second, division within Protestantism, especially with the advent of liberal Protestantism and its challenge to traditional Protestant ideas, also added impetus to pluralism and tension. The influence of traditional Protestantism has gradually receded under the challenges brought about by immigration and division. It remains to be seen whether the resurgence of conservative Protestantism will be anything other than a brief reassertion of a lost past.

Joining the Issue

The tensions within and between the major religious groups are magnified in the larger issue: Should life outside church walls be devoid of religious references? Should democratic society take religious principles into account?

At the one extreme stand humanists, who believe that human beings are capable of self-fulfillment without reference to a supreme being. Allied with them on what may be characterized as the liberal position are those who fear that any interface of politics and religion—even in favor of their own beliefs—would mean denying some Americans their right to religious freedom. At the other extreme stand those who believe that a godless society will fall because it has no moral foundation. In this light, all the individual issues—of education, abortion, sexual practices, clergy in politics, and so on—become rallying points for the much deeper debate and the fundamental tension. The two sides of this tension have different views of America's past, different perceptions of the present, and different visions for the future. They disagree about the nature of God and humanity and on what government should do and how.

By what standards should public policy decisions be made, and their results assessed, in a democracy? Should a democratic government respond solely to the will of the people, or should it look to an external reference point? These questions are much in dispute. Then, too, if there is an external reference point, who defines and applies it? In the name of a divinity, many conservatives and liberals have maintained that democracy should have higher ethical and moral measurements of divine origin as its ultimate guide for decision making and judgment. Jerry Falwell and Pat Robertson, Martin Luther King and Jesse Jackson have claimed they know what those ethical and moral principles are. Earlier in America's history, in an overwhelmingly

Protestant culture, consensus on such principles was easier to reach. The sociologist Robert N. Bellah tells us that

> any coherent and viable society rests on a common set of moral understandings about good and bad, right and wrong, in the realm of individual and social action. It is almost as widely held that these common moral understandings must also rest in turn upon a common set of religious understandings that provide a picture of the universe in terms of which the moral understandings make sense. Such moral and religious understandings produce both a basic cultural legitimation for a society which is viewed as at least approximately in accord with them, and a standard of judgment for the criticism of a society that is seen as deviating too far from them.[13]

Today there is intense competition among our values and life-styles. Religion, once a part of the glue holding American society together, now appears to be contributing substantially to society's breaking apart. American democracy now reveals religion as a divided and a divisive force in politics and government. Religious interests have come to compete on the same political terrain with nonreligious interests in trying to define American public policy, unlike what Alexis de Tocqueville found in the early 1800s when he said: "In the United States religion exercises little influence upon the laws and upon the details of public opinion, but it directs the customs of the community, and by regulating domestic life, it regulates the state." [14] Politically at least, religion now occupies a role no more exalted than any other interest. The secularization of American politics and society has generally reduced religion to another competing political force within America's pluralistic democracy.

Notes

1. Norman De Jong, "The First Amendment: A Comparison of Nineteenth and Twentieth Century Supreme Court Interpretations," *Journal of Political Science* 16 (Spring 1988): 69.
2. Robert Lee and Martin E. Marty, eds., *Religion and Social Conflict* (New York: Oxford University Press, 1964), 70; Peter L. Benson, "Religion on Capitol Hill," *Psychology Today* 15 (1981): 57.
3. Peter L. Berger and Richard John Neuhaus, *To Empower the People* (Washington, D.C.: American Enterprise Institute, 1977), 28.
4. Betty Glad, *Jimmy Carter* (New York: W. W. Norton, 1980), 337.
5. A special issue of *Humanities in Society* (Winter 1983), ed. Robert Booth Fowler, offered the first major collection of political science research on the subject. Later came Charles W. Dunn, *American Political Theology* (New York: Praeger, 1984); Robert Booth Fowler, *Religion and Politics in America* (Metuchen, N.J.:

Scarecrow, 1984); A. James Reichley, *Religion in American Public Life* (Washington, D.C.: Brookings, 1985); and Kenneth D. Wald, *Religion and Politics in the United States* (New York: St. Martin's Press, 1987). Almost three hundred political scientists now belong to the research section on religion and politics in the American Political Science Association.

6. Alexis de Tocqueville, *Democracy in America* (New York: Vintage Books, 1954), 311.

7. Charles L. Wallis, ed., *Our American Heritage* (New York: Harper & Row, 1970), 26.

8. Benjamin Perley Poore, ed., *The Federal and State Constitutions, Colonial Charters and Other Organic Laws of the United States* (Washington, D.C.: U.S. Government Printing Office, 1877).

9. Michael Novak, *Choosing Our King* (New York: Macmillan, 1974), 114.

10. De Jong, "The First Amendment," 62.

11. Robert S. Alley, *So Help Me God* (Richmond, Va.: John Knox, 1972), 21.

12. Timothy Dwight, *A Discourse on Some Events of the Last Century* (New Haven, 1801), as quoted in Charles W. Dunn, *American Political Theology* (New York: Praeger, 1984), 25, 26.

13. Robert N. Bellah, *The Broken Covenant: American Civil Religion in Time of Trial* (New York: Seabury Press, 1975), ix.

14. Alley, *So Help Me God*, 311.

Part I

THE TENSION OF INTERPRETATION: RELIGIOUS LIBERTY AND THE CONSTITUTION

The heart of most disputes about religion and politics centers in the Constitution and particularly the origins and intentions of the "free exercise" and "no establishment" clauses of the First Amendment. A. James Reichley places the contentious history of the First Amendment's religion clauses in perspective. Neal Riemer contends that religious liberty as provided by the First Amendment has been responsible for many of the most important solutions to major political and social problems during the history of the United States. Paul J. Weber outlines the major interpretations of the extra-constitutional idea of separation of church and state and suggests that "strict neutrality" or "equal separation" may be the developing dominant interpretation.

1. RELIGION AND THE CONSTITUTION

A. James Reichley

Shortly after the adjournment of the Constitutional Convention in 1787, Alexander Hamilton encountered on the street in Philadelphia a professor from nearby Princeton College who told him that the Princeton faculty were "greatly grieved that the Constitution has no recognition of God or the Christian religion." Hamilton replied, "I declare, we forgot it!" [1]

Hamilton's dodge was among the first in a long series of efforts by American statesmen to reconcile broad social support for religion with cultural pluralism and belief in the rights of individual conscience. In our own time, differences over the role of religion in public life have fueled important political issues and given rise to both fear and resentment among major social groups.

It is, therefore, worthwhile to reexamine the constitutional framework that undergirds relations between religion and civil society, which the founders eventually worked out through the First Amendment, and to trace the evolving interpretations through which this structure has since been applied.

Religious enthusiasm, buffeted by the winds of the Enlightenment, was at a relatively low ebb in America in 1787. The effects of the Great Awakening of the 1740s, which had remained strong at the time of the Revolution, had receded, and the beginning of the Second Great Awakening was still more than a decade in the future. Nevertheless, about 75 percent of Americans had their roots in some form of Calvinism, and most of the rest belonged to Anglican, Baptist, Quaker, Catholic, or Lutheran traditions. [2] A few Jewish congregations had gathered in places like Newport, Rhode Island, and Charleston, South Carolina.

The reason the framers of the Constitution avoided the topic of religion, except for the prohibition of a religious test for national public office in Article VI, was neither hostility nor indifference, but that they had not yet developed a conceptual means for relating religion to public life in a free society.

Enactment of the First Amendment

Most of the founders were not particularly pious men. Some, like Thomas Jefferson and Benjamin Franklin, were personally religious in only a very broad and loosely defined sense. But practically all were convinced that republican government rests on moral values that spring ultimately from religion. They shared George Washington's view that "of all the dispositions and habits which lead to political prosperity, religion and morality are indispensable supports." Even Jefferson, despite his personal skepticism, held that religion should be regarded as a "supplement to law in the government of men," and as "the alpha and omega of the moral law." [3]

Belief in the socially beneficial effects of religion led some of the founders, including Washington, John Adams, Patrick Henry, and John Marshall, to favor maintenance of established churches, directly supported by public funds, in their own states. Others, notably Jefferson and James Madison, argued that government should play no role whatever in direct sponsorship of religion. All agreed that there could be no established national church in a country already so culturally various and intellectually diverse as the new United States. [4]

Their common objective was to secure the moral guidance and support of religion for the republic, while escaping the political repression and social conflict with which religion had often been associated throughout history, and specifically in the public life of the former colonies. Since no scheme of generally accepted constitutional doctrine to achieve this end was available, the framers of the original Constitution ducked the subject almost entirely.

The need to define the relationship of religion to civil society, however, would not go away. In the bitter battle over ratification of the Constitution in the states, some opponents attacked the proposed federal charter's failure to include a guarantee of the free exercise of religion. Several of the state ratifying conventions, including those in Virginia and New York, passed resolutions calling for an amendment declaring the "unalienable right to the free exercise of religion according to the dictates of conscience," and assuring that "no particular religious sect or society" would be "favored or established by Law in preference to others." [5]

When the first Congress met in 1789, James Madison, who a few years before had led the fight for passage of Jefferson's bill for religious liberty in Virginia, quickly moved in the House of Representatives that the Constitution be amended to incorporate a Bill of Rights, including prohibitions against establishment of a national religion or infringement on "full and equal rights of conscience" by either the federal government or the states. When Madison's bill came to the floor of the House for debate, several members of Congress objected that it might be interpreted to undermine religion. The clause dealing with establishment, Peter Sylvester of New York warned, "might be thought to have a tendency to abolish religion altogether." Benjamin Huntingdon of Connecticut, one of the five states that still maintained an established church, asked if the amendment could be construed to prohibit state "support of ministers or building of places of worship?" Huntingdon said he favored an amendment "to secure the rights of conscience," but not one that would "patronise those who profess no religion at all." At Madison's suggestion, the bill was reworded to make clear that the prohibition against establishment applied only to the federal government. The entire Bill of Rights was then approved by the House without major change.[6]

In the Senate, the ban against infringement on rights of conscience by the states was dropped, presumably reflecting the Senate's particular concern for upholding the authority of the state governments, and the religion clauses aimed at the federal level were combined in a single amendment with provisions for freedom of speech and a free press. The language of the religious clauses was considerably watered down, requiring only that Congress "make no law establishing articles of faith, or a mode of worship, or prohibiting the free exercise of religion." Under this formulation, even the national government would be permitted to give direct financial support to the churches, and would be excluded only from meddling in matters of theology or ritual.[7]

A conference committee between the House and the Senate, which Madison is generally believed to have dominated, kept the Senate's textual framework combining the religion clauses with the free speech and free press clauses but toughened the religion clauses to read, "Congress shall make no law respecting an establishment of religion or prohibiting the free exercise thereof." This formulation was approved by two-thirds majorities in both houses of Congress, and later ratified by the required three-fourths of the state legislatures—giving us the First Amendment as we have it today.[8]

What Did the Fourteenth Amendment Do?

The first thing to be said about the First Amendment is that when enacted it clearly applied only to the federal government. Madison's proposed amendment to prohibit infringement by the state on individual rights of conscience would have done nothing to upset the established churches still supported by some of the states. (The last of the state religious establishments was finally terminated when Massachusetts disestablished the Congregational church in 1833.) But Congress did not approve even this modest prohibition. During the first half of the nineteenth century, the Supreme Court issued a series of decisions specifically placing the state governments outside the authority of the First Amendment.[9]

At the end of the Civil War, Congress proposed and the states ratified the Fourteenth Amendment, prohibiting the states from abridging "the privileges or immunities of citizens of the United States," or depriving "any person of life, liberty, or property without due process of law," or denying any person "equal protection of the laws." The chief purpose of the Fourteenth Amendment, everyone agreed, was to extend full rights of citizenship to the former slaves who had been freed under the Emancipation Proclamation or the Thirteenth Amendment. Beyond that, some of the principal sponsors of the amendment spoke vaguely of giving the federal government power to enforce "the personal rights guaranteed and secured by the first eight amendments to the Constitution." But the idea that the entire Bill of Rights might be extended to cover the states by the due process clause or the privileges or immunities clause of the Fourteenth Amendment played no significant part in the debates over the amendment in Congress or the state legislatures.[10]

For some years thereafter, neither the Supreme Court nor the governmental community at large showed any signs of believing that the states were now subject to the Bill of Rights. In 1876, the Grant administration sought enactment of a constitutional amendment that would have specifically prohibited the states from aiding church-related schools. Neither supporters nor opponents of the proposed amendment (which passed the House and failed in the Senate by only two votes) suggested that such aid might already be unconstitutional. When some imaginative jurists in the 1890s began to argue that the Fourteenth Amendment prohibited infringement by the states on some of the rights set forth in the first eight amendments, the majority of the Court at first rejected this claim.[11]

Beginning in the 1920s, however, the Supreme Court gradually discovered a growing portion of the Bill of Rights in the due process clause of the Fourteenth Amendment. In 1925, the Court ruled in *Gitlow v. New York* that the free speech and free press clauses of the First Amendment applied to the states. (Gitlow was the author of a left-wing publication that had been suppressed by the state of New York. He did not himself benefit from the new interpretation, since the Court held that his book was an active "incitement" to violence, and therefore not shielded by the First Amendment.)[12]

In 1940, the free exercise clause and the establishment clause were at last extended to cover the states. The court decided in *Cantwell v.*

Connecticut that the First Amendment prohibited the state from prosecuting a member of the Jehovah's Witnesses sect for breaching the peace by playing a recorded diatribe against the Catholic religion on a streetcorner in a neighborhood of New Haven heavily populated by Catholics.[13] From the legacy of *Cantwell* has sprung the large body of decisions through which the Court has defined and generally broadened the rights of citizens against infringement on religious liberty or establishment of religion by either the federal government or the states.

The line of decisions based on the free exercise clause, though often controversial, has produced a reasonably clear and consistent set of guidelines on how far religious liberty goes, and where other social values, such as public safety, the rights of children to education in basic skills and citizenship, and the need for discipline in the armed forces, must take precedence.[14]

The Meaning of "Establishment"

In contrast to the decisions on "free exercise," the Court's rulings based on the establishment clause—including the 1948 decision prohibiting the use of public school facilities for religious instruction, the 1962 decision banning organized prayer in the public schools, and the great tangle of decisions that forbid some but not all forms of public aid to students in parochial schools—have produced a disconcerting muddle. "We are divided among ourselves," Justice Byron White ruefully conceded in 1981, "perhaps reflecting the different views on this subject of the people in this country." A part of the reason for the Court's intellectual disarray on establishment clause issues may be the inherent difficulty of finding the prohibition of religious establishment in the Fourteenth Amendment's protection against deprivation of "liberty." [15]

Recently, some conservative scholars and public figures have suggested that the Court may have erred in the whole line of decisions descending from *Gitlow*. Some have even proposed returning authority over most First Amendment issues to the states. It is extremely unlikely that any foreseeable Court would abandon federal protections against infringement by government at any level on basic freedoms of speech, press, or religion. There is some possibility that a future Supreme Court might modify the current reach of the establishment clause. But civil libertarians argue that limiting the coverage of the establishment clause could encourage some states, such as Utah, where Mormons constitute about two-thirds of the population, actually to establish a church. Improbable though this result may be, the claim provides an effective last-ditch defense against limiting even the establishment clause to the federal government.[16]

In any case, even if the states were exempted from the reach of the establishment clause, many important church-state issues, such as federal aid to students in parochial schools and the many symbolic relationships that continue to exist between religion and the federal government, would still have to be decided at the federal level. From a practical standpoint, the most important question regarding the establishment clause now is not the extent of its coverage but what "establishment" means in the context of the First Amendment.

Some interpreters argue that the founders intended that the prohibition against establishment should do nothing more than prevent the government from singling out a particular church for support or recognition, as most of the colonies had done before the Revolution, and as many European governments still do today. (Whether the "intentions" of the founders should have any bearing on current interpretation is a question that I will turn to shortly.) In this view, the establishment clause presents no impediment against government giving support, financial or otherwise, to religious institutions, so long as such aid is distributed impartially among the several churches, or among churches and secular institutions supplying similar services.[17]

One trouble with this interpretation is that it does not go beyond what would have been permitted under the First Amendment in the form originally passed by the Senate in 1789. Since the establishment clause as finally enacted contains tighter language, it is reasonable to assume that Congress meant to require something more strict. Furthermore, as Freeman Butts has pointed out, the founders had before them examples of religious establishments in states like Maryland and South Carolina under which public support was authorized for a number of different denominations (all Protestant). Their understanding of establishment, therefore, must have included more than favoring a particular church.[18]

At the opposite extreme of interpretation are those who would apply literally Jefferson's phrase calling for a "wall of separation between church and state." (Jefferson's remark appeared in a letter written more than ten years after the adoption of the First Amendment, but it has been cited so often in Court opinions that many Americans have come to regard it almost as part of the Constitution.)[19]

According to these strict separationists, the establishment clause requires absolute neutrality by government, not only among religions, but also between religion and irreligion, and prescribes keeping all activities of government, including conduct of the public schools, sealed as tightly as possible against any hint of religious influence or contact. "Neither a state nor the Federal Government," Justice Hugo Black wrote in 1947, in an opinion still approvingly quoted by separationists, "can pass laws which aid one religion, aid all religions, or prefer one religion over another. . . . No tax in any amount, large or small, can be levied to support any religious activities or institutions, whatever they may be called, or whatever form they may adopt, to teach or practice religion." The Supreme Court has carried this line of reasoning to the point of prohibiting display of the Ten Commandments in the hallways of public schools, though the Court itself sits beneath a frieze depicting promulgation of the Ten Commandments, and of forbidding use of public school teachers to give remedial instruction to mentally handicapped children in parochial schools.[20]

It is difficult indeed to find mandate for such relentless exclusion of religion from publicly supported activities in the intent of the founders. The first Congress that enacted the First Amendment also appointed chaplains in both houses and adopted as part of the ordinance governing the Northwest Territory the directive, "Religion, morality, and knowledge, being necessary to good government and the happiness of mankind, schools and the means of learning shall forever be encouraged." Presidents Washington, Adams, and Madison, though not Jefferson, issued proclamations establishing national days of prayer and thanksgiving. Washington began the custom, continued by all his successors, of adding the phrase "so help me God" to the presidential oath of office.[21]

A Positive Freedom

Congress's decision to include the religious clauses in a single amendment with the free speech clause and the free press clause provides a useful indicator of intention. Clearly, Congress did not regard freedom of speech or of the press merely as privileges for the enjoyment of individuals. Both of these freedoms were justified, not only as personal rights, but also as essential supports for the conduct of a free society and republican government. There is every reason to believe that the founders saw the free exercise of religion in the same light: both as a guaranteed liberty to the individual and, in Washington's words, as an "indispensable" support for "political prosperity." Free exercise of religion, that is, was not merely to be permitted, like such unspecified general rights as travel or recreation, but positively to be encouraged, like the free expression of ideas, as a vital contributor to the public good.

Of course, the First Amendment includes no parallels to the establishment clause in the areas of speech or the press. Government, besides encouraging free discussion and a free exchange of ideas, may also, under the First Amendment, enter the marketplace of ideas with substantive arguments and policy proposals of its own. It has no such

right in the area of religion. The founders recognized the dangers to social harmony, personal freedom, and religion itself if government
attempts to sponsor its own versions of religious practice or belief. To
counteract these dangers, they enacted the establishment clause. They
specifically rejected any public religion—or civil religion, as it is now
sometimes called—for the United States. By prohibiting establishment
of religion, they intended that government should give no direct support
or sponsorship to any church, or any group of churches, or even to the
cause of religion in general. But they did not intend that prohibition of
establishment should extend to preventing symbolic acknowledgment of
the dependence of civil government, as of .all life, on transcendent
direction, or to impeding normal functions of government in areas like
education and health care that might indirectly benefit church-related
institutions.

The founders sought to maintain a society in which civil government would receive moral support and guidance from transcendent
values. To help promote continuing renewal of the source for recognition of these values, they enacted the free exercise clause. To assure that
the source would not be polluted by the narrow political interests of either government or the institutional churches, they added the establishment clause.

Judicial Activism

In recent times, a school of legal philosophers known generally as
judicial activists, or among legal scholars as "noninterpretivists" (because they do not believe the courts should be limited to interpreting the
text of the Constitution), has held that the intentions of the framers of
the Constitution are to a great extent unknowable, and in any case
should have little bearing on current understanding of basic law.
Lawrence Friedman, professor of law at Stanford, has argued that in
the modern United States part of the function of the courts should be to
act as "brooms," sweeping out legal anachronisms that "cannot now be
repealed" because of political blockages. In performing this cleanup
function, Friedman suggests, the courts should draw on a general sense
of where society currently stands. "The measuring rods are very vague,
very broad principles. These are attached loosely to phrases in the
Constitution. They are connected more organically to the general
culture." [22]

The question of what is meant by "general culture" as a standard
for judicial interpretation is particularly problematic with regard to
establishment clause issues. If general culture is equated with public
opinion, many of the Court's decisions in the 1960s and 1970s on
establishment clause cases were without ground. National opinion polls

have consistently shown a large majority of the public favoring return of organized prayer to the public schools, for example.[23] By general culture, Friedman may mean public opinion if the public were as well informed as Supreme Court justices, or opinion at the more refined levels of culture, or opinion elevated by judicial vision. There is something to be said for all of these as partial sources for judicial reasoning, but all hold obvious perils as standards to be relied on by the courts in a political democracy.

The activists surely are right when they argue that the Constitution should not be employed as a judicial cookbook, in which legal recipes can be found to apply to particular cases. As Laurence Tribe, a leading proponent of noninterpretivism, says, the courts should search out "the principles behind the words" in the written Constitution. But in doing so, they must, if their decisions are to be accepted as objectively valid, seek the principles that moved the authors of the Constitution and its amendments rather than impose standards derived from a vaguely conceived contemporary "general culture." Tribe concedes, "The Justices may not follow a policy of 'anything goes' so long as it helps put an end to what they personally consider to be injustice." [24]

During the 1960s and the 1970s, some of the Supreme Court's strict separationist decisions, perhaps reacting against an earlier period of excessive passivity, went well beyond any principles that can credibly be ascribed to the enactors of the First or Fourteenth Amendments. To claim otherwise is like suggesting that the enactors of the Fourteenth Amendment had a secret plan to reimpose slavery.

Return to Accommodationism

More recently, the Court has appeared to move back toward more traditional interpretations. In 1983, the Court upheld the constitutionality of the Nebraska legislature's employment of a chaplain and approved a scheme through which Minnesota permits parents to take a state income tax deduction for part of the costs of educating their children in parochial schools. In 1984, the Court found no implication of establishment in maintenance by the city government of Pawtucket, Rhode Island, of a nativity scene during Christmas season. And in 1986 the Court let stand on procedural grounds a policy instituted by the public schools in Williamsport, Pennsylvania, of making school facilities available for use by volunteer prayer groups on the same basis as other extracurricular clubs.[25]

The Court's apparent trend toward a more accommodationist stance has by no means been undeviating. In 1985, the Court ruled unconstitutional an Alabama statute authorizing a one-minute period of silence in the public schools "for meditation or voluntary prayer"—

though a concurring opinion by Justice Sandra O'Connor suggested that state laws calling for moments of silence without specific mention of prayer might "not necessarily manifest the same infirmity." Also in 1985 the Court issued the prohibition against use of public school teachers to give remedial instruction to handicapped children in parochial schools.[26]

Many of the Court's recent establishment clause decisions have been closely divided. To the extent that prediction is possible, it seems likely that the accommodationist trend will continue, though not nearly back to the point at which the previous trend toward strict separationism began in the 1940s. The principle of institutional separation between church and state will surely be maintained, though the line of separation is likely to be regarded more as a fence through which church and state carry on mutually beneficial interactions than as a grimly impenetrable barrier or wall. In any case, the question of what the Constitution intends for the relationship between religion and civil government will no doubt continue to cause much controversy—a tribute, after all, to the unquenchable vitality of religion in American national life.

Notes

1. Catherine L. Albanese, *Sons of the Fathers: The Civil Religion of the American Revolution* (Philadelphia: Temple University Press, 1976), 203.
2. Sydney E. Ahlstrom, *A Religious History of the American People,* vol. 1 (New York: Doubleday, 1975), 169.
3. *Annals of America* (Chicago: Encyclopaedia Britannica, 1968), vol. 3, 612; Thomas Sieger Derr, "The First Amendment as a Guide to Church-State Relations" (Paper delivered at the Conference of Roscoe Pound—American Trial Lawyers Foundation, Cambridge, Mass., 1981).
4. Paul J. Weber and Dennis A. Gilbert, *Private Churches and Public Money: Church-Government Fiscal Relations* (Westport, Conn.: Greenwood Press, 1981), 10, 11.
5. *Documents Illustrative of the Formation of the Union of American States* (Washington, D.C.: Government Printing Office, 1927), 716.
6. *Annals of the Congress of the United States* (Galen and Seaton, 1834), vol. 1, 444, 451, 729-731, 766.
7. *Journal of the Senate,* 77 (September 9, 1789).
8. Irving Brant, *James Madison, Father of the Constitution* (New York: Bobbs-Merrill, 1950), 271.
9. *Barron v. Baltimore,* 32 U.S. 487 (1833); *Permoli v. New Orleans,* 44 U.S. 609 (1845).
10. *Congressional Globe,* 39th Cong., 1st sess., 806, 1088, 2459; Charles Fairman, "Does the Fourteenth Amendment Incorporate the Bill of Rights?" *Stanford Law Review,* vol. 2 (December 1949), 76; Henry J. Abraham, *Freedom and the Court* (Oxford University Press, 1977), 36-48.

11. *O'Neil v. Vermont,* 144 U.S. 363 (1892).
12. *Gitlow v. New York,* 268 U.S. 625 (1925).
13. *Cantwell v. Connecticut,* 310 U.S. 296 (1940).
14. See particularly *Murdock v. Pennsylvania* 319 U.S. 112 (1942); *Prince v. Massachusetts,* 321 U.S. 296 (1940); *Sherber v. Verner,* 374 U.S. 404 (1962); *Wisconsin v. Yoder,* 406 U.S. 227 (1971); *Heffron v. International Society for Krishna Consciousness,* 452 U.S. 640 (1981); *Larson v. Valente,* 457 U.S. 1111 (1982); *Goldman v. Weinberger,* slip no. 84-1097 U.S. (1986).
15. *Committee for Public Education v. Regan,* 444 U.S. 646 (1981).
16. *Congressional Quarterly Weekly Report,* July 20, 1985, 1463.
17. Weber and Gilbert, *Private Churches and Public Money,* 185-189.
18. R. Freeman Butts, *The American Tradition in Religion and Education* (Beacon Press, 1950), 128.
19. Anson Phelps Stokes, *Church and State in the United States* (New York: Harper Brothers, 1951), vol. 1, 335.
20. *Everson v. Board of Education,* 330 U.S. 15 (1946); *Stone v. Graham,* 497 U.S. 39 (1980); *Aquilar v. Fenton,* slip no. 84-237 U.S. 11 (1985).
21. Walter Berns, *The First Amendment and the Future of American Democracy* (New York: Basic Books, 1970), 7-8; Paul F. Boller, Jr., *George Washington and Religion* (Dallas: Southern Methodist University Press, 1963), 53, 62; Stokes, *Church and State,* vol. 1, 335.
22. Lawrence M. Friedman, "The Conflict Over Constitutional Legitimacy," in *The Abortion Dispute and the American System,* ed. Gilbert Y. Steiner (Washington, D.C.: Brookings, 1983), 20, 21.
23. *Public Opinion,* June/July 1982, 40; *Religion in America: 50 Years, 1935-1985,* Gallup report no. 236 (May, 1985), 11.
24. Laurence H. Tribe, *God Save This Honorable Court* (New York: Random House, 1985), 43.
25. *Marsh v. Chambers,* slip no. 82-83 U.S. 5 (1983); *Mueller v. Allen,* slip no. 82-1256 U.S. 7 (1984); *Bender v. Williamsport Area School District,* slip no. 84-773 U.S. (1986).
26. *Wallace v. Jaffree,* slip no. 83-812 U.S. 7 (1985); *Aquilar v. Fenton.*

2. RELIGIOUS LIBERTY AND CREATIVE BREAKTHROUGHS: THE CONTRIBUTIONS OF ROGER WILLIAMS AND JAMES MADISON

Neal Riemer

What is the relationship between the idea of religious liberty and creative breakthroughs in American politics? My thesis is that the idea of religious liberty led to the first creative breakthrough in American politics in the theory and practice of Roger Williams, and that the idea played an important part in the second creative breakthrough in American politics in the theory and practice of James Madison. Moreover, I contend that future breakthroughs in American politics will continue to draw fruitfully from concepts, problems, and activities in the religious domain.

What is meant by the concepts of "creative breakthrough" and "politics," taken together? A creative breakthrough in politics is a significantly fruitful resolution of a major problem in connection with one or more of the major interrelated tasks of the discipline of political science.[1]

In connection with the breakthroughs to be examined in this article I shall, first, identify the problem that called for a breakthrough; second, articulate the theory that addressed itself to the problem; third, highlight the breakthroughs in their ethical, empirical, and prudential dimensions; and, finally, highlight the central or significant role that key religious ideas played in the breakthrough.

Roger Williams and the Breakthrough to Religious Liberty

The troubling problem that faced Williams in seventeenth-century America had been agitating Western thought and practice since at least the advent of Christianity, and it had become more acute with the Protestant Reformation: Is it possible to reconcile the dominant ideal of religious orthodoxy and political order *with* the facts of religious diversity, religious persecution, and political conflict? The facts of religious and political life underscored the realities of disagreement (primarily but not exclusively between Catholics and Protestants, and also between Protestants and Protestants) on who possessed the one true faith. The facts of religious and political life also underscored religious and political warfare rooted significantly, if not solely, in such religious disagreement.²

At the risk of making Williams's position more coherent and modern than it was, let me develop his related arguments (1) on behalf of religious liberty, and (2) on behalf of separation of church and state.³

Williams makes a religious and moral argument *and* a historical and expedient argument on behalf of religious liberty. Williams's religious and moral argument consists of two main points: first, persecution is contrary to the spirit, teaching, and deeds of Jesus; and, second, persecution is hypocritical.

Williams argues that persecution is contrary to the spiritual nature of Christ's gospel and kingdom. Is it not anomalous, Williams deftly asks, for Christians—in the name of Christ, the Prince of Peace—to persecute, to wield the sword, to spill blood, to divide person against person? Christ himself indicated that disbelievers must be allowed to live in this world, that their punishment would come in the next. People should come to God freely, not because of the fear of earthly persecution, punishment, and coercion. Rape of the soul— Williams's vivid image for religious persecution—is incompatible with God's message that people be drawn freely to divinity. Enforced uniformity, Williams holds, ravishes conscience and violates Christ's message.

Williams uses a famous New Testament parable—the parable of the wheat and the weeds (*tares*) in Matthew 13—to drive home his argument. The weeds (that is, the unregenerate, the impure, the faithless) may grow unmolested among the wheat (the elect) until harvest time— that is, death. Why? Because the wheat may be endangered by plucking (persecuting) the weeds. At harvest time (Judgment Day) the weeds can safely be gathered and burned; that is, at the time of Judgment Day, punishment can safely be meted out. God's battles in this world, Williams insists, must be fought with God's weapons—God's words— not with swords and prisons, not with persecution and civil disabilities.

A policy of persecution is malicious, vicious, and counterproductive; moreover, persecution is hypocritical. Individuals should not be forced to believe what their consciences forbid them to believe or to support a church (and beliefs) their consciences do not endorse. In an imperfect world how can we, Williams asks rhetorically, say we are godly and, therefore, have the right to persecute the ungodly who adhere conscientiously to their own beliefs?

In his historical and expedient argument Williams maintains that religious persecution both undermines civil peace, law, and order, and results in grave injury to true believers. He notes the alternating persecutions of Protestants by Catholics, Catholics by Protestants, and Protestants by Protestants. He contends that enforced religious conformity destroys the very prerequisites of civilized society, or true civility—law, order, peace, respect—and injures true believers. He also emphasizes that persecution for cause of conscience has not, in fact, produced the alleged "good" sought by the persecutors. Religious uniformity has not been achieved. Disbelievers persist. True believers, moreover, are clearly martyred; and civility is clearly damaged. On the other hand, Williams argues on the basis of the historical record that religious liberty is compatible with the teachings of Jesus and with true civility. This point is more fully developed in Williams's argument on behalf of separation of church and state.

Oddly, from a modern point of view, Williams's argument is rooted in the conviction that only one church-state (biblical Israel) ever possessed the legitimate power to persecute unbelievers. The key question for Williams in the seventeenth century thus became this: What is the proper conception of church and state since Israel and Christ?

The church, Williams argues, is spiritual in nature. It is concerned with souls. The weapons for its rightful defense must also be spiritual. Worldly props, he maintains, would undermine the church. Therefore, a spiritual church can make no use of a secular state for its spiritual purposes. God, he writes, has not "appointed the civil sword" as a "remedy" for the sores of His Body and His Church.[4] The church must be understood as a corporation with an independent existence. Dissent and division within the church need not endanger the peace of the political community.

The state is self-sufficient and has peace as its objective. The state is different in essence from the church. The state existed before corporations or associations and will remain when they are gone. The state does not need the church in order to preserve peace and order. The political community does not require enforced religious conformity for its continuance. The prince, civil magistrate, or state has limited responsibilities: to preserve peace and order in the political community. Religious uniformity is neither a necessary nor a sufficient condition for such peace and order. Indeed, when the civil magistrate persecutes for cause of conscience, he undermines peace and order. The sword and the prison should not, must not, be used to enforce the alleged one true religious faith. In brief, matters of religion are to be left to the individual and to God. The practice of religious faith is not to be a matter of concern to the civil magistrate. Religion is to be placed beyond the power of the state.

The most creative breakthroughs are breakthroughs along several fronts—ethical, empirical, and prudential—and are well illustrated by

Williams's religious and political philosophy. Ethically, Williams articulates an admirable philosophy of politics, of how we *ought* to live together. He affirms a philosophy of people of different religious faiths living together—freely, happily, harmoniously, civilly, peacefully, prosperously—in the same political community. For Williams, in practice, this community is to be a democratic political community. Religious freedom, the separation of church and state, a democratic and constitutional polity—these are for Williams preferred and crucial values. They become more strongly established in political American practice in the late eighteenth century (with help from philosopher-statesmen such as James Madison) and provide the basis of expanded notions of basic rights and republican rule, and thus serve to ensure a more generous democratic and constitutional regime.

Empirically, Williams articulates a new hypothesis, which will become a cornerstone for his "lively experiment" in what is later to be called Rhode Island, and which will (as already noted above) be subsequently tested more fully in the United States. The new hypothesis is that in the United States people of different religious faiths— enjoying religious liberty—can in fact live together without the evil effects that some feared (incivility, immorality, disrespect for law and order, war); that in fact religious persecution is the great enemy of society, of harmony, of peace, and of prosperity.

Prudentially, Williams makes the judgment that it is wise to ensure religious liberty and to separate church and state. He does so by calling attention to the ill-effects, hypocrisy, and illogic of persecution; by acting to limit the abusive power of the state in religious matters; and by establishing legitimate domains of operation for church and state.

Religious ideas clearly play a central role in the creative breakthrough to religious liberty and to the principle of separation of church and state. Williams, an orthodox Puritan in essentials, does not deny that there is only one true faith; but he does emphatically reject the proposition that it is the duty of the ruler of the state to maintain the one true faith. And he clearly rejects the conventional wisdom at key points. Those adhering to the conventional wisdom could only believe Williams's ethical recommendation on behalf of religious liberty to be outrageous; his empirical proposition that religious liberty and political peace are compatible to be false; and his prudential judgment that religious liberty and separation of church and state are wise to be absurd. However, when the decision on behalf of religious liberty is tested, it works. In time religious liberty would become enshrined in the First Amendment as a cardinal and admired value. Religious liberty serves in fact to advance social harmony. Both religious liberty and separation of church and state function to protect against the abuse of religious and political power. The way to democratic and constitutional pluralism is open.

Let me now turn to James Madison and note how he articulates in his theory of the extensive republic the second great breakthrough in American politics. This breakthrough, I will argue, owes a great debt to Madison's fundamental commitment to religious liberty and separation of church and state, and to his cardinal insight about the link between a multiplicity of religious sects and freedom.

James Madison and the Breakthrough to the "Extensive Republic"

The problem facing Madison and thoughtful Americans in 1787 was this: Is just republican government in a large state possible? Republican thinkers in America were struggling to avoid being impaled on either horn of a dilemma: either a despotic empire as a necessity of government in a large state; or faction, injustice, and weakness as the inevitable outcome in a confederate republic with major power residing in the thirteen American states.

The problem was not only theoretical but practical. Patrick Henry and other anti-Federalists—arguing that republican government is possible only in a small political community—opposed the new constitution of 1787 and the stronger government it created. They could not lift their sights beyond the loose political confederation of the Articles of Confederation. Alexander Hamilton, John Adams, and other advocates of "high-toned" government maintained—before the adoption of the new constitution—that only an empire, or a strong central government on the British model, could hold together a political community as large as the new American nation. Confederations, they insisted, were notoriously weak and unstable, plagued by faction, and detrimental to the interests of justice and the common good. Madison's great contribution was to demonstrate that the conventional wisdom— the testimony of history and previous political theory—was wrong.[5]

Madison's response to the problem required him to deal with four interrelated difficulties: disunion, large size, faction, and the anti-republican danger. The potent forces of disunion were strongly entrenched in the thirteen sovereign states. The large geographic size of the United States increased the threat to free and effective government. It did so, ironically, by encouraging both those who favored almost complete autonomy for each state and those who favored centralization of power. Selfish factional interests—groups opposed to the nation's common interest—operated within each of the states and obstructed the central government of the Union. Men and movements unsympathetic to republicanism were hostile to popular government in theory and disgusted with the weakness and degradation of republican government in practice.

Madison's goals required him to be at once a nationalist, a federalist, an empirical political scientist, and a republican. He was a nationalist who saw in a greatly strengthened, more nearly perfect federal union the instrument to cope with the danger of disunion. He was a federalist defending the new principle of federalism as the republican answer to the problem of large size. He was an empirical political scientist who articulated an explanation of how faction, the disease of liberty-loving republics, might be brought under control in an extensive, representative, federal republic. And, finally, Madison was a republican passionately concerned in 1787 with the anti-republican danger who (in the 1790s) worked his way toward a theory of democratic politics, a theory based on the significance of civil liberties, bold republican opposition, and a loyal republican opposition party.

Madison believed that a strengthened federal republic would enable the nation to cope with matters of national concern and yet would leave ample powers—and freedom—to the people in the several states. The new federalism would thus affirm: a unique division of powers between nation and states; key constitutional prohibitions on both the nation and the states; the direct operation of federal law on the individuals of the nation; a pragmatic and experimental federal system relying for its success upon a national consensus, a representative system, separation of powers, a resourceful presidency, and such organs as the Supreme Court. Madison argued decisively (and here we come to the heart of his empirical theory of the extensive republic) that the multiplicity, diversity, and conflict of factional interests, plus their larger sphere of operations, would diminish the possibility of factional agreement and unified factional action. Federalism would limit the spread of factional mischief and make it difficult for a factional majority to achieve power. What we today call pluralism would facilitate, not hinder, the pursuit of the common good. Madison sought in 1787, then in 1789, in the 1790s, and finally in the 1820s and early 1830s, to make his theory relevant to the central challenge of reconciling liberty and large size. His approach called for a keen analysis of the danger facing republican government, for political debate, for popular or party protest, and for a willingness to use radical constitutional means to secure necessary change.

Ethically, Madison's theory—particularly as fully developed— embodies a breakthrough to a broadened conception of how Americans ought to live: enjoying broadened conceptions of liberty, self-govern- ment, pluralist democracy, the good political life in a strengthened and more nearly perfect Union. He extolls the vision of religious and political liberty. He endorses the vision of just popular rule, operating through republican representation, and resistant to factional dominance. He accepts the value of the multiplicity and diversity of interests, of an informed and vigilant public opinion, and of competing political parties, including a loyal opposition. He fights for a republican Union and nation, operating under a more powerful, but still limited, constitution.

Empirically, Madison's theory of the extensive, federal republic constitutes another breakthrough. The large size of, plus the diversity and multiplicity of interests in, the new federal republic would defeat or inhibit the operation of factions and thus ensure greater success for the public good. The federal division of power would keep government at the local level close to the people, and yet give to the central government authority in matters of common national concern. Representation would operate to filter the evil effects of faction. Constitutional limitations on power and separation of powers would help to ensure the successful reconciliation of liberty and authority in the new republic. Moreover, a loyal republican and constitutional opposition party would guard against tyranny at the center. The constitutional operation of majority rule, a sound public opinion, a free press, a healthy two-party system, the federal judiciary, wise statesmanship that could distinguish between a usurpation, an abuse, and an unwise use of constitutional power—these features would protect against the evils of monarchy, plutocracy, tyranny in the central government and against anti-republicanism and anarchy in the component states of the Union.

Prudentially, Madison's theory illustrates practical breakthroughs in politics. In 1787 he sees the need to strengthen the powers of the central government but is willing to settle for a central government not as strong as he had originally wanted, because he perceives correctly that the new Constitution is a major step in the right direction. He articulates key features of the new federal republic in Philadelphia in 1787; explains the new Constitution brilliantly and effectively in *The Federalist* and in the important Virginia Ratifying Convention; works to establish the new Constitution on a firm foundation with a Bill of Rights and with other supporting legislation in the first Congress; and exercises leadership on behalf of a republican constitutional opposition party in the 1790s.

Madison's devotion to religious liberty strengthened his devotion both to constitutionalism and to federalism. This devotion enabled him to see that the same principle—of the salutary consequences of the multiplicity of sects—that operated to ensure religious liberty might also operate (now as the multiplicity of political, economic, and social interests) to ensure civil freedom. Human wit could, indeed, perceive that pluralistic diversity might advance freedom without interfering with civil decorum and harmony. As early as 1785 Madison had recognized that only a coalition between religious sects could endanger our religious rights.[6] Madison's *Memorial and Remonstrance Against Religious Assessments* (1785) testifies to his early great defense of religious liberty. His success in defeating such assessments was in no small measure to be attributed to the reality of the beginnings of religious pluralism in his native Virginia. In 1787 Madison again expressed his worry about a religious sect forming a majority and using its power to oppress other sects. And he noted that civil as well as religious rights could be endangered by an oppressive majority. To Madison the multiplicity of religious sects guarded against such oppression. In the Virginia Ratifying Convention of 1788 Madison drove home his point clearly and vigorously:

> If there were a majority of one sect, a bill of rights would be poor protection for liberty. Happily for the states, they enjoy the utmost freedom of religion. This freedom arises from that multiplicity of sects, which pervades America, and which is the best and only security for religious liberty in any society. For where there is such a variety of sects, there cannot be a majority of any one sect to oppress and persecute the rest.[7]

This idea, I am arguing, was in Madison's mind before, during, and after the writing of the Constitution. So, too, I am suggesting, was the link between religious plurality and freedom, on one hand, *and* economic, political, and social plurality and freedom, on the other. It was an easy step from the value of religious plurality for freedom to one of Madison's cardinal ideas—an idea central to his creative breakthrough in 1787—that the multiplicity and diversity of political, economic, and social interests would similarly constitute a safeguard for political freedom.

Thus Madison's religious convictions carried over into the political arena. Again, the concern for religious freedom would strike another great blow for democratic and constitutional government in American politics.

Conclusion

It is, I believe, no accident that key religious ideas—particularly the ideas of religious liberty, separation of church and state, and religious pluralism—have played such a prominent part in creative breakthroughs in American politics. Moreover, if we look to other reform movements in American history and politics—antislavery, women's suffrage, peace, economic reform, antidiscrimination—we can detect a comparably prominent religious role. Similarly, as we contemplate current and future problems we may well conclude that key religious ideas will play a prominent part in our efforts to deal with them. This, I would suggest, is bound to be the case because of the intimate connection between key religious ideas and a more prophetic politics. In taking key religious ideas seriously—belief in the divine, in freedom of conscience, in covenant, in commandments—people in politics take seriously the gap between religious values and existential reality. They are, moreover, sensitized to probe both the reasons for such gaps and what might be done to bridge them. Genuinely creative breakthroughs in politics are rare, but the two examples treated in this essay (and the links between religious ideas and other reform movements hinted at above) suggest that religious liberty and other key religious ideas will play a significant role in future breakthroughs in American politics.

Notes

1. See here Neal Riemer, *The Future of the Democratic Revolution: Toward a More Prophetic Politics* (New York: Praeger, 1984); and Neal Riemer, *Political Science: An Introduction to Politics* (New York: Harcourt Brace Jovanovich, 1983).
2. See Neal Riemer, *The Democratic Experiment* (Princeton, N.J.: Van Nostrand, 1968), chap. 2.
3. See here Riemer, *The Democratic Experiment*, and also Irwin H. Polishook, *Roger Williams, John Cotton and Religious Freedom* (Englewood Cliffs, N.J.: Prentice Hall, 1967), and William Lee Miller, *The First Liberty: Religion and the American Republic* (New York: Knopf, 1986).
4. Roger Williams, *The Bloudy Tenent of Persecution of Cause of Conscience* (1644) in *Roger Williams: His Contribution to the American Tradition*, ed. Perry Miller (Indianapolis: Bobbs-Merrill, 1953), 184.
5. See Neal Riemer, *James Madison: Creating the American Constitution* (Washington, D.C.: CQ Press, 1986).
6. See Riemer, *James Madison*, 105.
7. Ibid.

3. STRICT NEUTRALITY: THE NEXT STEP IN FIRST AMENDMENT DEVELOPMENT?

Paul J. Weber

In the world of church-state scholarship writers are usually grouped into opposing camps called absolute separationists and accommodationists. Both groups attempt to interpret the First Amendment religion clause but draw radically different conclusions about what the First Amendment requires of us today. Those who espouse other positions are either ignored or, worse yet, accused of being closet separationists or accommodationists (depending on the perspective of the accuser).

Yet there is another position gaining ground. In the twenty-five years since the concept of strict neutrality emerged, success has come almost inadvertently.[1] The Supreme Court, without adopting the concept of strict neutrality, has begun to use the terminology of neutrality on occasion, and the major casebook in the field has the intriguing title *Toward Benevolent Neutrality*, a term the authors conveniently leave undefined.[2] Unfortunately, *neutrality* has almost as many meanings as the more generalized concept of separation.

To understand the strict neutralist position it is helpful to begin with two presuppositions. (1) The founders did not write the First Amendment with either the clairvoyance or the specificity that would make it easy to apply their principles to problems arising in today's church-state relations. Various strands in the Founders' thought allow not only for conflicting interpretations but also for contemporary adaptation. (2) We live almost two hundred years after the First Amendment religion clauses were penned, and enormous changes have taken place, changes far beyond what the Founders could have imagined.

Granted these presuppositions, the challenge in constitutional theorizing is to create a principle of interpretation that (1) remains as faithful as possible to the language of the Constitution and the intent of the Founders; (2) is realistic, that is, acknowledges political and economic reality; and (3) resolves problems in a manner seen as just, fair, and required by the Constitution.

Varieties of Separation

The phrase "separation of church and state," although it never appears in the Constitution, has become so embedded in American consciousness that it seems to sum up what is meant by the First Amendment religion clauses. Small wonder. The term is broad enough to embrace a wide variety of beliefs and practices, and it allows groups espousing any one of several policy agendas to wrap themselves in the mantle of the Constitution. Our first task is to sort out the divergent meanings of *separation* and determine which best meet the challenges of constitutional theorizing.

Separation, in the First Amendment context, is a generic term that has at least five distinct varieties.[3] The most fundamental is *structural separation,* which distinguishes most Western systems from such organic systems as exist in Iran, Saudi Arabia, and other Muslim countries. The characteristics of structural separation are independent clerical and civil offices, separate organizations for government and religion, different personnel performing different functions, separate systems of law, independent ownership of property, and the absence of any officially designated church or religion. Jefferson, Madison, and most of the other Founders accepted the need for structural separation, and where they found remnants of organic relationships, as in parts of common law, they worked to remove them. It may be that this is as far as their thought had progressed at the time, although there are clues that they wanted something more.

Absolute separation is a type vigorously pursued by some interest groups in this country. It is more of a financial separation than anything else, holding that no aid of any kind should flow from government to religion or churches, and no financial support should flow from religion or churches to the government. Absolutists would take as normative Justice Black's description of the establishment clause in *Everson v. Board of Education:*

> The "establishment of religion" clause of the first amendment means at least this: Neither a state nor the Federal Government can set up a church. Neither can pass laws which aid one religion, aid all religions, or prefer one religion over another. Neither can force nor influence a person to go to or to remain away from church against his will or force him to profess a belief or disbelief in any religion. No person can be punished for entertaining or professing religious beliefs or disbeliefs, for church attendance or non-attendance. No tax in any amount, large or small, can be levied to support any religious activities or institutions, whatever they may be called, or whatever form they may adopt to teach or practice religion. Neither a state nor the Federal Government can, openly or secretly, participate in the

affairs of any religious organizations or groups and vice versa. In the words of Jefferson, the clause against establishment of religion by law was intended to erect "a wall of separation between Church and State." [4]

The difficulties facing the advocates of absolute separation are twofold. First, it is by no means clear that the Founders intended so specific a meaning of separation.[5] Second, historical practice in the United States, including contemporary practice, has included enormous amounts of aid, both direct and indirect, flowing to religion from government in return for enormous amounts of mostly indirect aid from religion.[6] This is a political and economic reality absolutists may rally against, but it is so imbedded in law and practice that it is unlikely to change in the foreseeable future. Absolutists are left in the awkward position of claiming as a constitutional principle something that has never existed and is never likely to. Absolute separation is an ideal, not a reality. Unfortunately for absolutists, the Constitution, unlike the Declaration of Independence, has the force of law and is meant to be obeyed as well as admired.

Transvaluing separation is less well understood in the United States, but the principle does have a devoted following. It holds that one objective of government is to secularize the political culture of the nation, that is, to reject as politically illegitimate the use of any religious symbols, or the appeal to religious values, motivations, or policy objectives in the political arena. Transvaluing separation would deny all aid to religious organizations under any circumstances. It is this type of separation that is touted in the Soviet constitution and law.[7] One American group that seems to express this position is the American Humanist Association:

> To promote the "general welfare," a particular measure may be favored by church interests, and consequently pressure and influence are brought to bear on the state's political machinery to assure its passage. Or a measure may be viewed with disfavor by the church with a resultant pressure on the state's political machinery to assure its defeat. This type of activity by the church harks back to pre-Revolutionary days both here and in Europe, where there was "cooperation" between government and church. But it was just that sort of religion-political interplay that the Founding Fathers tried desperately to prevent on American soil by adopting the First Amendment and the corresponding state laws.[8]

Thomas Jefferson's desire to provide access to the University of Virginia for neighboring schools of divinity is prima facie evidence that he did not favor this type of separation. I have argued elsewhere that Madison's *Memorial and Remonstrance* shows his opposition to this type of separation.[9] In any event, the Supreme Court has never accepted transvaluing separation, and it does not appear to have much promise as a constitutional principle in the United States.

What has traditionally been called "accommodation" I would call *supportive separation.* Those who hold this position acknowledge the need for structural separation but would not drive the principle to the extremes of the absolute or transvaluing types. To the contrary, supportive separationists favor aid and support for religion, holding only that government may not support one religion over another. This position takes as normative Justice William O. Douglas's dictum:

> We are a religious people whose institutions presuppose a Supreme Being. We guarantee the freedom to worship as one chooses. We make room for as wide a variety of beliefs and creeds as the spiritual needs of man deem necessary. We sponsor an attitude on the part of government that shows no partiality to any one group and that lets each flourish according to the zeal of its adherents and the appeal of its dogma. When the state encourages religious instruction and cooperates with religious authorities by adjusting the schedule of public events to sectarian needs, it follows the best of our traditions. For it then respects the religious nature of our people and accommodates the public service to their spiritual needs.[10]

Unfortunately for advocates of supportive separation, the history of the battle for religious liberty in Virginia and of the framing of the First Amendment undermines any claim that this is what the Founders intended. In addition, a whole series of decisions indicates very clearly that the Supreme Court does not believe this is what the Constitution requires. Finally, there has been strong political opposition to such a position throughout American history.

Equal separation rejects all political or economic privilege, as well as coercion or disability based on religious affiliation, belief, or practice (or lack thereof), but guarantees to religiously motivated or affiliated individuals and organizations the *same* rights and privileges extended to other similarly situated individuals and organizations. It provides protection to religion without providing privilege. It treats the right to religious belief and practice as a human right to be protected evenhandedly along with other human rights. It protects the right of religiously motivated groups and individuals to participate in the political process and the economic system in the same manner and to the same extent as it protects the rights of other similar groups and individuals to participate.

A difficulty facing proponents of equal separation is that it is a concept only recently developed and therefore unfamiliar to most Americans. It has been viewed suspiciously by advocates of other types of separation who fear that it will lead to a decrease in protection for religious liberty or an increase in aid to religion. Nonetheless, it is the basis for the strict neutrality approach to the religion clauses and will be further developed below. I have argued elsewhere that equal separation is the principle most consistent with the thought of James Madison.[11]

Historical Developments

Several developments of enormous proportions have made it impossible to apply the First Amendment religion clauses to contemporary problems in any simplistic fashion and still meet the requirements for constitutional theorizing posited above.[12]

The first development is the application of the religion clauses to the states through the due process clause of the Fourteenth Amendment by the Supreme Court. This is not something the Founders foresaw.

A second unforeseen development is the transformation of both federal and state governments from passive-protective, minimalist governments to active-expansive, pervasive administrative bureaucracies. This change from a laissez faire to a bureaucratic state with broad taxing, regulatory, and spending powers has enormous implications for church-state relations.

Parallel to the expansion of government has been the expansion of religious organizations in population, physical institutions, activities undertaken, and sheer variety of denominations, sects, and cults.

A fourth major change is the invention of technologies that make possible such new activities as mass education, mass communication, extensive impersonal fund raising, the fabrication of mind-altering drugs, and genetic manipulation.

Finally, the sheer growth in population density, mobility and diversity has profoundly altered the environment within which religious organizations operate and the laws affecting them are made. It is no longer easy for individuals to live solely among their own kind or to shelter their children from exposure to competing values.

Taken together, these five developments since the First Amendment was written pose such difficulties in terms of potential conflict, discrimination, and entanglement that legal theories that ignore them are doomed to failure. The task of the original Founders was to protect religious liberty *from* government. The contemporary task is to protect religious liberty *in the midst of* government. The same is true for preventing establishment while not discriminating against religion.

The Theory of Strict Neutrality

Strict neutrality was proposed a quarter century ago by Professor Philip Kurland of the University of Chicago:

> The thesis proposed here as the proper construction of the religion clauses of the first amendment is that the freedom and separation clauses should be read as a single precept that government cannot utilize religion as a standard for action or inaction because these clauses prohibit classification in terms of religion either to confer a benefit or to impose a burden.[13]

The thesis has been further developed since then, and some clarifications may be helpful. First, the purposes of the religion clauses can be summed up as freedom, separation, and equality. The application of the clauses in conjunction is both possible and necessary. It can be done by reading the clauses as an equal protection doctrine, or as Kurland explains:

> For if the command is that inhibitions not be placed by the state on religious activity, it is equally forbidden the state to confer favors upon religious activity. These commands would be impossible of effectuation unless they are read together as creating a doctrine more akin to the reading of the equal protection clause than to the due process clause, i.e., they must be read to mean that religion may not be used as a basis for classification for purposes of government action, whether that action be the conferring of rights or privileges or the imposition of duties or obligations.[14]

The equal protection doctrine is a well-developed component of constitutional law and can provide a firm foundation for dealing with current controversies in the church-state arena, providing both consistency and flexibility. Acceptance of strict neutrality is not a denial that religion can be used as a classification to identify a significant personal interest or social unit. It would be incongruous to hold that the Constitution can recognize the existence of religion but that the government based on that Constitution cannot. Recognition of an objective fact of personal value preference or of social organization would not be a violation of the neutrality principle. Examples might be recognition of the presence of a church or synagogue when planning traffic control signals or assigning personnel to expedite traffic. Such recognition implies that in relevant secular aspects individual religious interests and social groups are similar to other interests and groups, not based on religious content, but on the other public and secular aspects of a religion's social organization. Put in other words, strict neutrality is committed to the proposition that there is seldom a *legally significant* characteristic of religion so unique that it is not shared by similar nonreligious individuals and groups. The conclusion to be drawn is that in most aspects, religious individuals and interests are subject to the same laws as other similarly situated individuals and groups.

But what happens when there is a claim based on a uniquely religious belief, for example, when an Adventist cannot work on Saturday and requests unemployment compensation? Or a Mennonite refuses to have her picture on a driver's license? Or a Baptist church requires all its employees to be members of the church? Or what happens when a purportedly neutral law in fact imposes a significant burden on a religion or even prohibits a religious activity, such as an ordinance that prohibits door-to-door solicitations on weekends? In such cases religion may be treated as a *suspect classification* subject to strict scrutiny by the courts. A suspect classification is one in which there is "a presumption of unconstitutionality against a law implying certain classifying traits." [15] If religion is considered a suspect classification, any statute naming religion or specifically affecting religion is automatically suspect, will demand a very heavy burden of justification, and will be subject to the most rigid scrutiny. More than just a rational connection to a legitimate public purpose will be required. Nevertheless, if the standards of proof are met, the religious interest will be protected.

The suspect classification concept is used most frequently to prohibit racial and sexual discrimination, but it can equally well be used to preserve government neutrality with respect to religion. The question immediately arises, What are the principles that justify such a classification and define its limits? Donald Giannella several years ago offered two such principles. The first is the principle of free exercise neutrality that "permits and sometimes requires the state to make special provision for religious interests in order to relieve them of both direct and indirect burdens placed on the free exercise of religion by increased governmental regulation." [16] Such a provision is consonant with the "protected civil right" nature of religious liberty; but in accordance with the general neutralist position such provisions must be extended to other similar groups, if there are any.

The second principle is that of political neutrality. Its aim is "to assure that the establishment clause does not force the categorical exclusion of religious activities and associations from a scheme of governmental regulations whose secular purposes justify their inclusion." [17] Several examples might clarify the concept. If a local government is distributing excess cheese and bread to the poor through neighborhood organizations, church groups could be neither given exclusive rights to distribute the foodstuffs nor excluded from doing so. If government rents neighborhood buildings as polling places, churches could be neither preferred nor excluded from participation. Obviously, equal access legislation fits within the strict neutrality concept. At the same time, if a church did participate in secular programs, under the neutrality principle it would have to keep the same records and maintain the same standards as other participants.

Objections to the Strict Neutrality Principle

A number of objections have been raised to the neutrality principle. First is the objection that strict neutrality guts the religion clauses of any substantive meaning; this objection argues that if religious groups, individuals, and interests are to be treated equally with others then the religious clauses are irrelevant—surely not a situation the Founders intended.

It is true that very much of religious activity and all of religious thought are fully protected in the speech, press, and assembly clauses of the First Amendment, as well as by the due process and equal protection clauses, and so on. Double protection serves no additional function. Unlike the speech, press, and assembly clauses, however, the religion clauses are twofold, prohibiting the establishment of religion and guaranteeing its free exercise. The recognition of an independent liberty must be such that it offends neither one nor the other. Classification in terms of religion may tend to discriminate either by favoring religious interests at the expense of other similarly situated interests or by burdening religious interests in such a way as to have a chilling effect on religious liberty. The most equitable solution to this dilemma is to treat religious groups and interests like similar groups and interests. For example, a religious group seeking funds for its projects would have to conform to the same fund-raising rules and accounting standards as other nonprofit groups.

Precisely because religious liberty is *an independent, substantive right*, it functions as an indicator of the need to protect other groups and limit government intrusion into their affairs as well as into its own. Religious liberty is a protected legal right, but not a uniquely privileged one, that is, it gives no rights on the basis of religious commitment that do not extend equally to similar interests. In that sense it is a qualified legal right—qualified by the establishment clause.

A second objection holds that strict neutrality will limit religious liberty, that is, religious groups will be required to live under the same government regulations, abide by such things as affirmative action goals, file informational tax returns, and so on, in the same manner as other not-for-profit organizations. That objection is partially valid, by design. There is a cost to be borne for living in an organized society; although that cost is not borne equally under the neutrality principle, churches and other religious groups ought to be paying the same price and sharing the same burdens as other similar groups. If they do not, they are in a uniquely privileged position, a situation that is not something the Founders intended and that is a major objective of the establishment clause to avoid. Does this mean churches would have to pay taxes under the principle? No, not as long as other not-for-profit groups do not.

There is another side to this. Bureaucracies can be burdensome; regulations can be unreasonable. Religious groups may often find themselves resisting government intrusions, opposing new regulations or reporting requirements, and so on. Their input into the policy process is useful and healthy; churches can act as a brake on unnecessary government expansion and protect not only religious interests but the interests of others in society as well. Strict neutrality does not limit religious liberty; it only removes religious privilege.

A third objection is that strict neutrality is only a smokescreen behind which to usher in massive aid to religious schools at the expense of the public schools. Several considerations are relevant. Religious schools seeking funds would need to conform to the same hiring, certification, accrediting, admissions, and attendance standards; to accept the same curriculum and textbook requirements; and to submit to inspections and oversight at the same level as other publicly funded schools. This would not suit at all the purposes of the Religious Right or the interests of the parochial schools.[18] Under such conditions there would not likely be a rush for funding. The real advantage, if there is one in this area, is to stimulate competition and innovation in education by groups willing to accept government regulation, a competition many public schools desperately need.

A fourth objection is that acceptance of strict neutrality would undermine decades of court precedents and open the floodgates for a torrent of cases testing the limits of neutrality. The Supreme Court has increasingly been using the language of neutrality (although not consistently), and many of its holdings are in keeping with the principle. Acceptance would not, for example, undermine the three-pronged test for establishment clause cases, except that entanglement would need to be refined.[19] One advantage, if the principle were accepted, would be more consistently decided cases, a major dividend.

A fifth objection is that "similarly situated" is a vague term fraught with potential conflict and abuse. Similar in what? How broad must the category be? Who gets to decide? One model is nonprofit organizations under the Internal Revenue Service's 501(c)(3) category, which includes charitable, literary, recreational, fraternal, scientific, social, and educational groups. The neutrality principle is built on the realization that in most legally significant dimensions religiously motivated individuals and groups are similar to their secular counter-parts. Unfortunately, the use of a strict neutrality principle would not do away with lawsuits, but testing the contours of similarity is precisely what courts do best.

The Values of Neutrality

The values of adopting a principle of strict neutrality would appear to be the following:

1. The integration of free exercise and nonestablishment clauses into a coherent, consistent, comprehensible principle that is faithful to the intentions of the Founders, responsive to contemporary constitutional values of due process and equal protection, cognizant of current political and economic realities, and defensible as a fair and equitable rule of law.
2. Equal protection for nonreligious groups and individuals that are similar to religious groups and individuals.
3. Establishment of a principled reason for bringing the secular components of religious activities into conformity with the standards and procedures required for other not-for-profit groups and activities.
4. A stimulus for religious groups that currently seek to influence government policy to undertake the protection of rights for the larger society as well as for themselves.

Whether the courts will accept a neutrality principle depends in large measure on whether it is understood, analyzed, critiqued, developed, and ultimately accepted or rejected by the intellectual community that deals with church-state issues. For that to happen, the principle must be given far more attention than it has yet received.

Notes

1. The concept was first articulated by Philip Kurland, *Religion and the Law* (Chicago: Aldine, 1962).
2. Robert T. Miller and Ronald B. Flowers, *Toward Benevolent Neutrality: Church, State, and the Supreme Court* (Waco, Texas: Baylor University Press, 1987).
3. The five-part typology is adapted from an earlier article, Paul J. Weber, "James Madison and Religious Equality: The Perfect Separation," *Review of Politics* 44 (April 1982): 163.
4. *Everson v. Board of Education*, 330 U.S. 15 (1947).
5. For a credible discussion of this point, see Michael Malbin, *Religion and Politics: The Intentions of the Authors of the First Amendment* (Washington, D.C.: American Enterprise Institute, 1978).

6. For a discussion of the types and amounts of aid from government to religion, see Paul J. Weber and Dennis Gilbert, *Private Churches and Public Money: Church-Government Fiscal Relations* (Westport, Conn.: Greenwood Press, 1981).
7. See Paul D. Steeves, "Amendment of Soviet Law Concerning Religious Groups," *Journal of Church and State* 19 (1977): 37.
8. American Humanist Association, "In Defense of Separation of Church and State," in *Cornerstones of Religious Freedom in America,* ed. Joseph L. Blau (Boston: Beacon Press, 1949): 309.
9. Weber, "James Madison and Religious Equality," 168-173.
10. *Zorach v. Clausen,* 343 U.S. 310 (1952).
11. Weber, "James Madison and Religious Equality," 168-173.
12. For an elaboration of this section, see Paul J. Weber, "A Wavering First Amendment Standard," *Review of Politics* 46 (October 1984): 483-501.
13. Kurland, *Religion and the Law,* 18.
14. Ibid.
15. Joseph Tussman and Jacobus TenBroeck, "Equal Protection of the Laws," *California Law Review* 37 (1939): 354.
16. Donald Giannella, "Religious Liberty, Nonestablishment and Doctrinal Development," part 2: "The Nonestablishment Principle," *Harvard Law Review* 81 (1968): 518.
17. Ibid.
18. William K. Stevens, "Fundamentalists Pledge to Press Drive on Schools," *New York Times,* August 29, 1987, 1.
19. See Weber, "A Wavering First Amendment Standard," 483-498.

Part II

THE VALUE OF TENSION: RELIGIOUS PARTICIPATION IN AMERICAN POLITICS

Of what value is religion to politics and politics to religion? What role should religion play in politics? These questions arouse heated debate. Robert Booth Fowler argues that in a liberal society that appears to be aloof from, if not at odds with, religion in many ways, religion still performs very useful and necessary roles—not the least of which are a sense of certainty and community within the larger society's insecurity and impersonality. Clarke Cochran points out that religion and politics teach one another many things to the benefit of both and that they function better when they are neither totally separate nor totally unified. Anne Motley Hallum offers a case study of the political position adopted by a mainline Protestant denomination to illustrate one form of politico-religious activity. Mary Hanna examines the political role of American Catholic bishops. And Roger Hatch studies the influence of religion on Jesse Jackson's politics.

4. RELIGION AND THE ESCAPE FROM LIBERAL INDIVIDUALISM

Robert Booth Fowler

There are two areas in which religion, especially organized religion, constitutes a temporary alternative or escape from popularly perceived limitations of our liberal culture. It is a refuge from liberal skepticism and from liberal individualism, our peculiar and relentlessly demanding moral ideal for the human person. As a refuge from skepticism (and expansive, expanding tolerance), churches remain places where absolute, spiritual truths are still (sometimes) affirmed, places in which there are certainties, no matter how much they may evaporate when one thinks about them in terms of concrete morality or public policy (though for many of the religious they do not evaporate then).

More debatable, perhaps, is my second claim, that religion commonly functions as an alternative to liberal individualism. This is the subject of this essay. My view is that even in America, religion is popularly associated by the larger society with "community" in contrast with the rigors of liberal individualism. In this instance *alternative* means compensation, not rejection of liberal individualism in all its expressions. The churches' interest in community is as an addition, one might say, to liberalism. It is to function as a kind of socializing of normal liberalism, sought by large numbers of Americans far from ready to repudiate liberal values or institutions, but seeking the community they find so rarely in liberal culture.

The basic tenets of modern liberalism I take to be roughly the following: (1) commitment to skeptical reason, affirmation of pragmatic action, and uneasiness over both abstract philosophical thinking and nonrational modes of knowledge; (2) enthusiasm in principle and sometimes in practice for tolerance in political terms and, increasingly, in lifestyle and social norms; (3) affirmation of the individual and individual freedom; (4) commitment to some sort of democratic government. That these values are widely held within our culture is well established.[1]

By *liberal culture* I mean not just the values of modern American liberalism but also the practices that exist in our political order, our schools, our media, and the major institutions (except, to some extent, religious institutions) of our society. Culture is not only ideas but practice, and in those institutions liberal values ordinarily reign.[2]

The Endurance of American Religion
and of Liberal Individualism

Intellectuals long predicted that religion would all but disappear. As Daniel Bell has observed, "From the end of the nineteenth century to the middle of the twentieth century, almost every sociological thinker . . . expected religion to disappear by the onset of the twenty-first century." [3] That this has not taken place, especially in the United States, and gives no sign of taking place, is now obvious. This fact does not deny that some of the forms, influences, and expectations of religion have changed and will continue to.[4]

That religion continues to be important in American lives is undeniable—far more important, as Kenneth Wald notes, than politics.[5] More than half of the adult population rates religion as very important to them (56 percent). Close to 70 percent claim to be members of organized religious groups, and 40 percent claim to attend services weekly.[6]

Equally alive is religion's uneasy and unintended partner in American society today, liberal individualism. The pervasiveness of individualism in America needs constant underlining. The evidence is indisputable that individualism and freedom are the values Americans treasure.

Often enough, "the meaning of one's life for most Americans is to become one's own person, almost to give birth to oneself." Nor is there much doubt of the power of individualism in our culture, of the commitment to "self-actualized" existence, with its tension with ideas of duty, obligation, or community.[7]

This is even true to a considerable degree in the world of American religion, a realm where individualism is no stranger. After all, religion is not isolated from the larger culture. Much of classic American Protestantism had a large element of individualism in it from the start. Emphasis on individual relations with God, individual salvation, individual prayer, and personal spiritual journey have long been a staple of religion in America. These ideas continue their sway today as much as ever. Also relevant here is the decided pluralism present among American religious groups. So is the continuing strength of the idea in Protestant and Jewish circles that each congregation is sovereign.[8]

Community and American Religion

At the same time organized religion is also a locus in the United States for a continuing yearning for community, a condition of closeness among people which may have spiritual, social, or broader participatory dimensions—in the case of religious community, usually all three. The longing for community in this sense is powerful, perhaps especially in a liberal culture such as ours where human relations are casual and spontaneous, utilitarian and affective, rather than formal, binding, and long term, and where interest groups are second nature but the public good is hard to conceive. No matter how much we think of Americans as speaking only the language(s) of individualism, students of American culture consistently find that Americans retain a "second language," the language of community and commitment.[9]

The desire for spiritual community refers particularly to what is often called the search for a "community of believers," the interest in finding a group of persons with whom one may share spiritual concerns, feelings, and rituals. This search very frequently leads people to church as they search for something deeper in life than individual lifestyles. It is not the only alternative available or used, but in America it is the most common. This quest for depth often takes the form of individual spiritual journeys, but its usual form involves joining a religious group or church, to seek a community of shared believers and belief.

Closely related is the urge toward social community, the fact that people turn to a church to find a congenial social circle, quite apart from an interest in "spiritual" community. These two cannot easily be separated, since experience in churchly social communities strongly influences attitudes about the reality and appeal of larger communities of believers.

In any case, the evidence is overwhelming on the linkage of organized religion and community in these senses. *Religion* attracts those seeking transcendence from skeptical liberalism, but *organized religion* is much more intimately connected with community. After all, more Americans belong to a church or synagogue (70 percent) than to any other private association, by an immense margin, and they often are looking for social and/or spiritual community in joining.[10] Consider the evidence, for instance, regarding Catholics. The Notre Dame Study of Parish Life has documented how characteristic active Catholics' definition of their image of church as "the community of believers" is. Many Catholics look to church in terms of individual spiritual growth, but more think of it as a spiritual community. Indeed, given a range of possible images, this was chosen most often, by 42 percent of active Catholics.[11]

The social dimension of community is also important for Catholics, symbolized above all perhaps by the continuing popularity of bingo at the church hall. No parish activity attracts more participation, except mass itself. The social function of bingo is obvious, but the fact is that social activities in general are important "as a vitalizing force" in churches even as they satisfy the individual layperson's social needs.[12]

Systematic interviewing of Roman Catholic converts and returnees has confirmed the close link between the family community and the church as community. Why do people join the Roman Catholic Church? Why do they return after a period of indifference or alienation? The answers are overwhelmingly connected with marriage and family. One study established that fully 83 percent converted for reasons of marriage and/or family. For converts, marriage to a Catholic makes the difference. For returnees, the act of marriage, a turn from an individualistic lifestyle to a more communal one, brings many back to church.[13]

All of this applies generally, not just to Roman Catholics, for whom both church doctrine and ethnic loyalties (diminished today, except for the important Hispanic and Asian-American elements of the church) self-consciously promote community. A significant illustration may be found in Jewish circles in the United States. Although the current strength of Judaism in a religious sense is under intense debate,[14] we know that Jews who "return" to Judaism strongly emphasize desire for community as an essential motivation. Judaism attracts many Jews in a characteristically American fashion. Desire for community and desire for a more vibrant Judaism in one's life rarely lead to an all-or-nothing decision. Instead, individual Jews in individualistic America pick and choose in a spirit of freedom how much Judaism they want in their lives. They are individuals not rejecting liberalism, on the whole, but reaching out for an element of religious community to fill an important space in their lives.[15]

No doubt the search for community and the tradition connecting churches and community have their roots largely outside any given church. But how well religious groups address the need will influence their numbers, because a crucial motivating factor leading people to any church, *indeed the most common factor,* is desire for more community— both in the family and in one's life in general. Churches and denominations that tap this association of religion and community are likely to grow.[16]

Though the connection between children and church involvement is controversial, there is no doubt that the arrival of children in a family is often crucial to forming church ties. Just as for adolescents departure from church is routine on the road to self-reliance and affirmation of their American individualism, so an interest in church among young couples with children reflects a reborn interest in community. A definite life cycle rhythm is at work in American organized religion.[17] Since church is associated with family, often through an individual's own past, it is part of a package of family-community values. It is also assumed to be a family-promoting institution. Parents are commonly in favor of church as a place for their children. In our terms, they see it as an alternative not to life in liberal America but to the unchecked dominance of liberal individualism and relativism.[18]

There is no evidence that how well a church satisfies the interest in community has the slightest thing to do with grand declarations on the subject by the church's denominational leaders or headquarters staff. The relevant testing ground is, as always, concrete experience, in this case the actual life of local churches, not abstract moral or political declarations. This is one important reason why religious denominations not noted for their strong foundation beliefs, vigorous evangelism, or firm morality continue to retain large memberships. Wherever one goes in religious precincts in America, people belong to their local church, parish, or synagogue, often as much, usually more, than they do to their particular denomination or, in some cases, even their specific religion. Whatever the image of a denomination, a local church of that denomination that has a reputation for addressing community needs will attract members. There are numerous such churches in every denomination.[19]

Conflict at church or synagogue is very unpopular. And the perception of intrachurch conflict leads directly to membership declines.[20] People do not go to church for the excitement of conflict. They go in good part for community defined as harmony with the universe and fellowship with others. People commonly perceive conflict at church as a statement that the institution has failed in a basic way, that it cannot fulfill a need that led them there in the first place.

We can also draw on data from intermarriage and its effect on one's connections with organized religion. Greeley notes that intermarriage is a leading explanation for religious/church "disaffection." What this says in our terms is that in the interest of community (family unity), people will leave a given church or religion. Indeed, they are more likely to disaffiliate for this reason than for any other.[21] This is what we would expect, as it underlines that people are community seekers who assess the organized religion they encounter in good part on its ability to speak to this need.

People who experienced a turbulent family life as children and/or experience considerable tension with their family today frequently view their family's church, and any type of organized religion, with either ambivalence or hostility. From another side, this repeats what we already know, that there is a close association between church and family among Americans, and documents again that "communities" associated with family will pay a price when family does not model the community people expect from it.[22]

Mostly, though, organized religion benefits from the popular perception that it is a realm in which community is affirmed. People look for community in religious activity. Very often they find enough of it to satisfy them. Of course, we have to be careful not to exaggerate the part organized religion plays as a source for the alternative view of community in liberal America. Community is pursued in many places in America.[23]

Many "lifestyle enclaves" may not fulfill the type of community that some intellectuals define (yearn for?). But for many people their neighborhood bar, soccer club, PTA, bridge club, or what have you— even if temporary and built around fluid circles of friends—are the outlets for their need for community, *outlets they like*.[24]

Community and Participation

The data reported here support the idea that people think about organized religion as a place of community and in many cases go to church to experience community, or at least a respite from the individualism of the larger liberal society. So much of this association of religion and community is perceptual. It refers to feelings. What community means as a result varies enormously from person to person, including in terms of behavior.

The degree of participation in organized religion, beyond the three-quarters or so of the population that claims membership in a religious group, is hard to document. There is evidence on the most obvious measure, attendance at services. The data here, while self-reported, are extensive and the patterns are plausible. Evangelical and fundamentalist Christians are by far the most active in this sense. While Catholic attendance at mass has fallen since Vatican II (1962-65), still in a given month most Catholics appear at mass, and a sizable minority attend every week. The lowest attendance comes among liberal or mainstream Protestants: the majority do not attend in a given month. Attendance at services is not emphasized among non-Orthodox Jews, so the rare appearance of Jews at synagogue except at special holidays means little.[25]

Of course, participating in one way or another guarantees nothing, not even a sense of community. Indeed, participation can damage a strong sense of spiritual community by bringing one into conflict with other church members. But participation does often lead to an increased sense of community for an individual and for a religious body. That is why success in generating a sense of community in a local church or parish correlates importantly with opportunities for participation. Only open, active churches allow community to grow. Opportunities for participation will not necessarily breed community unless participants find among themselves people who care about others. But where caring and opportunity abound, the ideal of community people seek in religion will actually exist in specific local churches.[26]

Formal religious services are hardly the sole outlet for participation for any religious group, of course. There are numerous other opportunities, one might say numerous opportunities for creating or participating in community at church. Indeed, the chances for going beyond community as a spiritual ideal have long been extensive at churches and synagogues. Organizations abound: women's groups, men's groups, scripture study, social action, charity, church governance, music, youth, and education; the list is long.

But the fact is that, given the opportunities, actual participation is modest. It appears closely correlated with overall attitudes toward one's religion and each church's general cohesiveness. Thus in evangelical and fundamentalist churches most members are involved beyond merely attending. Among Catholics about half claim to be. Among liberal Protestants, far less than half are.

The most extensive data on any one group we have comes from the Study of Catholic Parish Life. This contemporary study found that of the half or so of Roman Catholics active beyond attending mass, the largest group (26 percent) participate in church social/recreational groups and activities. Almost as many are active in the church liturgies, as readers, choir members, and the like. More than 10 percent work in church educational programs (including evangelism efforts, helping to run the parish, and so on).[27]

Jewish patterns of involvement beyond the synagogue are impressive. To be sure, 25 percent of American Jews have no connection with organized Judaism. Yet the vast majority are at least occasionally involved in the considerable range of Jewish organizations, 10 percent or so intensely, another third actively, the rest more infrequently.[28]

The amount of activity or participation—of real or potential community—inside religious groups is large in comparison with the degree of participation in outreach to the larger world. Community with the outside world continues—even in this day of supposedly politicized religion—to be low on people's agendas, as indicated by practice. To be sure, most organized religious groups have one or more forms of outreach. They make some effort to build paths of community beyond their walls. A great proportion of these efforts concentrates on the larger community of the religious denomination to which they belong. A typical Catholic church, for example, makes many efforts in a year to connect with local, national, and even international communities. But it does so mostly in terms of help in local Catholic schools or the apostolate to the handicapped or to a religious order abroad. Moreover, even including the sometimes remarkable (but very parochial) outreach programs of the Knights of Columbus, the numbers of laity active are very small. This pattern is repeated by many Jewish synagogues insofar as a great deal of their outreach is directed toward Israel, and certainly by many conservative Christian groups whose tension toward the outside world beyond the "born again" is evident.[29]

Moreover, lay opposition to community outreach, if that means involvement in social/political causes or groups, has been and continues to be common.[30] It is simply the case that few people join an organized religion or go to church to get involved in social/political action. This is not the kind of community involvement they are after. Some people do become busy in charitable activities—in community meal programs, community pantries, and the like—though in proportional terms not many. Community in this broader sense of a relationship between the faithful and the larger community is a regular if quite small part of almost all organized religious groups' activities.

The fact that only modest numbers of people reach out from their religious community to the larger community underlines my point. These numbers are predictably small given my hypothesis that people go to church in large part to escape (for a time) the larger liberal culture. That participation inside religious "communities" is higher is equally predictable.

Concluding Reflections

One must concede that we do not yet have evidence that establishes directly that religion serves as an escape hatch from excessive cultural liberal individualism, a place where one can find at least the idea of community. But I think the pieces of evidence I have put together, the studies of joining and leaving organized religions, the evidence about participation, the conception of religion in terms of community, and the like should be read to mean just that. The point is that religion, organized religion especially, is viewed as an alternative to the liberal individualism which is basic to our culture. That contrast does not work out to religion's disadvantage on the whole. Nor, it is my thesis, to liberal society's, though showing the connection of religion and community is not quite the same thing as establishing that the consequence is unintended support for liberal culture.[31]

Interest in community could be interpreted as a statement of nonsupport for liberal culture. It could, for instance, reflect nonsupport through the growth of a religious subculture which is intensely sympathetic to "community" and hostile to the larger American culture, and trying to change it in radical ways.

The major case against this type of possibility is simply that most Americans do not reject liberal individualism, as we have noted. They do not ordinarily see religion and liberal culture as mortal enemies at war in society or within themselves. That they rarely see such a war means it does not exist for them. Church and culture, though about different values, fit together.

There may be a case for arguing that those who seek to escape liberal culture by entering separatist religious settings are growing, such as the substantial numbers involved in the Christian school movement among Protestant fundamentalists.[32] Still, all our evidence suggests that for the average churchgoer there is no yearning to have community replace individualism.[33] Apparently Americans do believe they can have it all. As long as this holds true, then organized religion will continue to serve, as I suggest it does, as a backhanded supporter of a liberal culture it must necessarily view ambivalently. This is the irony of organized religion in American life today.

Notes

1. The poll data back up this popular liberalism again and again. But I think one learns the most about it through such qualitative studies as Robert Bellah et al., *Habits of the Heart: Individualism and Commitment in American Life* (Berkeley: University of California Press, 1985); Jennifer Hochschild, *What's Fair? American Beliefs about Distributive Justice* (Cambridge: Harvard University Press, 1981); Richard Merelman, *Making Something of Ourselves: On Culture and Politics in the United States* (Berkeley: University of California Press, 1985); Richard Reeves, *American Journey* (New York: Simon & Schuster, 1982).
2. Two good sources here are Merelman, *Making Something of Ourselves,* and Daniel Bell, *The Cultural Contradictions of Capitalism* (New York: Basic Books, 1978).
3. Daniel Bell, "The Return of the Sacred? The Argument on the Future of Religion," *British Journal of Sociology* 28 (December 1977): 419-449.
4. Mary Douglas and Steven Tipton, eds., *Religion and America: Spirituality in a Secular Age* (Boston: Beacon, 1983), 3-13.
5. Kenneth Wald, *Religion and Politics in the United States* (New York: St. Martin's, 1987), 9.
6. *Religion in America: 50 Years, 1935-1985,* Gallup Report no. 236 (May 1985), 11, 13.
7. Ibid., vii-viii, 82, 97-107.

8. In developing the overall theory, I have been influenced by Herve Varenne, *Americans Together: Structured Diversity in a Midwestern Town* (New York: Columbia University Press, 1977).

9. Bellah, *Habits of the Heart,* 85, 154, 191, 206.

10. *Religion in America,* 40.

11. David C. Leege and Thomas A. Trozzolo, *Religious Values and Parish Participation: The Paradox of Individual Needs in a Communitarian Church,* Notre Dame Study of Catholic Parish Life, no. 4. (June 1985), 1-8.

12. David C. Leege, *Parish Organizations: People's Needs, Parish Services, and Leadership,* Notre Dame Study of Caholic Parish Life, no. 8 (July 1986).

13. Dean R. Hoge, *Converts, Dropouts, Returnees: A Study of Religious Change among Catholics* (New York: Pilgrim, 1981), 44, passim.

14. See Charles E. Silberman, *A Certain People: America's Jews and Their Lives Today* (New York: Summit Books, 1985), and Arthur Hertzberg, "The Triumph of the Jews," *New York Review of Books,* November 21, 1985, 18-22.

15. Silberman, *A Certain People,* 250, 270, chap. 6 and 7.

16. For a vigorous challenge to the neodeterminists who dismiss internal church factors as an influence on growth or decline, see: Dean M. Kelly, "Commentary: Is Religion a Dependent Variable?" in *Understanding Church Growth and Decline 1950-1978,* ed. Dean R. Hoge and David A. Roozen (New York: Pilgrim, 1979), 338-339. On the growth of certain churches, see, for example, Edmund A. Rauff, *Why People Join the Church* (New York: Pilgrim, 1979); George Gallup, Jr., and David Poling, *The Search for America's Faith* (Nashville: Abingdon, 1980).

17. Bellah, *Habits of the Heart,* 62.

18. There is no shortage of skepticism of the theory that having children increases participation in organized religion; for example, for liberal Protestants, see David A. Roozen, "The Efficacy of Demographic Theories of Religious Change: Protestant Church Attendance, 1952-1968" in *Understanding Church Growth and Decline 1950-1978,* ed. Hoge and Roozen, 135-136; for a contrary view regarding Roman Catholics, see Jay Dolan and David C. Leege, *A Profile of American Catholic Parishes and Parishioners: 1820s to the 1980s,* Notre Dame Study of Catholic Parish Life, no. 2 (February 1985), 6.

19. See David C. Leege, *The Parish as Community: Developing Community and Commitment,* Notre Dame Study of Catholic Parish Life, no. 10 (March 1987).

20. Dean A. Hoge and David A. Roozen. "Some Sociological Conclusions About Church Trends," in *Understanding Church Growth and Decline,* 324-325; Wade Clark Roof, Dean R. Hoge, John E. Dyble, and C. Kirk Hadonay, "Factors Producing Growth of Decline in United Presbyterian Congregations," in *Understanding Church Growth and Decline.*

21. See, for example, the argument of Hoge, *Converts, Dropouts, Returnees.*

22. Andrew Greeley argues this in several places; one is Andrew Greeley, "Religious Musical Chairs," in *In Gods We Trust: New Patterns of Religious Pluralism in America,* ed. Thomas Robbins and Dick Anthony (New Brunswick, N.J.: Transaction Books, 1981), 101-126.

23. For disagreement on this broad interpretation of "community," see Bellah, *Habits of the Heart,* 72-73.

24. Varenne, *Americans Together,* a very stimulating essay, explores the kind of prevalent "community," chap. 4, 7. This view of fluid, multiple social interest groups as Americans' life is partly based on Varenne's *Americans Together,* and on Bellah, *Habits of the Heart,* 71-75, from which the central term "lifestyle enclave" comes.

25. *Religion in America,* 11, 42; Dolan and Leege, "A Profile of American Catholic Parishes and Parishioners," 6.
26. Leege, "The Parish as Community."
27. David C. Leege and Thomas A. Trozzolo, *Participation in Catholic Parish Life: Religious Rites and Parish Activities in the 1980s,* Notre Dame Study of the Catholic Parish Life, no. 3 (April 1985), 6.
28. Daniel Elazar, *Community and Polity: The Organizational Dynamics of American Jewry* (Philadelphia: Jewish Publication Society, 1976), 70-77.
29. Leege and Trozzolo, *Religious Values and Parish Participation,* 5, presents the Catholic data, the best we have on any branch of American religion.
30. For summaries of the data, see: James Reichley, *Religion and American Public Life* (Washington, D.C.: Brookings Institution, 1985), chap. 6; Robert Booth Fowler, *Religion and Politics in America* (Metuchen, N.J.: Scarecrow, 1985), chap. 4.
31. As Kenneth Wald has pointed out to me.
32. Though Christian schools come in many, diverse forms. See the following: John C. Carper and Thomas C. Hunt, eds., *Religious Schooling in America* (Birmingham: Religious Education, 1984); James C. Carper and Neal E. Devins, "The State and the Christian Day School," in *Religion and the State: Essays in Honor of Leo Pfeffer,* ed. James E. Wood, Jr. (Waco, Texas: Baylor University Press, 1985), 211-232; Alan Peshkin, *God's Choice: The Total World of the Christian School* (Chicago: University of Chicago Press, 1986).
33. Even if Christianity were somehow to push forward the idea of community into the larger American society, would it come in a form which necessarily stressed individualism? This is the query and suspicion of Bellah in *Habits of the Heart,* 232, 236.

5. NORMATIVE DIMENSIONS OF RELIGION AND POLITICS*

Clarke E. Cochran

Government seems to me a part of religion itself, a thing sacred in its institution and end. For if it does not directly remove the cause, it crushes the effects of evil and it is as such (though a lower yet) an emanation of the same divine power that is both author and object of pure religion. . . . But that is only to evil doers, government itself being otherwise as capable of kindness, goodness, and charity as a more private society. They weakly err that think there is no other use of government than correction which is the coarsest part of it. Daily experience tells us that the care and regulation of many other affairs, more soft and daily necessary, make up much of the greatest part of government and [this] must have followed the peopling of the world had Adam never fell and [it] will continue among men, on earth, under the highest attainments they may arrive at by the coming of the blessed Second Adam, the Lord from Heaven.

William Penn, 1682[1]

Penn's rather sanguine view of government assimilates it to both religion and private life. Yet there is something to be said for his view. Government does outlaw (some) sin, and it does regulate (not always softly) matters of food, clothing, and shelter. Government acts on the border of private and public life; yet it forms its own border with religion. I intend here to examine the dynamics of the transactions across these borders. These transactions at their best reflect a creative tension between religion and politics.

General Considerations

This tension is often misunderstood as strain between private and public life. Yet religion is a constant reminder of the unity of public and private, as well as of the boundary between them. Private and public

* I am grateful to the Earhart Foundation for a Fellowship Research Grant and to Texas Tech University for a Faculty Development Leave, which supported the research for and writing of this article.

life need each other, but they are different realms. The validity and the distinctive character of each contributes to a healthy society. Religion affirms the public/private distinction, but also the need to cross the boundary.

Because religion suggests that culture is not divine (at the most, it is the direct will and creation of the divine), religion more directly than other systems of value insinuates the tension between culture and something higher than culture. Although religion is linked to culture and frequently coopted by it, the "higher" religions and religions with more reflective traditions more emphatically suggest tension with culture. The inherent dynamic of religion's orientation to a transcendent source of being, independent of human control, opens the path toward cultural conflict. As much as culture takes upon itself divine color, it cannot hide its human roots.

The individual person, where the competing attractions of culture and the sacred intersect, really is the locus of tension.[2] Machiavelli, for example, denouncing Christianity's public effects, clearly understood that the strain was not between private religion (Christianity) and public good (the republic), but between the different public demands of Christianity and the republic on the individual. Machiavelli rejected Christianity for its cultural consequences. The unique perspective of religion reveals the person as a field of cross-cutting tensions between the divine and culture in private and public life.

Because religion touches (sometimes unconsciously) the core of a believer's character, it bears upon the moral boundaries of public and private life. The role of politics in creating social peace and justice depends upon personal interior peace and justice. Government and politics cannot bring men and women to virtuous living or inner tranquility, for they cannot prescribe all virtuous actions or proscribe all vice. Moreover, political life cannot bring final beatitude.

Although religion and public life intersect, religion fundamentally reminds us of the limits of politics and of the nonequivalence of politics and public life. In the American tradition, for example, the Bible has reminded us "that public spirit will always be opposed by private interest," that law and coercion must supplement public virtue and participation, and that "the larger the political society, the greater the tension between body and spirit, private feelings and public duties."[3] We must remember that religion points resolutely to life beyond politics. It reminds us that public problems and their solutions are not entirely political. Indeed, the distinctive contribution of religion to public and private life, to individuals and to culture, is to refer them to what is beyond politics.

Two (or more) forces pulling in different directions define a tension. Sometimes its stress holds things together, for example, as a rubber band does. But sometimes it causes things to break apart, as when a spring snaps from being wound too tightly. To understand the religion/politics tension, we must define the directions in which each pulls. We must also show how tension between them permits each to work better.

Religion brings politics to awareness of the highest, lowest, and most mysterious, sometimes lofty, features of life. Politics, better acquainted with the lowest, brings religious passion and self-assurance to awareness of the middle ground between the highest and the lowest; that is, it teaches religion the necessity and the art of compromise. Moreover, some of the highest and lowest things are already at home in politics—honor, bravery, lust for power, and the passions of blood and soil. Politics can make religion alert to these, and to their danger.

Religion pulls toward the transcendent, toward principles, virtues, ideals, and perfection. Unrestrained by tension this religious dynamic produces fanaticism. Religious passion finds it difficult to compromise, to acknowledge how striving after perfection founders on human weakness. Politics, however, demands compromise, for the key fact of politics, especially of participatory public life, lies in confrontation with the ideas and the interests of others, with the mosaic of human frailty and plurality.

Just as religion would avoid compromise, politics would avoid righteousness. Politics pulls toward the vague middle ground, toward indifference and cynicism. Left to itself, politics seeks the easy, painless way. High principles make for difficult political choices, for it is painful to confront higher things, to acknowledge the possibility of something better and to accept the discipline necessary to reach it. Religion in public life can teach politics about the higher things and stimulate, even embarrass, politicians and citizens to discover them.

The tension produced by these conflicting natural tendencies defines their relationship as both competitive and cooperative.[4] The danger of misunderstanding the relationship between religion and politics comes when we forget that it must include *both* cooperation and competition. When the tension is lost, the two either fly apart or, worse, collapse together. The latter is the world's too frequent condition. As Roland Robertson observes, "Religion is being politicized and politics (as well as economics) is being sacralized intrasocially and globally." [5] The agendas of the New Christian Right and the National Council of Churches exemplify politicized religion; sacralized politics takes form in totalitarian ideologies. Both of these forms of lost tension obscure the border between religion and politics. These territories should remain distinct but mutually interactive.

What Religion Teaches Politics

In a skeptical and relativistic age religion challenges easy moral relativism and indifference. As Hadley Arkes remarks, "Moral 'relativism' has become the secular religion these days among those with a college education." [6] Religion contests the cynical and egoistic political consequences of this relativism by advancing in public debate principles claiming sacred roots.

Thus, despite the exaggerated claims and extreme lengths to which some religious groups have gone in policy debates, it is healthy for a political system (and for citizens) dangerously close to "interest group liberalism" to face demands for unilateral disarmament, feeding the hungry and taking care of the sick, full employment, action against cocaine, marijuana, teen pregnancy, and pornography, cessation of abortion, and an end to capital punishment. The debate sparked by religious campaigns to confront the political system with these issues is uncomfortable, but the debate at least revives substantive political issues and principles and pushes fundamental questions of justice and peace to the forefront of attention in a system characterized by self-satisfied, cynical boredom with any but self-interested political concerns. [7] Similarly, instead of deploring the debate over the judicial principles and substantive views of Robert Bork, President Ronald Reagan's 1987 Supreme Court nominee, we should welcome such debate as the true substance of public, political life.

Neither politics nor political theory is to judge the truth of competing religious claims. I recognize that religious groups disagree on matters of principle and policy and that they themselves pull in multiple directions. However, even their advocacy of conflicting principles is vital, for genuine public life depends on matters of character and virtue and pertains to substantive issues over which citizens interact and confront each other to create a common good out of conflicting interests and principles. Politics must not deplore or dismiss religious competition, but rather moderate its worst passions.

The approach to justice in the 1986 pastoral letter on the economy issued by the United States Catholic Conference illustrates my point. I do not intend to analyze the strengths and weaknesses of that statement or the debate it occasioned or even to reveal my agreement or disagreement with its positions. The point I wish to emphasize is Gerald M. Mara's contention that the letter contains an account of justice superior to such liberal, political treatments as Rawls's, for the letter addresses the urgency of justice. [8] Political theorists' accounts of justice tend to be abstract and categorical. They supply no urgent motivation to act against injustice. The bishops' statement is substantive and sensitive to historical conditions. Moreover, it furnishes for those who agree with it urgent motivation to political action.

The bishops' theory of justice is not philosophically unchallenge-able. Yet their account of justice, like that of the Hebrew prophets, resonates with the passion for justice. A religious dimension advances in policy debate the passion for justice neglected by "neutral" theories and interest group politics. Justice touches the heart as well as the head, and religion can push the public to take that fundamental emotion into account.

Similarly, the radical activity of those religious groups and individuals acting outside ordinary politics—such as Gandhi, Mother Teresa, Dorothy Day, Mitch Snyder, and Dietrich Bonhoeffer—can goad formal, bureaucratic political institutions to take account of a higher spirit and a good greater than rules, efficiency, and the letter of the law.[9] Sparks often fly in such encounters, just as they fly in the cre-ative tension of a steel blade pressed against a sharpening stone.

Let me advance an even more controversial example of the kind of contribution religion can make to politics in a liberal democratic society. Though religious groups may take obedience too far, liberal society needs religion's lessons in obedience. For liberalism tries to abolish obedience by making the legitimacy of rules depend upon the satisfac-tion of interests. Rousseau, no liberal but here in the liberal spirit, wanted to find a way to make it possible in civil society to obey only oneself.

Liberalism tends to undermine the public grounds of obedience, leaving it only, for example, for the private life of the family. Even in private life, however, increasing public requirements for procedural rights hedge obedience. Yet, as Milgram's experiments show, a deep human propensity to obey authority remains even in liberal society.[10] "Blind" obedience, frowned upon by liberal principles, goes under-ground and emerges in strange places, not least of which are cultic forms of religion, such as that of Jim Jones, and claims of obedience to demons in cases of strange, often violent behavior. Though I realize that these brief illustrations do not constitute proof, traditional Western religions could perform a public service in reemphasizing discipline and obedience with respect to religious principles, rules, rituals, and behavior. Bringing obedience above ground makes it more likely to find appropriate outlets.

If religion enters policy debates on politics' terms, it gives up its claim to uniqueness, becoming one more interest group trapped within the limited alternatives offered by modern ideologies. To accept these alternatives would be to resolve the tension between religion and politics by surrender. It would abandon the cold, lonely marches of religion's border with politics for the warmth of the political capitol. I contend, on the other hand, that religion must maintain its claim to a truth higher than politics. This perspective does not mean that politics can or should judge that truth, only that religious claims should force politics to a higher level than it otherwise would discover. Its truth claims do not relegate religion to the private sphere. The proper ground of these claims is the public/private border, not the heartland of private or of public life.

This argument suggests that religious persons should approach politics from their particular faith perspectives, from their own truth-claims. Politics will water down those claims sufficiently without religious groups themselves attempting to find a lowest common set of religious or moral beliefs. Religious groups become properly political and place the necessary pressure on politics when they advocate their distinctive principles *on matters of public concern* and when they live faithfully their distinctive beliefs about the transpolitical.[11]

Religions should not promote all of their beliefs in political debate. Doing so confuses the territory of religion with that of politics. Rather, those religious beliefs and principles that most touch public concerns, for example, justice, freedom, respect for life, peace, the place of sin, death, and the meaning of human sociability, should enter political debate in order to draw politics beyond the level where it otherwise would settle. Privatization of religion is dangerous, because it allows politics itself to become privatized and self-absorbed. As George Armstrong Kelly observes, "If privatization has pushed religion out of the public sphere, it is currently turning politics into an I-Thou relationship or a sphere of indifference." [12] Reduced to administration and interests, politics becomes as secularized and squeezed of meaning as private religion. Politics without high principles is a dull but dangerous business for anyone not driven by consuming ambition, greed, or need for recognition.

What Politics Teaches Religion

But religion without politics is also dangerous. I have alluded previously to religious fanaticism. Messianism without a messiah sweeps all principle before it. Religious persons often divide the world into two camps, fellow believers and those outside the faith. Toward the former the appropriate attitude is familiarity and community, including both affectionate feelings and (at times) discipline. Attitudes toward the latter, however, include attempted conversion, conquest and enslavement, and withdrawal. Relationships with outsiders governed solely by their lack of faith allow no public bond between believers and nonbelievers. What remains are only the deadly, dichotomous categorizations: us and them, believers and heathens, friends and enemies.

Public life creates other possibilities. The first is "stranger." [13] The fellow believer is known as one of the group, and the heathen is known through stereotypes. The stranger, however, is mysterious and unknown. He may be one of us or one of them, a potential friend or enemy. Or, the most radical possibility of all, he may just be himself, different from us, but related nonetheless. Public life, especially in the form of politics, requires interaction with strangers. For politics is full of strangers, people with ideas, customs, interests, emotions, and beliefs different from, and sometimes at odds with, our own. Entry into a political relationship with strangers dispels some mystery but does not eliminate it. Strangers still remain different. Nevertheless, politics opens a middle camp between friends and enemies, and, because both friends and enemies trade with that camp, the world seems less black and white, the grounds of fanaticism less solid.

Indeed, politics requires everyone to spend some time among strangers and to discover their own strangeness. Politics is self-discovery as well as self-display. Believers who enter politics enter the strangers' camp and discover things about strangers and about themselves that alter their frame of reference and call for less singlemindedness, for more tolerance and civility. Ultimately, believers might even learn that they are strangers to themselves and that God is also a stranger, for the God completely known does not transcend human control. Politics can teach religion humility and the tolerance that is humility's natural partner. It may teach the believer the limits of his or her belief.[14]

Politics can teach religion how to live with pluralism. As religion can reconcile politics to mysterious forces beyond its control, so politics can reconcile religion to facticity, to the hard places against which the tide of religion crashes. Religious ideals meet recalcitrant political reality and the strangers who live there. The principles, values, excellences, and virtues of religious life cannot suffuse public or private life with the wave of a wand or a word of blessing. Use of coercion is always a temptation for frustrated virtue, a temptation to which even the most perceptive (witness Augustine) can succumb. In authoritarian, totalitarian, or oligarchic regimes, use of coercion finds ready justification. A democratic regime, however, supports resistance to imposed religious ideals, blunts the weapon of coercion, and teaches religion other methods for dissemination of belief. As William Penn suggested, coercion is the coarsest part of government; so political regimes restrict its availability.

When politics involves the encounter of strangers on a common ground where they must interact peaceably, it learns compromise. Compromise is a lesson religion too must learn, though it does not like the name and tries to find synonyms, such as "prudence" or "pastoral solutions." The full excellence of religious ideals is seldom achieved. As J. Budziszewski argues, "Real excellence is apt to be a rare item, more like leaven than like flour. Cultivating the excellences will always be of the first importance, but we should also be prepared to curb and channel the flows and eruptions of passion." [15] Compromise is one way, a distinctively political way, of resolving the tensions between religious ideals and recalcitrant facts.

This role for politics allows religion to be religion; it allows all religions to advance their views strongly. Religion entering politics should not be wishy-washy. But politics and the necessity of compromise force religious groups to recognize the plurality of the political world, especially the plurality of religious groups strongly advancing distinctive views. The point is not for religious groups to compromise their principles in order to enter the fray, but for politics to force compromise at the level of policy.[16] When religious groups recognize and acknowledge both politics as a form of public life and the recalcitrant facticity of political life, they can begin, not to change their principles, but to find ways of applying them to policy that are acceptable to other citizens. They can begin to learn political civility, tolerance, and the art of compromise. Observe the course of the Reverend Jerry Falwell in moderating his policy proposals on abortion and other agenda items of the New Religious Right from the late 1970s to the late 1980s.

In the previous section I used the Catholic bishops' pastoral letter on the economy to illustrate the contribution religion can make to politics in introducing high conceptions of justice into political debate. Let me use the same example to illustrate what political life can teach religion. The bishops' letter is particularly vulnerable to criticism in light of the social and economic realities of modern, postindustrial society. The pastoral letter does not address these realities creatively, nor does it reflect the limitations of social and economic resources for realizing the principles of justice.[17] The passionate concern for justice that is the bishops' special contribution must meet the social realities that are politics' special concern. Both are necessary for creative policy making.

There are two fundamental dangers of public religion: religious domination of public life and the affiliation of religion with political ideology. Both dangers stem from religious passion. The first occurs when religion is able to use government as a means for realizing its vision. The second occurs when religious passion is coopted (often willingly) by a political ideology and used for the ideology's ends.

The realities of participatory politics moderate the proclivity of government and political ideology to inflame or coopt, and sometimes to be coopted by, religious passion. First, politics tames religious passion for reasons suggested above. Passion must put on decorous clothes to appear in public. Moreover, religious passion encounters the seawall of interest group reality and of counterpassions in other religious and nonreligious groups. Religious passions must seek more moderate, tame expressions and more limited goals. The realities of pluralism make it less likely that government or ideologies will be able to enflame religious fervor or to be coopted by such emotions more than temporarily.[18] There are too many influences on the state for religion to dominate more than briefly.

This is as it should be. Religion should expect to be only one voice (though actually itself many) in political life. It can help to move policy in certain directions, but it cannot expect to determine the outcome of political debate.

One unfortunate, but unavoidable, consequence of the political taming of religion is that both good and bad religious passions are tempered. Politics is, in this sense, indiscriminate. Given politics' haphazard effect, what counts is the character of citizens. Ultimately, the people must separate the wheat from the chaff of religious ideals and passions.

There is no guarantee of popular virtue, but preservation of the good and discarding the bad finally depend upon it. The mechanisms of public life cannot make such judgments; they can only furnish the space, time, and civility needed for character to work. The many political devices for channeling passion known to the ancients and moderns are prone to fail, to lose sight of excellence.[19] Compromise itself cannot be a final ideal, for compromises must be judged better and worse. We come full circle from what politics teaches religion to what religion teaches politics. Religious vision can help to judge and call to account political compromise, keeping the aspiration toward excellence before citizen attention.

Conclusions

It seems to follow that, if religion is public in the ways I have specified and if it makes the political contributions I have described, then it should be admitted to political life on precisely the same terms as other groups. Yet an important consideration militates against this simple conclusion. Religion is fundamentally private as well as public. Religion is a distinct realm from politics. Inviting it too far into political territory runs the many risks of politicized religion and chances dilution of its distinctive qualities.

Religion should be not excluded from politics but kept at arm's length. The relationship between religion and politics should imitate that of partners in a dance of approach and flight, a ballet expressing the tension between attraction and repulsion. Neither partner must dominate, if the dance is to continue. Religion and politics challenge and test each other; that is their special dynamic.

Let me return to the metaphor of the border. What is vital is that religion and politics meet, not in the center of each other's territory, but at the border. This leaves sufficient mystery for mutual attraction. Religion beckons from the periphery for politics to come seek its ideals; politics cajoles religion to shed its unrealistic ideals and recognize the goods of plurality, civility, and tolerance. Such transactions across the border also produce just enough knowledge for mutual repulsion. Religion knows well the temptations of power.[20] Politics recognizes the fanaticism of religion and flees it.

Religion exists on a double border: the boundary between private and public life and the boundary with politics. Life on the border is never easy, but religion should remain there. To confront politics wholeheartedly, though not to enter it fully, constitutes its political mission. To abandon either private or public life is to betray its essence.

The lines of influence between religion and politics do not run one way. Politics, and culture generally, shapes religion as much as religion shapes politics. Not every political influence on religion is beneficial. Evidently, religion can learn the worst aspects of politics as well as the best. The point is that the debate about religion and politics, and the speculations of political theorists, have neglected the positive influences in each direction, the creative tensions characterizing this encounter.

Notes

1. Preface to the Frame of Government of Pennsylvania, quoted in Sydney E. Ahlstrom, *A Religious History of the American People* (Garden City, N.Y.: Doubleday Image, 1975), vol. 1, 166.
2. The perspective of this paragraph was suggested by H. Richard Niebuhr's discussion of the tension between Christ and culture, *Christ and Culture* (New York: Harper Colophon, 1975), esp. chap. 1.
3. Wilson Carey McWilliams, "The Bible in the American Political Tradition," in *Religion and Politics,* ed. Myron J. Aronoff, vol. 3 of *Political Anthropology* (New Brunswick, N.J.: Transaction Books, 1984), 19.
4. George Armstrong Kelly, *Politics and Religious Consciousness in America,* 1-2, passim.
5. Roland Robertson, "Church-State Relations and the World System," in *Church-State Relations: Tensions and Transitions,* ed. Thomas Robbins and Roland Robertson (New Brunswick, N.J.: Transaction Books, 1987), 50.
6. Hadley Arkes, *First Things* (Princeton: Princeton University Press, 1986), 5.

7. I do not contend that religious groups alone keep substantive, principled issues before the public. Nor do I contend that religious groups are the most important actors in this respect. Rather, my point is that religion can and should contribute by pushing politics to confront such principled issues, even though a democratic politics oriented toward compromise finds them disturbing.

8. United States Catholic Conference, *Economic Justice for All: Pastoral Letter on Catholic Social Teaching and the U.S. Economy* (Washington: United States Catholic Conference, 1986); Gerald M. Mara, "Poverty and Justice: The Bishops and Contemporary Liberalism," in *The Deeper Meaning of Economic Life: Critical Essays on the U.S. Catholic Bishops' Pastoral Letter on the Economy,* ed. R. Bruce Douglass (Washington, D.C.: Georgetown University Press, 1986), 157-178.

9. See Glenn Tinder, "Christianity and the Welfare State," unpublished paper. To say this is not, of course, to endorse Fawn Hall's theory of action outside the law.

10. Stanley Milgram, *Obedience to Authority* (New York: Harper & Row, 1974).

11. This perspective is similar to that advanced by Stanley Hauerwas, *A Community of Character* (Notre Dame, Ind.: University of Notre Dame Press, 1981), and *A Peaceable Kingdom* (Notre Dame, Ind.: University of Notre Dame Press, 1983). David Walsh makes similar points in "The Role of the Church in the Modern World," *Journal of Church and State* 29 (Winter 1987): 63-77.

12. Kelly, *Politics and Religious Consciousness,* 186.

13. On public life as the realm of strangers and its significance for religion, see Parker J. Palmer, *The Company of Strangers: Christians and the Renewal of America's Public Life* (New York: Crossroads, 1981).

14. On God as stranger, see Palmer, *Company of Strangers.* I argue not that humility and moderation are learned only in politics but that in regimes with a genuine public and political life politics is a readily available teacher.

15. J. Budziszewski, *The Resurrection of Nature* (Ithaca, N.Y.: Cornell University Press, 1986), 153.

16. With respect to the idea of politics welcoming the sharp advocacy of religious views, I am indebted to the remarks of Sen. John Danforth and Rep. Lindy Boggs during an interreligious forum on religion and politics at St. Alban's Church, Washington, D.C., March 17, 1987.

17. For criticism along these lines, see Henry Briefs, "The Limits of Scripture: Theological Imperatives and Economic Reality," in *The Deeper Meaning of Economic Life,* 57-96.

18. These points are difficult to prove conclusively, but the actual political behavior of American religion suggests their truth. Religious groups rise and fall in influence, and the virulence of their expression wanes as it breaks against the hard rock of competing interests and the labyrinthine ways of lawmaking.

19. See Budziszewski's account of these devices in *The Resurrection of Nature,* chap. 5.

20. The temptations of Christ, especially the third, are instructive in this respect. See Matthew 4:1-11. (In Luke 4:1-13 the most political temptation is the second.)

6. PRESBYTERIANS AS POLITICAL AMATEURS

Anne Motley Hallum

An article in the Reverend Jerry Falwell's monthly magazine, the *Fundamentalist Journal,* recently boasted that "The Mainline Is Becoming the Sideline." [1] Mainline denominations, which include the Presbyterian, Episcopalian, Methodist, and United Church of Christ churches, have been challenged by their own loss of members coupled with the ascendency of conservative fundamentalism and Roman Catholicism. From a religious and ecumenical perspective, a shift from one denomination to another is of only passing significance, but surveys indicate that many members are simply dropping out of established churches altogether rather than moving to other denominations. [2] Thus, the concern for mainliners becomes not only a certain rivalry with the fundamentalists, but also the decline of interest in religion among the current membership.

Scholarly assessments highlight the seriousness of this trend for denominations once considered the stalwarts of middle- and upper-class America. James Reichley refers to the situation as "mainline Protestants in crisis"; Benton Johnson in a 1986 article concludes that the "liberal Protestant community remains mired in depression"; and historian William Hutchison states that liberal Protestantism "has become a minority movement and must accept sectarian status." [3]

The Presbyterian Church (PCUSA), for instance, has lost fully one-fourth of its total membership since the late 1960s. The denomination remains a significant national institution with just over three million adherents. Yet in 1985 another 43,000 members left, continuing the downward trend. [4] Many long-time Presbyterians insist that the political activism of the church leadership has become so radical that members have no choice but to leave.

In reality, the precise reasons certain members are deserting Presbyterianism are varied and difficult to measure. Nevertheless, this article examines the political activism thesis because it reveals much about the attitude of a church leadership that sometimes seems bent on self-destruction. We will focus on a recent political debate among

Presbyterians, examining how the established church differs from other political groups. Finally, options for the Presbyterian leadership—and for other mainline Protestants—will be clarified.

One political distinction should be made before we progress further. The PCUSA, as a mainline Protestant denomination, endorses the social activism approach to politics. This approach is defined as the promotion of a variety of social and political causes by church activists without sliding into direct intervention in campaigns or legislation.[5] This middle-of-the-road strategy protects the tax exempt status of the denomination but ironically tends to exacerbate political tensions within the church. This occurs because the church is not involved in the pragmatic tasks of winning an election, lobbying to pass specific legislation, or even enhancing the political influence of the organization. Rather, the political role left to the social activist church is that of political amateur.

The concept of political amateurism has been used in analysis of the weakening of the political party system.[6] However, it is also a revealing concept in the present analysis. The *style* of the political amateur stresses uncompromising statements of principle even at the risk of losing a broad base of support or long-term participation. Certainly the resolutions and protest rallies of many liberal Protestant churches demonstrate a "purist" dedication to principle, which is reinforced by religious beliefs. George Chauncey, the Washington lobbyist for the PCUSA, notes that faith provides the motivation and purpose for engaging in politics, as well as a distinctive style of political action:

> Christians ought to be in the vanguard of those asking the hard questions. Confidence in God's love and grace . . . should free us to take risks, to support hopeless causes, even to fail. Some people are compulsively careful in their politics. . . . Their main preoccupation is with what is "politically feasible." They would rather stay out of the fight than lose . . . But surely, faithfulness to the cause of peace and justice rather than the feasibility of political proposals ought to be the primary concern of believers.[7]

This statement is a clear rejection of political professionalism and an endorsement of political amateurism, a stance we will now examine more closely.

A Resistance Church?

In 1986 a remarkable document was distributed to 202 local presbyteries, 1,400 requesting congregations, and the top governing body of the PCUSA, the General Assembly.[8] The document is entitled *Presbyterians and Peacemaking: Are We Now Called to Resistance?*

The General Assembly's Advisory Council of Church and Society commissioned it as a study paper for the whole church. In June 1988, the council presented a policy statement based on the document to the General Assembly.

Even in this preliminary stage, the essays contain the most radical recommendations made to date for the institutional Presbyterian church. The paper discusses such topics as "just war" theory and nuclear weapons; U.S. militarism; and the religious tradition of resistance to government authority. After political and theological analysis, the authors call for a variety of responses to U.S. policies: the withholding of war taxes; occupational withdrawal from nuclear weapons industries; noncooperation with the military, including disassociation with ROTC programs and military chaplains; and civilly disobedient protests. Significantly, the authors do not simply address the individual consciences of church members but urge the General Assembly to provide corporate encouragement for such actions as well as financial support. They defend their aggressive position by noting that since 1945 General Assemblies have called on the U.S. government at least twelve times to seek arms reduction and disarmament. Such resolutions, letter-writing campaigns, and petitions to government officials have had negligible effect. Therefore, the authors now feel compelled to recommend a resistance stance for the Presbyterian denomination.[9]

The strongest response to the study paper has come from a small organization called Presbyterians for Democracy and Religious Freedom (PDRF). The PDRF published and circulated a study paper in rebuttal to *Presbyterians and Peacemaking* which concluded with instructions on how congregations could repudiate the resistance recommendations.[10] The PDRF booklet was written by ten Presbyterian scholars who attack in strong terms the theology, political analysis, and recommendations of the original paper. But whereas *Presbyterians and Peacemaking* was commissioned and funded by official church structures, the PDRF operates outside the official church, and its study paper was financed by donations and receipts from the sale of ordered copies.[11]

Many of the PDRF articles are essays on foreign policy. For example, the authors argue for the need for nuclear deterrence, deny that the U.S. is militaristic, list the atrocities of Stalinism and communism, and criticize the position of pacifism. They often begin with assumptions about U.S. policy and totalitarianism that are so at odds with the assumptions of the liberal position as to be almost totally unpersuasive.

The language of both studies is inflammatory and does not appear to be an attempt to persuade or even educate church members. Rather, the authors are apparently seeking to mobilize those who already agree with their basic political beliefs. In the manner of political amateurism, they eschew compromise and accommodation while sharply articulating the divisive issues.

The debate between supporters of the PDRF and those advancing the Advisory Council's paper is a microcosm of broader dissension within the mainline Protestant churches. In fact, many members of the PDRF originally met as members of the interdenominational Institute on Religion and Democracy (IRD).[12] The IRD is a controversial mainline Protestant organization that has adopted the narrow agenda of promoting anticommunism in the churches, and it often stands opposed to the established liberal hierarchy.

Reichley and others have already documented the political dissension that exists between the Protestant leadership and the majority of their moderate or conservative members. In 1984, for example, exit polls indicated that 32 percent of Presbyterians voted for Walter Mondale and 68 percent voted for Ronald Reagan. A survey in that year of 3,700 Presbyterians found that twice as many church ministers as laypersons labeled themselves liberal as opposed to conservative. Eight times as many clergy in specialized ministries (higher education, church bureaucracy, and so on) said they were liberal rather than conservative.[14] In regard to the Presbyterian "resistance" paper, only 7 percent of members polled approved of the specific recommendation to withhold income tax payments equivalent to the military's percentage of the national budget. Eighty-six percent of the denomination's members disapproved.[15]

The Church Is Not a Democracy

In the face of such figures, in combination with membership losses of 40,000 to 50,000 each year, why does the Presbyterian leadership persist in adopting liberal political positions offensive to many Presbyterians? The 1986 General Assembly, for instance, condemned the militarization of space, strongly opposed aid to the contras in Nicaragua, offered aid to the illegal sanctuary movement for Central American refugees, and passed other resolutions regarding political events in India, Korea, Lebanon, and South Africa.[16] We have already noted that the resistance paper is the most liberal—some would say radical—position yet put forth by the church. The recommendations were ultimately rejected by the full 1988 General Assembly, yet the paper itself indicates that the church elite are not intimidated by controversy or a shrinking denomination.

In the writings of the liberal hierarchy, little if any reference is made to the loss of members, whereas the PDRF opposition is quite blunt: "Already thousands of Presbyterians are snapping their pocket-books firmly shut and edging toward the exits, suspecting that their church has political bats in its belfry. Do we need to convince them totally? The temporal health of the church is not everything, but it is something." [17]

This is not to suggest that conservative activists care more about the denomination than liberals, but they are using the statistics and the current conservative mood of the nation as one argument in their case. However, if PDRF adherents come to dominate the church hierarchy, many liberal members and church professionals might correspondingly feel compelled to leave. Both ends of this polarity are currently making divisive political statements—one group from within the official church structure and one from outside.

The rationale for the self-defeating stance of the liberal Presbyterian leadership provides a special challenge for political scientists. Kenneth Wald suggests that the decision by clergy to be activists began in the 1960s with civil rights, Vietnam, and social justice issues, and was a strategic move to be relevant and attractive to young, progressive members.[18] Two problems arise relative to this somewhat cynical interpretation. One is that social activism by Protestants is not recent. Rather, religious historians have noted that "throughout their history the mainline denominations of connectional Calvinism have been deeply involved in political life." [19] This involvement seldom, if ever, included the majority of Protestants and was restrained by affirmation of the doctrine of separation of church and state. Still, Presbyterians made their presence known in support of the Revolution, opposition to the War of 1812, support for temperance, sabbath observance, and (for northern Presbyterians) abolition of slavery. As early as 1909, missionary work in the Congo brought Presbyterians into the international arena in widespread protest against colonial atrocities.[20] True, the General Assembly considers more political issues now than in the past, but this could reflect the complexity and interrelatedness of the modern world. It is not simply a trend that began in the 1960s.

Second, and most obviously, if Presbyterian leaders became activists to attract young liberal members and remain in touch with societal trends, why have they not been as savvy in the 1980s in pursuit of conservative members? The national conservative direction has been as evident in the 1980s as was the liberal mood in the late 1960s and 1970s. Yet Presbyterian leaders have become *more* adamant in their leftist positions and are losing members in greater numbers than at any time in church history. Opportunism is not a sufficient explanation for the motives behind the clergy's political outspokenness.

Presbyterian minister and author Richard Hutcheson asserts that "a managerial revolution" in the mainline denominations took place in the 1970s, which explains their unpopular liberalism. Structural reorganizations put church bureaucrats in charge of governing bodies such as the General Assembly. If church managers control the budget, communication channels, and lengthy denominational agendas, they also are likely to control the pronouncements of the annual General Assembly meetings.[21] Hutcheson's view that the managerial mentality tends to be secular and liberal is debatable, but his assertion that many Protestant governing bodies are not strictly representative is valid.

In the General Assembly, for instance, the laity are allocated 50 percent of the delegates' seats although they represent 99 percent of Presbyterians. The remaining 50 percent of delegate slots go to the other 1 percent: Presbyterian clergy, who generally take more liberal political positions. Thus, liberal church staff shape the agenda and provide position papers to an assembly in which their viewpoint is already disproportionately present. Political scientist Whitfield Ayres offers a political science solution to this biased organization. He suggests structural reform with proportional representation of the laity and more lay participation in preparing assembly resources.[22]

The Presbyterian leadership and staff sometimes react to this suggestion with the practical consideration that laypeople have careers outside the church. They would not be able to devote sufficient time and study to church issues for wise decisions to result, and therefore guidance from clergy and staff is needed. In addition, the church hierarchy often points proudly to the constitutional duties of the General Assembly. The church constitution clearly states that delegates (presbyters) in governing bodies "are not simply to reflect the will of the people, but rather to seek together to find and respect the will of Christ." [23] Dean Lewis, the director of the Advisory Council on Church and Society, elaborates on this point: "If we waited on every issue until there was consensus in the church, the General Assembly would never say anything about anything important. The task of a governing body is to try to find out what obedience to God requires, not what people want." [24] Compare this statement with Edmund Burke's description of the concept of trustee representation in government: "Your representative owes you, not his industry only, but his judgment, and he betrays, instead of serving you, if he sacrifices it to your opinion." [25]

Presbyterians have historically stressed the importance of an educated clergy, and they also demonstrate an elitist predisposition in the makeup of the General Assembly and in their preference for trustee rather than delegate theories of representation. Thus, the Presbyterian

hierarchy would not dispute Hutcheson's claim of managerial dominance but would point to the traditional and constitutional practices of
Presbyterian governing bodies. Most mainline denominations have
never claimed to operate as democracies. In any case, Hutcheson's
organizational emphasis is an explanation of *how* controversial resolutions are passed by the General Assembly but does not address *why*
such positions are taken in the first place.

Why Political Amateurs?

One reason for the ideologically extreme positions of the current
leadership already has been mentioned. Protestant social activists
endorse strict institutional separation between church and state, but
they feel a religious obligation to be involved in political and social
issues. Rather than playing the role of "professionals" who compromise
and make deals to win political victories, social activists play the part of
"outside agitators" and, because this is a limited role, they often play it
as noisily as possible.

However, the underlying frustration with the limitations of this
stance is evident in the Presbyterian resistance paper. After citing
numerous General Assembly declarations and programs for arms
reduction, the authors ask, "How long can we continue to bear witness
and seek change in the familiar ways while the nuclear arms race goes
on and on?" [26] They discuss the importance of symbolic witnessing for
peace but long for political effectiveness. They write of the overriding
importance of being faithful without expectation of success but advocate
forming coalitions with peace groups and adopting "politically astute
strategies for impacting public policies." [27]

The dilemma for liberal social activists is clear. Denominational
resolutions can be passed without much dissension from conservative
members and without much effect on national politics. When the
church leaders experiment with more radical strategies for engaging in
politics, they arouse the opposition within the church. The denomination then becomes weaker politically because of the obvious lack of
political cohesion and the gradual loss of members. At this point, the
liberal leadership denies the need for consensus and asserts that they
are speaking *to* the church, not *for* the church. However, risky political
endeavors require not only commitment but some measure of consensus
in order to be meaningful. Martin Luther King's successful model of
civil disobedience is often cited by mainline leaders, but King's
leadership came at a time when a consensus for change was already
present among blacks. The 1955 Montgomery bus boycott by 40,000
black citizens was set in motion by the churches in two days!

Thus, the social activism stance itself forces church leaders into an amateurish position in which they have limited effectiveness, whether they choose to be mildly reformist or dramatically radical. To find the rationale for their persistence in the face of such discouragement, we must turn to theology. An intriguing article by sociologist Benton Johnson focuses on the writings of Reinhold Niebuhr during the 1930s as a turning point for liberal Protestantism.[28] Niebuhr gave the liberal churches a sense of mission in his powerful call for Christians to aid the politically oppressed peoples of the world. He combined this call with a scathing criticism of middle-class values and a preoccupation with social sin. Protestant intellectuals adopted both elements of Niebuhrian thought wholeheartedly. In the present analysis, note the unrelenting self-criticism in the theological interpretation of "enemy" found in *Presbyterians and Peacemaking:* "Perhaps the key biblical insight is that we are our own worst enemy. The sin is in us. The chief builders of walls and hostility are ourselves. Perhaps we are even God's worst enemy as we pervert God's humanizing intention for the world into a rigid division of the world into friends and enemies." [29]

Many liberal Protestant leaders, however, add a crucial element to Niebuhr's theology which intensifies their social activist commitment: a sense of martyrdom sustained by belief in divine grace.[30] They acknowledge universal sinfulness but feel they still can take actions against sin in the world because all are forgiven by God's grace. Niebuhr's recognition of the pervasiveness of sin led him to be a Christian realist, recommending *effective* political action, not symbolic acts of risk and sacrifice. Since sin is inescapable, Niebuhr felt that Christians may as well engage in selective sinning in order to prevent greater evils on earth. Thus, for example, Niebuhr provided justification for the nuclear arms race as a necessary evil, whereas many social activists in the church today protest the existence of nuclear weapons as a matter of religious principle. The effect of their protest is not as important as being faithful in their actions regardless of personal consequences. Consider the martyrdom inherent in the following biblical interpretation by a professor of theology:

> The Gospel suggests that we locate the ultimate battle-line *wherever obedience to the commands of Jesus arouses the most violent hostilities* . . . the devaluation of wealth, the liberation of the helpless, the scorn for national security . . . the love for enemies, the repudiation of violence, fearless facing of death, unwavering trust in God. [31] (Emphasis added)

Choices for Liberal Protestants

This brief look at theology reveals certain possibilities for the future of liberal Protestantism, which we will now examine.

First, church leaders may continue the present course of political activism, even at the risk of offending many members and eventually becoming a "marginal church" like the Quakers and Unitarians.[32] This is the path of least resistance for many leaders because they already have control of hierarchical structures and, more importantly, because it fits the theological concept of faithfulness to God regardless of the personal consequences. In a few optimistic writings, liberal Christians postulate that political activism is at the forefront of a dramatic renewal in the church.[33] Exciting developments *are* occurring in the liberal church, particularly in the rise of liberation theology in Third World countries. But in the United States, the polarization surrounding the "resistance" paper we have seen in the Presbyterian church does not presage renewal in that denomination. In addition to fruitless political debate between two extreme groups, the rhetoric often spills over into theological disputes, and common ground is increasingly difficult to find.

A second possibility for strengthening mainline Protestantism is for the liberal leadership to confront its conservative opposition in the spirit of political compromise. It could, for example, support President Ronald Reagan's recent initiatives in arms negotiation with the Soviets and drop calls for unilateral disarmament. Perhaps a restructuring of governing bodies to allow more lay representation would result in such accommodation in political resolutions. Before we proceed further with this suggestion, let us concede that the groans from the church leadership are almost audible. That most mainline Protestant leaders reject the role of political professionalism should be evident by now. For them, the task of the church is to offer a prophetic critique of the state and to ask fundamental questions about policies, not to strike political deals. Even when the clergy express a desire for political effectiveness, they seldom recommend the perhaps obvious tactic of political compromise. Political amateurism is inherently controversial. But the stubborn, moral insights of the church are perhaps valuable in a time when political pragmatism usually crowds out idealism.

Is it possible, then, to retain social activism in the mainline church, however amateurish, without crippling the church itself? At this point we need to look more closely at why members are leaving. Studies show that the primary reason for membership decline is the failure of the grown children of mainline members to affiliate with their parents' church. A few older members are leaving because of political activism, but most of them remain loyal in spite of their complaints.[34] Reasons for the lack of commitment by a younger generation are beyond the scope of this article, but young members appear to be drifting away from religion rather than leaving in protest. That is, the decline in affiliation is caused not by what the church is doing but by what it is failing to do for members.

If this analysis is correct, the Protestant leadership does not need to ignore the call to political activism that they heed so fervently. However, the clergy must also be attentive to the private needs of church members. These needs include such things as pastoral counseling, meaningful symbolism, spiritualism, a sense of community, and guidance for modern lifestyles. Such a shift in emphasis could begin in the seminaries, which now tend to be sterile and overly intellectual.[35] Well-educated clergy often criticize middle-class values and call on members to make sacrifices, without stressing the more positive aspects of religion. Surely the task of faithfulness to God requires more than sacrifice; it also requires support, spiritual vitality, and self-confidence.

The General Assembly of the Presbyterian church recently adopted an evangelism program entitled "New Age Dawning." The program is designed to assess and try to meet the needs of modern Americans. The church is not abandoning its political involvement by any means, but it is finally recognizing an additional calling closer to home. Whether a new age is beginning for troubled mainline Protestants remains to be seen.

Notes

1. Quoted in "From 'Mainline' to Sideline," *Newsweek*, December 22, 1986, 55.
2. Ibid.
3. A. James Reichley, *Religion in American Public Life* (Washington, D.C.: Brookings Institution, 1985), 267; Benton Johnson, "Liberal Protestantism: End of the Road?" *Annals of the American Academy of Political and Social Sciences* 480 (July 1985): 40; Quoted in "From 'Mainline' to Sideline," 54.
4. Richard G. Hutcheson, "Leaving the Mainstream," in *Peacemaking? Or Resistance?* ed. Ted M. Dorman (Nashville: Presbyterians for Democracy and Religious Freedom, 1986), 53; and Reichley, *Religion in American Public Life*, 278.
5. Reichley, *Religion in American Public Life*, 3-4.
6. David E. Price, *Bringing Back the Parties* (Washington, D.C.: CQ Press, 1984), 25-32.
7. George A. Chauncey, "Faith and Politics: The Differences," in *Reformed Faith and Politics*, ed. Ronald H. Stone (Washington, D.C.: University Press of America, 1983), 28-29.
8. "General Assembly Report," *Presbyterian Survey*, July/August 1987, 31.
9. Dana W. Wilbanks and Ronald H. Stone, *Presbyterians and Peacemaking: Are We Now Called to Resistance?* (New York: Advisory Council on Church and Society, 1985), esp. 2-3 and 48-57.
10. Dorman, *Peacemaking?*, 66-69.

11. "Study Paper on Resistance Stirs Support and Opposition," *Presbyterian Survey,* April 1987, 34.
12. "Chapter 9 Organizations," *Presbyterian Survey,* April 1987, 30.
13. Reichley, *Religion in American Public Life,* 275; Kenneth D. Wald, *Religion and Politics in the United States* (New York: St. Martin's Press, 1987), 244-246; and Jeffrey K. Hadden, *The Gathering Storm in the Churches* (Garden City, N.Y.: Doubleday, 1969).
14. Q. Whitfield Ayres, "Disagreeing about the General Assembly," *Presbyterian Survey,* May 1987, 28.
15. Hutcheson, "Leaving the Mainstream," 54.
16. *Minutes of the 198th General Assembly of the Presbyterian Church USA: Part I, Journal* (New York: Office of the General Assembly, 1986).
17. Ervin S. Duggan, "Presbyterians and Peacemaking: Are We Now Called to Be Irresponsible?" in *Peacemaking?* 13.
18. Wald, *Religion in American Public Life,* 245.
19. Louis Weeks, "Faith and Political Action in American Presbyterianism, 1776-1918," in *Reformed Faith and Politics,* ed. Ronald H. Stone (Washington, D.C.: University Press of America, 1983), 102; and John T. McNeill, *History and Character of Calvinism* (New York: Oxford University Press, 1960).
20. Weeks, "American Presbyterianism," 111.
21. Richard G. Hutcheson, *Mainline Churches and the Evangelicals: A Challenging Crisis?* (Atlanta, Ga.: John Knox Press, 1981), 42.
22. Ayres, "Disagreeing about the General Assembly," 29-30.
23. *The Constitution of the Presbyterian Church (U.S.A.): Part II, Book of Order* (New York: Office of the General Assembly), G-4.0301d.
24. "Study Paper on Resistance," *Presbyterian Survey,* April 1987, 35.
25. Quoted in David V. Edwards, *The American Political Experience,* 3d ed. (Englewood Cliffs, N.J.: Prentice Hall, 1985), 314.
26. Wilbanks and Stone, *Presbyterians and Peacemaking,* 4.
27. Ibid., 39.
28. Johnson, "Liberal Protestantism," 44-49.
29. Wilbanks and Stone, *Presbyterians and Peacemaking,* 23.
30. See Bill Kellerman, "Apologist of Power," *Sojourners,* March 1987, 14-20, for a liberal critique of Niebuhr.
31. Paul S. Minear, "My Peace I Give to You," in *Reformed Faith and Politics,* 47.
32. Hutcheson, "Leaving the Mainstream," 52-55.
33. Jim Wallis, ed., *The Rise of Christian Conscience* (New York: Harper & Row, 1987).
34. Johnson, "Liberal Protestantism," 42.
35. Interviews with Janet Parker, Princeton Theological Seminary; Dr. Jack Walchenbach and Rev. John S. McCall, First Presbyterian Church, DeLand, Florida, August 14 and 20, 1987.

7. BISHOPS AS POLITICAL LEADERS

Mary Hanna

With the recent promulgation of the bishops' pastoral letters on war and peace and on the U.S. economy, the fact that American Catholic bishops are more and more acting as political leaders has to be acknowledged. It therefore seems appropriate that we look at them in the terms we ordinarily apply to political leaders.

Political scientists have devised a wide variety of approaches and criteria to define and measure political leadership. Most of these fall into two broad categories: those that focus on personal characteristics of a leader or leaders, and those that focus on the contextual situation against which leadership is played out. Scholars who take the former approach analyze personality traits, socioeconomic background data, career patterns, the degree of congruency between leaders and their constituents, and so on. Scholars who take the latter approach examine political leadership in terms of the institutional and organizational framework in which it must operate—the constraining and catalyzing effects of ideology, culture, law, and particular political institutions and processes. Aspects of both of these approaches can be applied to an analysis of bishops as political leaders.

The Context

American Catholics and their church had come of age by the early 1960s. No longer a largely working-class people encapsulated in the Catholic ethnic ghettos of our big cities, they had risen steadily in educational and economic status, especially in the postwar period, with its G.I. Bill.[1] The suspicion and hostility with which Catholics had long been viewed by many of their Protestant fellow citizens had also diminished greatly, as John F. Kennedy's election demonstrated. By the 1960s, therefore, conditions were ripe for increased Catholic activism. The fact that the 1960s was such an activist decade in general—a time when many new groups entered the political arena and when widespread participation became a rallying cry—made acceptance of intensified Catholic political activity easier.

These changes in the political culture in general facilitated church activism when contextual circumstances impelling political activity took place within the Catholic Church. The first important development was the new ideology that came out of the Second Vatican Council, the great assembly of all the world's bishops summoned by Pope John XXIII in 1962. Vatican II, which met over a four-year period, was one of the most active councils in the church's entire history. It reformed liturgy and ritual, but it also moved the church into far greater participation in social and political affairs. The council stressed that the church as an institution and Catholics in general had a positive obligation to involve themselves in the problems of the world; it issued a series of documents that denounced various political, social, and economic ills—poverty, illiteracy, political repression—as morally wrong under Christian doctrine; and it urged Catholics to work to alleviate them. A new political movement, if it is to emerge and act, needs an ideological basis, both to catalyze it and to give it a framework around which to develop positions. The speeches and documents of the Second Vatican Council, and the accompanying encyclicals of Popes John XXIII and Paul VI, provided the ideological framework necessary for a far more activist Catholic Church and a far more activist hierarchy.

This ideological development catalyzed the church as a whole and the bishops in particular. One New York bishop, musing on the effects of the council, said, "We had been too isolated from reality. . . . We were focused on eternal life. . . . The Second Vatican Council stressed the great obligation we have to address ourselves to the needs of the world." Another bishop stressed the way in which council documents provided ideological principles for himself and his fellow bishops, calling the documents "licenses," and "blueprints for action." [2]

The importance of this new ideological development is also evident in the actions bishops have taken. The very first line of the bishops' letter on war and peace is a quotation from a Vatican Council document on modern warfare. In the pastoral on the U.S. economy, the bishops explain that they were moved to act on issues so far outside what many would think their responsibility by the Vatican Council's insistence that Christian communities have a responsibility "to analyze with objectivity the situation which is proper to their own country, to shed on it the light of the Gospel's unalterable words and to draw principles of reflection, norms of judgment and directives for action from the social teaching of the Church." [3] The hierarchy has also attempted to link the church's anti-abortion efforts to its peace and justice issues by advocating what Cardinal Bernardin calls the philosophy of the "seamless garment": opposition to anything that ends, demeans, or diminishes human life. The bishops' seamless garment approach is directly tied to the council's principles calling for a broad definition of what the right to life entails.[4]

If Catholic political activism had rested on the basis of ideology alone, it might have disappeared along with many of the other movements of the 1960s. Instead, Catholic activism continued, and the bishops themselves actually came more and more to act as political leaders, in large part because they set up an institutional framework that facilitated political activity.

American Catholic bishops had had a small-scale national organization since World War I, the National Catholic Welfare Conference (NCWC). This attempt at a national organization was weak, however. The NCWC had only a small staff and was poorly financed. Its existence was always precarious, since some American bishops and much of the Vatican Curia viewed it with suspicion—as an attempt to set up a national church and to undercut the ties between individual bishops and the pope.

In 1966, acting on a Vatican Council decree calling for national councils through which bishops could "jointly exercise their pastoral office to promote the greater good which the Church offers mankind," the bishops set up a much stronger national organization. Dissolving the old NCWC, they erected in its place on January 1, 1967, the National Conference of Catholic Bishops/United States Catholic Conference (NCCB/USCC). These two agencies are vital to the political role the bishops are now playing. They provide intense interaction among the bishops themselves, give them experience in dealing on a regular basis with all kinds of political as well as religious issues, and furnish them with a pool of professionally trained experts to help them research problems, draw up policy statements, and communicate their concerns to the general public and to government officials.

The National Conference of Catholic Bishops is the national organization of all the bishops in the country. Under its aegis the bishops meet together every November for discussions of political and social, as well as pastoral, problems and for joint decision making. At their 1983 meeting the bishops passed the letter on war and peace, and at their 1986 meeting they approved the economics letter. At other national meetings, the bishops have condemned capital punishment, called for a national boycott in support of Cesar Chavez's United Farm Workers union, and urged amnesty for Vietnam War resisters and deserters.

As important as the annual meetings is the fact that the NCCB is a permanent, year-round organization. The bishops elect their own president and other officers by secret ballot. The organization also has a dense network of committees of bishops that meet regularly. The NCCB today has twenty-six standing committees, many with jurisdictions encompassing social and political issues as well as religious and internal church affairs. The human values committee, for example, meets with scientists to explore the relationship between religion and science. The Church in Latin America committee is concerned with evangelization but also with the problems of poverty and peace in that troubled region.

In addition to the standing committees, there are currently twenty-one ad hoc committees. These are largely concerned with social and political issues. The migration and tourism committee, for example, in 1986 was involved in evaluating both the sanctuary movement and the new immigration bill then before Congress. The committee on the moral evaluation of deterrence is examining progress on arms control and the president's Strategic Defense Initiative ("Star Wars") program.

The committees meet periodically throughout the year. Cardinal Bernardin told the November 1986 bishops' conference that his deterrence committee was holding day-long meetings once each month. While it was preparing its economics pastoral, the ad hoc committee on Catholic social teaching and the U.S. economy held twenty-two days of hearings alone, not counting the time the bishop-members spent together writing and considering the three drafts the letter went through. One hundred and ninety-five of the 288 bishops in the church in 1986 served on at least one NCCB/USCC committee; many had served on several. The bishops serving on these committees conduct investigations, report to their brother bishops, and propose policies for the American church. This means that bishops today, through their own organization, become acquainted with one another and knowledgeable about various subject areas in a way unavailable to most of their predecessors.

The bishops can also draw on their own professional staff for help—the United States Catholic Conference, their "operational secretariat." The USCC performs research, liaison, educational, communication, and administrative tasks on a year-round basis under the direction of the officers of the NCCB.

Although the Catholic Church historically had been led almost entirely by clerics with seminary educations, the bishops, from the beginning in 1966, staffed the USCC with highly trained professionals, many of them with advanced degrees from the country's most prestigious secular universities. In an interview, Ronald Krietemeyer, USCC director for domestic social development, explained that the influx of professionals was vital to the bishops. "To put Vatican II into practice, you needed people with specific knowledge—theologians, but others as well, liturgists, religious educators, fiscal managers, group process specialists. The bishops *needed* technicians to effect renewal." [5]

The USCC is divided into three major departments: communications; education; and social development and world peace, for which the mandate is almost entirely social and political. The department is specifically designed to help the bishops develop policies and programs involved with economic development, peace, and justice issues. The social development and world peace division epitomizes the new professionalism to come into the church with the establishment of the NCCB/ USCC. The division's director, J. Bryan Hehir, studied at Harvard under both Henry Kissinger and Stanley Hoffman. Ronald Krietemeyer, director of its domestic policy sector, holds master's degrees in both ethics and public policy from the University of Minnesota. The adviser on East Asian and European political issues is Edward Doherty, who served for years with the U.S. State Department. The bishops who wrote the peace letter and the economics letter drew heavily on this division: Hehir served as chief of staff for the war and peace letter, for example, and Krietemeyer as chief of staff for the economics letter. The USCC as a whole has a professional staff of almost fifty people, including public relations specialists and government lobbyists. In 1986, the NCCB/ USCC had a budget of $26,582,848.[6] For years the budget of its NCWC predecessor was under $125,000.

Any political scientist can understand the importance of this kind of organizational development to a political leadership role. The bishops, now armed with an ideology insisting upon political activism, set up an organization designed to facilitate that activism by providing themselves with a national assembly and forum; specialized committees organized around specific sets of issues, just as congressional committees are organized; and a professional staff to help design policy, publicize that policy, and administer programs.

Personal Characteristics

Although an ideological framework and an institutional structure were in place by the late 1960s and would later become important in the politicization of the hierarchy, bishops were not in the forefront of Catholic political activity when it first erupted in the late 1960s and early 1970s.

Catholic political activism first burst on the American public's attention through the nuns, priests, and young laypeople who were suddenly marching in civil rights demonstrations, burning their draft cards, leading protests of the urban poor, and organizing boycotts to support Chavez's union. Not the bishops, but priests and laypeople like the Berrigan brothers, Father James Groppi, Cesar Chavez, and Dorothy Day were the leaders of the Catholic political activism of the 1960s, at least by public perception.

These "prophets" were quickly joined and eventually subsumed by the "experts." Rising Catholic social, economic, and educational achievement levels meant that a large pool of highly educated, professionally trained young Catholics was available just as the Vatican Council declared that Catholics had an obligation to get involved in the problems of the world. In the late 1960s and early 1970s, this new Catholic educated class flooded and transformed traditional church organizations and created new ones, most with political and social as well as religious goals. Their influence, for a while, was so great that when I began my interviews in 1973 a priest cautioned me, "Interview bishops to find out what bishops are like, but don't think that's where the power is. . . . Influence and power lie with the professionals who aid them." [7]

If the 1960s was the decade of the "prophet" and the 1970s the decade of the "expert," however, the 1980s has become the decade of the bishops. The words and actions of the bishops now dominate the news, and these clerics now provide the most demonstrable political leadership in the American Catholic world. This seems clear from the reactions of both the media and political leaders to the bishops' letters on war and peace and the economy and from an examination of the continuing struggle over abortion and the developing conflict over other sexual issues—AIDS, homosexual rights, and biogenetics, for example. During our interview last year, Krietemeyer remarked, "They [the bishops] don't believe any more that the experts are the descendents of the four evangelists." The change came about, in his opinion, because the bishops themselves are now "more and more expert in leadership, coordination, communications."

The bishops had to learn to use their new institutional arrangements and to accustom themselves to the idea of political activity. Perhaps even more important, before political leadership could develop in the hierarchy a new generation of bishops had to come to power in the church. This happened in the 1980s. Half of all the bishops who voted on the war and peace pastoral in 1983 came to their bishoprics after the end of the Vatican Council in 1965. More than two-thirds of those voting on the economics letter in 1986 had been appointed since 1972.

We do not have the necessary data to do a political-psychological study of the bishops, à la James Barber. We do have demographic and career pattern data, however. Analysis of these kinds of data demonstrates that the new generation of bishops is much better adapted to the political role than were bishops earlier in the century. These men had been formed in large part by the often narrow subculture of an earlier, immigrant, ghettoized, working-class American Catholicism. They were largely educated in seminaries—sometimes of poor quality given the church's limited resources—and their exposure to general American society was further limited by the fact that most spent their priestly lives encased in their diocese's own administrative apparatus.

The new generation of bishops differs from its predecessors in age, ethnicity, education, experience, and outlook. The new breed of bishop was formed by the Vatican Council and by the tumultuous decade of the 1960s. These bishops benefited both from the upward mobility and acceptance Catholics had achieved in American society and from the council's insistence that the church and churchmen should be involved in the world.

Bishops today are somewhat younger than their predecessors, in part because Pope Paul VI instituted a mandatory retirement age of seventy-five for bishops and in part because men now seem to be appointed to the hierarchy at somewhat earlier ages. As recently as 1953, diocesan bishops in the United States averaged sixty-four years of age. The bishops who voted on the nuclear war letter in 1983 and the economics letter in 1986 averaged sixty years of age, and a tenth of the 288 bishops in the United States in 1986 were under fifty. The trend toward a younger hierarchy should continue, since 38 percent of all the new bishops appointed from 1983 to 1986 were in their forties.

The hierarchy has also become more ethnically diverse. For a hundred years, from roughly the time of the Civil War until after the Vatican Council, the American hierarchy was what men I interviewed called "an Irish Catholic Club." This began to change only after the Vatican Council, and particularly after 1970. A comparison of the American hierarchy in 1953 and in 1986 shows immediately a much higher number today of Italian and Slavic names. Even more dramatic is the presence now of Hispanic and black bishops. In 1986, the American church had ten black bishops; only one had been appointed before 1970, four were appointed in the 1970s, and five in the 1980s. It had eighteen Hispanic bishops, all appointed since 1970.[8] At its November 1986 meeting, the NCCB welcomed the first native American bishop into its ranks, Donald Pelotte.

Bishops today also differ markedly in education from even their fairly recent predecessors. Biographical data on bishops ruling dioceses as late as 1953 revealed only six who had received any part of their education from a secular college or university. Although all of today's bishops have a seminary education, as one must for priestly ordination, a surprising number also have degrees from secular institutions. The range is wide, from Ivy League colleges (for eight bishops) to specialized technical institutions and a conservatory of music. Many other bishops are graduates of the country's state colleges and universities, and some have degrees from major private universities and colleges.[9] The much wider and more secular education of many of today's bishops is indicative of their greater exposure to our heterogeneous society and the greater variety of men and experience now within their ranks.

When we turn to examine career paths, we see again a new breed of bishop, one made up not of monastic or parochial men, but of men who have been personally involved in the general, often tumultuous issues of our time and in the reforms that swept their church after the Vatican Council. Earlier in their careers, many present-day bishops were part of the "prophet" and "expert" sectors of the church and thus on the cutting edge of change in the country and the church.

As a young priest, Bishop Roger Mahoney helped mediate the bitter labor struggle between Cesar Chavez's United Farm Workers union and the California grape growers. In the early 1970s, Bishop Thomas Gumbleton uncovered the "tiger cages" in Vietnam, the underground bamboo cells where the South Vietnamese government was secretly holding political prisoners. Bishop John McGann, who recently came to public attention for his criticisms of the late CIA director William Casey in a sermon delivered at Casey's funeral, earlier in his career was both an antiwar and an antinuclear activist. Cardinal Joseph Bernardin helped to organize the rescue and resettlement of Vietnamese refugees after the fall of Saigon. Even Cardinal Bernard Law, generally considered a church conservative, shows a similar career pattern. After earning a degree in medieval history from Harvard University, he served as a priest in Mississippi. During the 1960s, he joined the fight against segregation, marching in civil rights demonstrations when that was still a very dangerous thing to do in that state.

The attitudes of today's younger bishops were formed by their participation in the general problems of an American society in turmoil, and also by their apprenticeship in a changing church with a much more complex organizational network and a much more participatory ethos. Certainly this is true of the bishops who voted to pass the war and peace and economics pastorals. Nine of them, for example, had been members or officers of priests' senates—groups of priests elected by their colleagues to represent them before their diocese's bishop and to act as an advisory body to him. Two had served as presidents of the Conference of Major Superiors of Men, a liaison body uniting church officials and men in religious orders—the Benedictines, Dominicans, and so on. Two were executive directors of the Campaign for Human Development, the church's antipoverty agency, formed in 1969. Two had served with the National Office of Black Catholics and one as president of the National Black Catholic Clergy Caucus. A number of today's bishops earlier were part of the USCC's professional staff. Bishop John McCarthy had been assistant director of the USCC's social action department, for example, and Bishop Raymond Lucker, director of the USCC's department of education. Cardinal Joseph Bernardin and Bishop Thomas Kelly had both served as general secretary, in effect the chief executive officer, of the NCCB/USCC.

The bishops' assumption of a political leadership role becomes explicable when we see how that role evolved in the contextual situation of a new ideology and a new institutional framework and when we examine the men themselves who are now in the hierarchy.

Political Leadership Criteria

To examine the bishops' conduct of their political leadership role and some of the problems it involves for them and for American society, we need to analyze their political leadership according to the major criteria we use to judge political leadership in general in a democratic society. The two most important and relevant criteria, I believe, are accountability and legitimacy.

A basic presumption of a democratic society is that those who exercise political leadership must in some way be held accountable to, or responsible to, the people of that society. The accountability criterion poses problems for any religious-political leadership, but perhaps especially for Catholic bishops, given the hierarchical, supranational nature of the Catholic Church.

Bishop Rembert Weakland chaired the bishops' committee that wrote the pastoral on the U.S. economy. In 1986 he told reporters that the bishops could afford to take a long-range view of problems and address difficult issues because "we don't run for office." This same factor poses a major problem in accountability for them. Catholic bishops are appointed by the pope, usually in consultation with other bishops and with his papal legate, or representative, in a country. American bishops are not chosen by the American people or even, except very informally, by lay Catholics or clergy in the United States. Although the elective principle is very important in American society, for bishops as political leaders the selection process raises the question of accountability at only one level. Examining the record of their words and actions indicates that the bishops themselves view the accountability issue in a much more complex way.

First, the bishops aver a "prophetic" responsibility, superseding more ordinary claims. That is, they insist that human society has an absolute need for a few people committed to the role of moral outsider, divorced from and unbeholden to ordinary institutions and roles, prepared to remind people and rulers of the transcendent values inherent in political and other actions. In their economics and war and peace letters, the bishops explicitly claim the right to speak on the basis of the prophetic tradition. In the peace letter, for example, the bishops declare that as bishops of the American church they have "both the obligation and the opportunity to share and interpret the moral and religious wisdom of the Catholic tradition by applying it to the problems of war and peace today." [10]

In what might seem a somewhat contradictory argument, bishops would also claim that they fulfill the accountability criterion because, although they are teachers and leaders, they are so in a church that over the past two decades has increasingly emphasized the doctrine of co-responsibility. A USCC official said that the best effect of the Vatican Council was that "it called for shared responsibility." A bishop, in talking about co-responsibility, insisted, "When we [bishops] speak now in a common voice, it's after we've consulted with all kinds of people." [11]

In writing the war and peace and the economics pastorals, the bishops developed a new system: they went through a long process of consultation with both ethicists and public policy experts. Then drafts were widely circulated in dioceses across America and the comments of ordinary Catholics solicited. At the 1986 NCCB meeting, Bishop Malone heralded the consultative/critical process as "a new and collegial method of teaching. . . . For the first time, the people of God have been involved in their [the pastorals'] formation." [12]

If the accountability criterion is complex and difficult for the bishops as political leaders, so is the criterion of legitimacy. Nothing is more important under our democratic political system than that political leaders be recognized as having legitimacy. Most scholars agree that legitimacy means more than simply having the legal or constitutional right to act as our leaders. Political leadership, to be recognized as legitimate, must be legal but also, more nebulously, must be perceived as "right," moral, licit.

Some of the most famous passages in Alexis de Tocqueville's classic study *Democracy in America* are concerned with the interrelationship of religion and politics. Tocqueville insisted that religion was profoundly influential in American life because it helped to form character and community and also because "the American clergy stand aloof from secular affairs. . . . They take no share in the altercations of parties, but they readily adopt the general opinions of their country and their age: and they allow themselves to be borne away without opposition in the current of feeling and opinion by which everything around them is carried along." [13]

The argument over the legitimacy of religious-political activism has become volatile, because today the religious connection to politics differs greatly from the situation Tocqueville described. Religious leaders now are more often challenging "the general opinions of their country," and they are even doing what most clergy long eschewed, sharing "in the altercations of parties."

The bishops in their pastoral letters challenged deeply held American values—individualism, the free enterprise system, patriotism, and anticommunism. The bishops argue that they are only asking that these values be examined in the light of moral principles and teachings; but the sense that the bishops are challenging basic "Americanisms" is widespread in the media and among Catholics as well as the general public.

The bishops, and other religious leaders, would surely question the value of being accorded legitimacy as actors in American political life only when they follow the civil religion patterns described by Tocqueville and being denied that legitimacy when they go beyond those patterns. The fact is, however, that their legitimacy as political leaders is challenged by some people on the basis of the Constitution's separation principle and by others on the generic charge of being un-American.

The abortion issue, also, brought the bishops directly into conflict with political leaders over the issue of participation in partisan politics, which again belies the Tocqueville patterns and raises questions of legitimacy. During the 1984 elections, when Cardinal O'Connor and other prelates challenged the licitness of Catholic politicians who took the position that they opposed abortion personally but felt they must uphold the law and could not impose their beliefs on others, the stage was set for an intense debate on the role of religion in politics. The Catholic governor of New York, Mario Cuomo, insisted on the right of politicians to separate their personal beliefs from their wider duties to the law and to their pluralistic constituencies. Bishop Malone, speaking for the NCCB, asserted the right and responsibility of the church and its bishops to "discuss the relationship of religion, morality and politics." He further insisted that political leaders, to be morally consistent, "had to try in accordance with democratic procedure, for public policy of some kind" which would accord with the moral precepts to which they were bound through their faith.[14]

The debate revealed how complex the interrelationship of religion and politics is today and how blurred the line of separation continues to be. Determining that line will have much to do with determining the legitimacy of Catholic prelates and other religious leaders in exercising a political role.

Issues with serious moral and ethical as well as political implications are more and more coming into the political arena. Their presence
will probably bring, and perhaps necessitate, increased involvement by
religious leaders in politics. It also necessitates serious, sustained, civil
analyses of the development and implications of religious-political
leadership by political scientists.

Notes

The information on which this article is based comes primarily from two sources.
The first is a series of interviews with Catholic Church leaders, which I did between
1973 and 1975 for my book, *Catholics and American Politics*. Interviewees were
promised anonymity. Therefore, these earlier interviewees are referred to not by name
but by interview number—church leader interview no. 12, and so on. Additional,
updated information came out of my attendance at the November 1986 National
Conference of Catholic Bishops annual four-day meeting. This gave me the opportunity to observe proceedings as the bishops debated and voted, to gather documentary
materials, and to interview church officials.

1. Mary Hanna, *Catholics and American Politics* (Cambridge, Mass.: Harvard
   University Press, 1979), 110-116. See also Andrew Greeley, *The American
   Catholic* (New York: Basic Books, 1977), 52-58.
2. Church leader interview no. 14; church leader interview no. 13.
3. National Conference of Catholic Bishops, "Economic Justice for All: Catholic
   Social Teaching and the U.S. Economy," *Origins,* November 27, 1986, 415.
4. National Conference of Catholic Bishops/United States Catholic Conference,
   Documentation on the Right to Life and Abortion (Washington, D.C.: USCC
   Publications Office, 1974).
5. Ronald Krietemeyer, interview with the author, Washington, D.C., November 12,
   1986.
6. NCCB/USCC, *Agenda Report: Documentation for General Meeting, Action Items
   1-19* (Washington, D.C.: NCCB/USCC, 1986), 253.
7. Church leader interview no. 5.
8. *Catholic Almanac 1987* (Huntington, Ind.: Our Sunday Visitor, 1986), 481.
9. Information on the bishops' educational backgrounds and their earlier careers was
   gathered from a variety of sources: *Catholic Almanac, Who's Who in America,* and
   the *New York Times Biographical Service;* press releases from the NCCB/USCC
   public affairs office; and various newspaper and magazine articles.
10. NCCB, "The Challenge of Peace: God's Promise and Our Response," *Origins,*
    May 19, 1983, 2.
11. Church leader interview no. 15; church leader interview no. 14.
12. Bishop James Malone, "The Church: Its Strength and Its Questions," *Origins,*
    November 20, 1986, 395.
13. Alexis de Tocqueville, *Democracy in America,* ed. Richard D. Heffner (New
    York: New American Library, 1956), 154-155.
14. Kenneth Briggs, "Bishops Describe View of Politics," *New York Times,* October
    16, 1984, 1, 13.

8. JESSE JACKSON IN TWO WORLDS

Roger D. Hatch

Jesse Jackson's campaigns for the presidential nomination of the Democratic party have raised important questions about the relationship between religion and politics in the United States. An ordained Baptist minister, Jackson freely uses religious language and imagery in his political speeches.[1] His campaigns used parts of the black religious infrastructure on both local and national levels. In his 1984 campaign, it was members of the black clergy, rather than black elected officials, who were Jackson's most prominent and active supporters. In both campaigns, Jackson held political rallies in black churches, as well as preaching there.

In this essay, I examine some of the problems Jackson's political activities pose, all of which involve the question of the role religion plays in his politics. First I examine the problem of understanding Jackson's purpose in running for the Democratic party's presidential nomination. Has he, as some charge, simply been attempting to use his religion and the religion of his fellow black Americans as a basis for advancing his own personal or political agenda? In this chapter I attempt to find an appropriate framework for understanding Jackson's political activities; then I explore the content of Jackson's approach, examining the role religion and religious ideas play in his approach to politics; finally, I take up some of the problems that Jackson's religion poses for electoral politics. Politics, after all, must be open to compromise and adjustment; successful electoral politics in America has always been a politics of the middle, able to balance the interests of one group with the interests of others. Politics deals with the hard realities of the here and now. Religion, on the other hand, deals with claims of truth, asks people to rise above their self-interests, and entertains ideas about ultimate reality.

The Contexts of Jackson's Political Activities

Although Jesse Jackson has been in the public eye for two decades, Barbara Reynolds's 1975 biography was the only book-length treatment of Jackson available until recently; it focused on Jackson's personality to explain his activities. Since his presidential candidacy in 1984, however, Jackson has been the subject of several books.[2] Thomas H. Landess and Richard M. Quinn drew heavily on Reynolds's work to analyze Jackson's twenty-year public career. They interpreted his political activities in the context of the Southern racist populist politics of the 1890-1940 period, arguing that Jackson and earlier white Southerners attempted "to paint themselves as leaders who had arisen out of the ranks of the oppressed, in order to speak for 'the people' in corrupt political forums controlled by the rich and powerful." Political scientist Adolph L. Reed, Jr., examined Jackson's 1984 campaign in the context of black electoral politics. Reporters Bob Faw and Nancy Skelton chronicled it as just another—although a highly interesting and certainly enigmatic—campaign for the presidency; Sheila D. Collins also wrote about Jackson's 1984 campaign, but from the standpoint of a participant-observer.[3] She viewed it in the context of a variety of twentieth century movements for social change, which she termed "underground streams in American political life."

Although each of these interpretive perspectives has some validity and utility, none explores the one institution to which Jackson is most indebted—the black church. James Melvin Washington, however, has examined Jackson from this vantage point; he concludes that Jesse Jackson's "roots are planted deeply within the black church's rich tradition of social, political, and economic activism."[4] I agree and would also observe that Jackson does not understand himself to be the heir of any particular American *political* tradition. Instead, he understands himself to be part of two other kinds of traditions: the activist tradition of the black church and the tradition of seeking racial and social justice exemplified by several American social movements.[5] In recent years, these two traditions came together in the civil rights movement.

Thus it is the black church and the civil rights movement from which Jackson comes and continues to draw as he participates in electoral politics. Religion, politics, and the quest for social and racial justice converge in this arena. Martin Luther King, Jr., was active in this same arena, and Jackson clearly understands himself to be following on the path blazed by King.

Near the end of his life, King advanced an analysis of American society and advocated a program for action very much like Jackson's. In his last book, *Where Do We Go From Here: Chaos or Community?*, published in 1968, King argued for "a radical restructuring" of American society aimed at eliminating the interrelated evils of racism, poverty, and militarism. He observed that, with the passage of the 1965

Voting Rights Act, the struggle for racial justice had entered a second phase, seeking equality rather than freedom and opportunity. This new phase demanded a reassessment of strategy. While it had been important for the civil rights movement to break down centuries-old social and legal barriers erected to keep blacks from having equal opportunities, more fundamental changes were demanded of American society if equality and racial justice were to be achieved. Achieving racial justice included getting black people "out of poverty, exploitation, [and] all forms of degradation." King believed that the real costs lay ahead: "Jobs are harder and costlier to create than voting rolls. The eradication of slums housing millions is complex far beyond integrating buses and lunch counters." [6] But he recognized that these are necessary if racial justice is to be achieved.

King also outlined the agenda of the newly formed Operation Breadbasket of the Southern Christian Leadership Conference (SCLC) in this book; Jackson had just become its first national director. Its primary aim, King said, was to secure more and better jobs for blacks by using the economic power of black people. Boycotts and demonstrations were directed at businesses operating in black communities that did not give a fair share of jobs to blacks. These businesses were encouraged to deposit money in black-owned banks, to stock products from black-owned and -operated firms, and to utilize services from black firms. The key word, he noted, was *respect:* "If you respect my dollars, you must respect my person." [7] Thus by the mid-1960s King and SCLC were turning their attention and efforts toward the economic dimensions of racism.

King also described how blacks should employ their newly won political power by moving into every level of political activity. His outline, written in 1967, could have served as a blueprint for Jackson's own entry into electoral politics in the 1980s.

> The new task of the liberation movement, therefore, is not merely to increase the Negro registration and vote; equally imperative is the development of a strong voice that is heard in the smoke-filled rooms where party debating and bargaining proceed. . . . We shall have to create leaders who embody virtues we can respect, who have moral and ethical principles we can applaud with an enthusiasm that enables us to rally support for them based on confidence and trust. . . . We shall have to master the art of political alliances. . . . They are the keys to political progress. . . . Everything Negroes need—and many of us need almost everything—will not like magic materialize from the use of the ballot. Yet as a lever of power, if it is given studious attention and employed with the creativity we have proved through our protest activities we possess, it will help to

achieve many far-reaching changes during our lifetimes. . . . The scope of struggle is still too narrow and too restricted. We must turn more of our energies and focus our creativity on the useful things that translate into power.[8]

In the final chapter of his book, King analyzed the role of the United States in world affairs. Because he concluded that racism, poverty, and militarism are the principal problems that make stable international relations difficult, King called for a revolution of values, followed by a restructuring of national and international relationships.

Thus the understanding by Martin Luther King, Jr., of the issue of racial justice at the end of his life went far beyond the notion of equal rights under the law or equal opportunity and included political, economic, and even international dimensions. He believed that the Public Accommodations Act of 1964 and the Voting Rights Act of 1965 were simply phase one of the struggle for racial justice. In effect, then, Jesse Jackson has been dealing with phase two for the past twenty years. His movement into national electoral politics in the 1980s, rather than being a diversion from his civil rights activities, constitutes an integral part of those activities.

The Content of Jackson's Message

At the core of Jesse Jackson's approach to every aspect of life is a religious-political vision for America that has its roots in the black church. It is important to note that this black church tradition is not simply a black counterpart to the white Christian tradition; it combines religion and politics in a unique way. At its base is an affirmation that is simultaneously religious *and* political. This is the affirmation that racism is not true, that all human beings are made in God's image and hence have value. Peter J. Paris has put it well: "The fundamental principle of the black Christian tradition is depicted most adequately in the biblical doctrine of the parenthood of God and the kinship of all peoples." [9]

This principle is religious because it is an affirmation about the nature of reality—in this case about human nature, human association, and the relation of human beings to God. This principle underlies Jackson's ubiquitous affirmation, "I am somebody," and his belief in the interrelated, interdependent nature of reality. This principle (especially the "kinship of all peoples" portion) also provides the basis for criticizing all racist arrangements in society. Thus it has a political as well as a religious character: all social policies and social arrangements that deny or devalue the worth of people because of their race are wrong. Racially oppressed people can retain their own self-worth only by resisting racist arrangements.

The history of black people in America shows that blacks have affirmed their own worth by resisting racism in a variety of ways. Forms of resistance have run the gamut from the private refusal to believe the degrading things said to be true about black people to armed attempts to overthrow various institutionalized forms of racism in America, including the federal government.[10]

Black churches, regardless of their theological stance or the social class of their members, have always addressed politics. They have always engaged in social criticism, at least to the extent of repudiating racism in its many embodiments. Sometimes this has taken the apparently nonpolitical form of emphasizing another world in the future and eschewing conventional political involvements. Yet the emphasis by black people on another, better world than this one constitutes a powerful religious and political indictment of this present world. This view often has been coupled with the judgment that no human activity—be it reform or even revolution—can adequately institute the kinds of social and political changes necessary to establish justice and peace; it will take the intervention of God.

Others have believed that conventional political activities are essential because they can help establish a measure of justice and peace. In this view, religious beliefs about the worth of all people need to be embodied throughout society, not just affirmed in the activities of churches. It was ministers and churches taking this latter stance who became involved in the civil rights movement. Jesse Jackson fits into this tradition: "My religion obligates me to be political, that is, to seek to do God's will and allow the spiritual Word to become concrete justice and dwell among us. . . . Religion should *use* you politically to do public service. Politics should not *misuse* religion. When the Word (the spiritual) becomes flesh (the actual) and dwells [among us], that's called good religion." [11]

But religion is more than a source of personal motivation for Jackson; it is intrinsic to social and political issues. He begins the preface to a collection of his speeches by noting: "In my preaching, teaching, and activism over the past quarter of a century—and hopefully in this book—I have tried to illustrate that the issues of life flow primarily from the heart, not from the head, and that at the center of every political, economic, legal, and social issue is the spiritual, moral, and ethical dimension." [12] Thus he argues that politics, at the most fundamental level, deals with choosing which of several competing views of reality and the future will be embodied in public policies. In 1984, for example, he told Democrats that it was not sufficient to be anti-Reagan; they had to offer a "superior vision": "Reagan has offered the American people a coherent vision, an ideology based on fighting communism and promoting the growth of American corporations around the world. We must offer an equally coherent vision based on fighting poverty, disease, and oppression and promoting economic development that meets the needs of people around the world." [13]

When Jackson's thought and his approach to issues are examined carefully, it is clear that his view of the world is deeply religious. Three general ideas form the core of his belief: the worth of each individual, the interrelation of all people and of all aspects of life, and the importance of vision.

Jackson's view of reality begins with his conviction that every human being is important because each person is God's child:

> I believe that the lack of self-esteem—the feeling that "I" do not count, that "I" cannot make a difference—is one of the important losses of our day. I always begin my speeches to students with a chant entitled, "I Am Somebody." [This] litany is designed to say to all of us, I may be poor, uneducated, unskilled, prematurely pregnant, on drugs, or victimized by racism—whether black, brown, red, yellow, or white—but I still count. I am somebody. I must be respected, protected, and never neglected because I am important and valuable to myself and others. I am a unique and significant person with hopes, dreams, and aspirations that must be encouraged and developed, rather than crushed or ignored. [14]

Self-respect "is the most fundamental factor in one's mental and spiritual health" and is the basis upon which mutual respect can be established. [15] Although self-respect has psychological value, it is the theological or spiritual value that finally matters. Racism is wrong theologically because it denies the idea that all people are valuable because they are God's children. As Jackson sees it, a black person's act of resisting racism is an affirmation of self-worth that is both religious and psychological. But resisting racism also is a highly political act in whatever context it occurs because it denies the legitimacy of all social arrangements based on racism.

Jackson believes that although individual differences are important and must be recognized, in the end, all people and all institutions and all dimensions of life are interrelated. As he noted in his speech at the 1984 Democratic National Convention, "America is not like a blanket, one piece of unbroken cloth—the same color, the same texture, the same size. It is more like a quilt—many patches, many pieces, many colors, many sizes, all woven and held together by a common thread." [16] The image Jackson most frequently uses to express this interrelatedness is the rainbow. In quilts and rainbows both the individual parts and the larger patterns can be seen and are important.

In a 1984 campaign speech in Akron, Ohio, Jackson outlined the relationships he saw between several apparently separate issues: the loss of twenty-five thousand jobs in the rubber industry in Akron; U.S. tax policy; multinational corporations' search for higher profits by exporting jobs abroad to cheap labor markets; U.S. foreign policy; the federal government's budget deficits; the abdication of governmental responsibilities for domestic needs such as education, cleaning up the environment, and rebuilding cities and roads; resistance to affirmative action programs; and the current hostility toward labor unions.[17]

However, because Americans have forgotten their relationship to each other and the interrelated nature of the world, they often are unable to deal effectively with many social problems. In order to bring about change, Jackson argues, these interrelationships must be rediscovered: "The tasks before us—a new foreign policy, a new domestic policy, decent schools, a clean environment, a safe and inexpensive energy program—look impossible if we face them one at a time, if we face them alone. . . . Each problem that we face as a nation is related to every other problem. It is our task to define that relationship." [18] These various interrelationships between people and between issues provide the possibility for forming coalitions, which is at the heart of Jackson's approach to politics.

"Vision," the third of Jackson's core beliefs, is crucial because it is necessary for human fulfillment. Jackson frequently quotes Proverbs 29:18: "Where there is no vision, the people perish." As he understands it, vision serves two main purposes: it provides insight by allowing people to see beyond the present situation, and it provides the basis for individual and societal fulfillment.

In his political campaigning he says, "Our party must not only have the courage and the conscience to expose the slummy side. We must have the conviction and vision to show America the sunny side, the way out." [19] Vision thus points beyond the current problems and realities of life to the enduring nature of reality itself, a reality which, for Jackson, includes a God of justice who is in control of the universe.

Vision also helps people see reality without distortion. In his 1984 campaign, for example, Jackson argued that Americans' sight was being distorted by racism, nationalism, and false religious appeals: "We must remove the cataracts of race from the eyes of our people and lift them out of poverty, ignorance, disease, and fear. . . . We must not blind them with prayer clauses, drape them in flags, and give them hot feelings of false racial pride when they remain hungry, ignorant, and diseased in the wealthiest nation in the history of the world." [20]

Finally vision provides the standards for evaluating both individual and national fulfillment. To individuals, Jackson offers this challenge: "Live beyond the pain of reality with the dream of a bright tomorrow. Use hope and imagination as weapons of survival and progress. ... Young people, dream of a new value system. Dream of teachers, but teachers who will teach for life, not just for a living." [21]

Jackson argues that America's "greatness must be measured by our ideals ... and how closely we approximate them." [22] He describes his vision of a transformed American society most forcefully when he calls for redefining "national greatness":

> It's not the size of our GNP. It's not our military might. It's not our educational and technological achievements—as great and as necessary as each of these may be. More fundamental to greatness, by my definition, is how we treat children in the dawn of life, how we treat poor people in the pit of life, and how we treat old people in the sunset of life. If we treat them with respect and dignity, we'll be a great nation. If we care for our young, insuring their proper nutrition and educate them to work in tomorrow's world, we'll be a great nation. If we provide decent, safe, and sanitary housing and food for the poor, then we'll be a great nation. If we provide health care and food and show respect for our elderly and allow those who are able and willing to continue to contribute something meaningful to our society, then we'll be a great nation. Greatness is in how we value and care for our people. [23]

Jackson's view of reality is highly religious, although he rarely articulates it in specifically religious terms. It rests upon a belief in a God of justice who finally is in charge. [24] This God can be seen only if people have vision. This same God also is the source of worth for individuals (because they are children of God) and is the basis for the interrelationship between individuals and groups (because all are God's children).

The changes Jackson seeks in America through electoral politics grow out of this religious perspective. As he explained in 1984:

> Our campaign is a moral and political crusade to transform the quality of American life. We want to restore a moral quality to the political decisions that affect our lives at home and the decisions that affect the lives of our brothers and sisters around the globe. We want to set our nation on a course where the full spiritual, moral, and physical resources of our people can be realized. We want to end the exploitation and oppression of the many by the few. [25]

The first two sentences, emphasizing conversion and moral values, could have been spoken by Jerry Falwell or Pat Robertson. But Jackson's social analysis from the point of view of the disinherited, present in the last sentence, sets him apart both from white conservative religious leaders active in politics and from conventional political liberals. This dual emphasis on conversion and moral transformation, usually characterized as "conservative," and on social action, usually characterized as "liberal" or "radical"—while not unusual among black Americans, particularly black Christians—rarely exists among white Americans. Thus it often befuddles political analysts, who tend not to know the realities of black America. Accordingly, Jackson prefers the term "progressive":

> Black America has always been on the cutting edge of progressive politics in America. We are not conservative, nor are we liberals. We are progressives. We don't seek to keep things as they are [as conservatives do] or to modify things as they are [as liberals do]. We seek to change our nation. We don't want cruel slavery or modified slavery, we want freedom—no slavery at all.[26]

It should not be surprising that most political analysts fail to understand either Jesse Jackson's place in American politics or the role of religion in his political activities. It indeed is true that Jackson does not fit into normal political or religious categories—as long as *normal* refers to American electoral politics, from which blacks have been excluded until recently, or to white American religious traditions. These are not the relevant contexts for understanding Jackson and his political activities. His political roots lie in extrapolitical movements for social and racial justice, such as the civil rights movement, and his religious roots clearly are in the black church, which has a long tradition of relating religion and politics in ways quite different from white American churches. The confusion—even consternation—among political analysts about "what Jesse Jackson wants" reveals more about their own lack of knowledge than it does about any uncertainty on Jackson's part.

Vision and Politics

Although Jackson recognizes that self-interest is the first principle of political activity, he argues that politics finally must be informed by something more than self-interest—by vision.[27] Without this, Jackson could be viewed as a typical interest group politician (although a black one), advancing the interests of the particular group he represents. Indeed, most political analysts believe that self-interest is the only reality in politics, which makes Jackson enigmatic and controversial. They cast Jackson as an outsider, someone who seems to be playing the game of politics by a different set of rules.

Some view Jackson as a naive idealist, as a man out of his depth, as a preacher who talks of ideals and speaks only in generalities. For example, the *New Republic* described Jackson in a 1984 editorial as "content with the most vapid of cliches, indifferent to questions of concrete policy."[28] Similar views were voiced following Jackson's electoral victories in the primaries in the middle of the 1988 campaign. Any examination of his activity, however, will reveal that Jackson routinely, almost instinctively, speaks in detail about the specific events of the day, offering instant commentary, as it were, on questions of concrete policy. His approach to black economic development, for example, involves the general themes of equity and reciprocity, but it also involves attention to specific details.[29] While he was president of Operation PUSH (People United to Serve Humanity), the moral covenants he negotiated with businesses included attention to the companies' advertising, banking, insurance, legal services, accounting, philanthropy, and purchasing practices as well as to the composition of their general work force.[30] Jackson uses ideals as the basis for judging current events, as a way of gaining perspective, not as an escape from the specific and concrete. As he says of his own Rainbow Coalition: "We must not measure our own identity by our proximity to the [Democratic party's] campaign. Rather, we must measure [it] by its proximity to our ideals. . . . We must remain consistent with our . . . mission."[31]

Others view Jackson as a charlatan. They believe that he is simply using this appeal to "moral higher ground" as a way to disguise or legitimate advancing his own or his group's own self-interests. Typical of these observers are Julius Lester, who claimed that Jackson's 1984 presidential campaign was "a race for power (disguised as a presidential campaign)," and William Safire, who claimed that Jackson "is not running for president of the United States, but is using the campaign for president to run for leadership of blacks in America."[32] It is this kind of view that often lies behind the question, "What does Jesse Jackson want?"

Others think Jackson really does believe what he is saying about the relation of ideals and politics and therefore view him as a dangerous ideologue. Much of this kind of thinking stems from problems growing out of the "modern bargain" between religion and politics: Civil and religious authorities are to be separate, and all manner of religion is to be tolerated as long as it does not subvert the political order.[33] This bargain has always been an uneasy one and often is misconstrued to read: religion and politics are to be separate, and all religion is acceptable as long as it is confined to the realm of private belief. All religion, however, has social (and thus political) implications; no religion is merely private. But if the modern bargain is misconstrued, confining religion to the private sphere, then any interrelation between religion and politics appears illegitimate. Accordingly, many political analysts have condemned with a single judgment the diverse political activities of Jerry Falwell or Pat Robertson, Jesse Jackson, and Robert Drinan, a former member of Congress and a Catholic priest.

The appropriate questions to ask about any religious or religion-based activity in the general political arena concern its *public effects*.[34] Let us consider questions about the role of religion in two areas of Jackson's political activity: (1) his goals for America and (2) the way judgments based on religious principles affect his politics.

Mainstream American politicians treat all interests as if they were equivalent. To act otherwise, they argue, is to destroy the possibility of compromise and adjustment, which is essential to democratic politics.[35] Jackson, however, speaks about the priority of the "least of these" and advocates measuring America's greatness by how it treats its young, its old, and its poor. These, critics argue, are simply rhetorically pleasing ways of advancing one group's interests over another's. This might be the case *if* these groups possessed sufficient political power to advance their own interests effectively. But this is precisely Jackson's point: these people are America's disinherited and thus do not enjoy a normal degree of political power. Accordingly, meeting their needs is not so much to prefer one *group* (and its interests) over another as it is to prefer one *kind of values* over another—to prefer "meeting basic human needs" over such values as "private property" or "to the (political) victor go the spoils." [36] Jackson's general goal—"to set our nation on a course where the full spiritual, moral, and physical resources of our people can be realized" [37]—is inclusive and does not give special place to certain groups on the basis of their religious beliefs or practices.

As Barry Commoner has observed, Jackson "makes people feel better about themselves because they can see how they are linked to others." But this feeling better is neither self-serving nor narcissistic: "Jackson's talent for challenging each group to look beyond the limits of its own, intense concerns is enormously important." [38] The coalitions Jackson seeks to form are not simply for the purpose of advancing their own self-interests; they are to be "progressive coalitions," coalitions seeking fundamental changes in American life. Their focus is on creating a new America, characterized by the quest for "humane priorities at home and human rights abroad." [39]

Such an approach is reminiscent of Martin Luther King, who urged:

> Let, us, therefore, not think of our movement as one that seeks to integrate the Negro into all the existing values of American history. Let us be those creative dissenters who will call our beloved nation to a higher destiny, to a new plateau of compassion, to a more noble expression of humaneness. . . . Our economy must become more person-centered than property- and profit-centered. Our government must depend more on its moral power than on its military power.[40]

Jackson says that his religion "obligates" him to be political, and that being political involves "seek[ing] to do God's will." [41] This makes it appear as if religious reasons may play an important—even decisive—role as Jackson chooses one political option or approach rather than another. Are religious principles legitimate bases for determining public policy?

Again, we must inquire about the *political effects* of employing religious principles in the political arena. First, even a cursory examination of Jackson's campaign speeches reveals that he consistently appeals to people as fellow citizens, not as adherents of a common Christian religious tradition.[42] Therefore he is not employing religious principles as a way of compelling people to agree with him. Since Jackson is genuinely interested in coalition politics, such a tactic would undermine his efforts to build coalitions. Second, insofar as he appeals to religious principles, he appeals to them as public, not private, principles. This means that these principles are not his private possession and were not the result of a direct revelation to him from God. Other citizens can obtain them in a variety of ways. Some can be obtained from other religious traditions, others from parts of the American tradition, and still others by employing reason. Thus the principles that Jackson obtains from his own Christian tradition are potentially available to everyone, even those not connected with Christianity. These principles are open to criticism and challenge; they do not enjoy a kind of privileged status because of their religious origin.

Thus Jackson adheres to the modern bargain between religion and politics because his religious principles have no special authority or standing in the political arena. They are legitimate insofar as they are open to reasoned argument and examination, and they are effective insofar as they are persuasive to voters, thinking and acting as citizens. Thus Jackson's religion does not undermine the general political process, even though his religion and politics are inseparably related.

Notes

1. For instance, in announcing his presidential candidacy in 1983, he called for the creation of "new covenants" between the dispossessed and the Democratic party, organized labor, and corporate America ("The Quest for a Just Society and a Peaceful World," Presidential Announcement Speech, Washington, D.C., November 3, 1983: "The new covenant we seek with the trade union movement is one that would provide for the swift elimination of all the remaining vestiges of racial discrimination in apprenticeship programs, seniority structures, and union staff and leadership opportunities. . . . The new covenant we seek with corporate America is one that would end the current restraint of trade practices that lock

blacks, Hispanics, and other elements of the rainbow out of business opportunities and jobs. . . ."). In that same speech he also described his campaign's purpose as "defending the poor, making welcome the outcast, delivering the needy, and being a source of hope for people yearning to be free everywhere." Here Jackson paraphrased Luke 4:18-19, which is an account of Jesus in the synagogue in Nazareth reading Isaiah 61:1-2.

2. Barbara A. Reynolds, *Jesse Jackson: The Man, the Movement, the Myth* (Chicago: Nelson-Hall, 1975), reissued as *Jesse Jackson: America's David* (Washington, D.C.: JFJ Associates, 1985); Thomas H. Landess and Richard M. Quinn, *Jesse Jackson and the Politics of Race* (Ottawa, Ill.: Jameson Books, 1985), 238; Adolph L. Reed, Jr., *The Jesse Jackson Phenomenon: The Crisis of Purpose in Afro-American Politics* (New Haven: Yale University Press, 1986). Reed observes that the campaign "was a ritualistic event—a media-conveyed politics of symbolism, essentially tangential to the critical debate over reorganization of American capitalism's governing consensus" (p. 1). Because he believed it was "not so much a political campaign as a crusade" (p. 35), Reed concluded that Jackson's presidential campaign actually undermined electoral politics within the black community.

3. Bob Faw and Nancy Skelton, *Thunder in America: The Improbable Presidential Campaign of Jesse Jackson* (Austin: Texas Monthly Press, 1986); Sheila D. Collins, *The Rainbow Challenge: The Jackson Campaign and the Future of U.S. Politics* (New York: Monthly Review Press, 1986). Collins concluded: "Jackson's genius lay in linking nonelectoral forms of political mobilization and protest with traditional electoral politics. . . . Although embryonic and fragile, the Rainbow Coalition represents the construction of a new kind of politics appropriate to the history, cultural realities, and changing socioeconomic context of late twentieth-century America" (p. 19).

4. James Melvin Washington, "Jesse Jackson and the Symbolic Politics of Black Christendom," *Annals of the American Academy of Political and Social Sciences* 480 (July 1985): 96.

5. I offer a longer interpretation of Jackson along these lines in *Beyond Opportunity: Jesse Jackson's Vision for America* (Philadelphia: Fortress Press, 1988). Collins's interpretation is similar, but she does not explore his roots in the black church or the religious basis of the social movements she identifies as the antecedents of his political activities. It is instructive to note that she identifies the black power movement of the 1960s, but not the civil rights movement, as one of Jackson's antecedents.

6. Martin Luther King, Jr., *Where Do We Go From Here: Chaos or Community?* (New York: Harper & Row, 1967), 157, 4, 6.

7. Ibid., 168-172.

8. Ibid., 173-183.

9. Peter J. Paris, *The Social Teaching of the Black Churches* (Philadelphia: Fortress Press, 1985), 10.

10. See, for example, Vincent Harding, *There Is a River: The Black Struggle for Freedom in America* (New York: Random House, 1983). Harding argues that any way of denying the validity or truth of racism is a form of resistance. Accordingly, he includes actions often characterized as "romantic" or "escapist" and argues that suicide has been a form of resistance (see, for example, p. 20).

11. Jesse L. Jackson, Preface to *Straight from the Heart*, ed. Roger D. Hatch and Frank E. Watkins (Philadelphia: Fortress Press, 1987), ix. This is the only collection of Jackson's speeches that is generally available. In his speech to the Democratic National Convention in 1984, he contrasted his own approach to

relating religion and politics with that of Ronald Reagan, whom Jackson says has used religion to obscure or confuse political issues: "In his appeal to the South, Mr. Reagan is trying to substitute flags and prayer clauses for jobs, food, clothing, education, health care, and housing. But apparently President Reagan is not even familiar with the structure of a prayer. . . . He has cut energy assistance to the poor, he has cut food stamps, children's breakfast and lunch programs, the Women, Infant, and Children (WIC) program for pregnant mothers and infants, and job training for children; and then says, 'Let us pray.' In a prayer, you are supposed to thank God for the food you are about to receive, not the food that just left" (*Straight from the Heart,* 9).

12. Ibid., ix.
13. Jesse L. Jackson, "The Keys to a Democratic Victory in 1984," Position Paper, 1984.
14. Jesse L. Jackson, "Politics as an Educational Forum," Ford Hall Forum, Boston, March 27, 1983.
15. Jesse L. Jackson, "The Rejected Stones: The Cornerstones of a New Public Policy," National Press Club, Washington, D.C., May 10, 1983.
16. Jackson, *Straight from the Heart,* 5.
17. Jackson, *Straight from the Heart,* 312-313.
18. Jesse L. Jackson, "Set a New Agenda: Justice at Home, Peace Abroad," *New York Times,* February 27, 1984.
19. Jackson, *Straight from the Heart,* 17. Jackson made a similar point in speeches before joint sessions of the Louisiana and South Carolina legislatures: "I want to suggest another definition of our fundamental problem. The dominant characteristic and common ailment in our society today is a sense of hopelessness. . . . We think our racial divisions are too deep. . . . We cannot communicate with our young people. . . . The fundamental issue confronting America today is not so much that Americans need *help*—jobs, curbing inflation, balancing the budget, etc. No, the issue is the restoration of hope. . . . If leaders provide hope, people can help themselves. . . . We must not let . . . external problems and circumstances break our internal spirit. . . . We must revive the spirit of hope and optimism in our people" (December 13, 1983, and January 24, 1984).
20. Jackson, *Straight from the Heart,* 143.
21. Jackson, *Straight from the Heart,* 17-18.
22. Jesse L. Jackson, "The Quest for a Just Society and a Peaceful World," Presidential Announcement Speech, Washington, D.C., November 3, 1983.
23. "Why I Want to Be President of the United States," Position Paper, 1984. Note that this quotation contains all three of Jackson's basic ideas: (1) we must respect ourselves and others; (2) nutrition, education, housing, health care, and meaningful employment are all interrelated; and (3) greatness lies in acting on the basis of a vision beyond self-interest.
24. See, for example, Jackson, *Straight from the Heart,* 18, 147, 186.
25. Jackson, *Straight from the Heart,* 307.
26. Jesse L. Jackson, "The Unfinished Business of the Democratic Convention," Operation PUSH Saturday Morning Community Forum, July 28, 1984.
27. See Jackson, *Straight from the Heart,* 78.
28. "The Third Candidate's World," *New Republic,* July 30, 1984, 12.
29. See my discussion in *Beyond Opportunity,* 45-51.
30. See Jackson, *Straight from the Heart,* esp. 280-281.
31. Jesse L. Jackson, "The Unfinished Business of the Democratic Convention," Operation PUSH Saturday Morning Community Forum, July 28, 1984.

32. Julius Lester, "You Can't Go Home Again: Critical Thoughts About Jesse Jackson," *Dissent* (Winter 1985): 21; William Safire, "Why Jackson Won't Disavow His Separatist Supporter," *New York Times*, April 10, 1984.

33. On the "modern bargain," see Sidney E. Mead, *The Nation with the Soul of a Church* (New York: Harper & Row, 1975), esp. chap. 3, 5, and 6; and see Joseph Tussman, ed. *The Supreme Court on Church and State* (New York: Oxford University Press, 1962), for important Supreme Court cases addressing this problem.

34. Alan B. Anderson and George W. Pickering, *Confronting the Color Line* (Athens: University of Georgia Press, 1986), 396-401.

35. Arthur Cohen long ago put the matter succinctly: "The fundamental problem of religion in a free society arises from the fact that religion tends to assert absolute claims and judgments, whereas the free society tends to insist that freedom can only thrive where all claims are treated as if they were relative" ("The Problem of Pluralism," in *Religion and the Free Society*, ed. William Lee Miller et al. [New York: Fund for the Republic, 1960]). In *The Jesse Jackson Phenomenon: The Crisis of Purpose in Afro-American Politics* (New Haven: Yale University Press, 1986), Adolph L. Reed, Jr., offers a related kind of criticism of the black church in general and of Jackson's 1984 campaign in particular. He argues that "an essential incompatibility, if not antagonism," (p. 60) exists between the church and politics. This is due to "the church's intrinsically antitemporal eschatological orientation" (p. 57) and its "model of authority that is antithetical to participatory representation" (p. 56).

36. Reinhold Niebuhr argued much the same way in "The Ethical Attitudes of the Proletarian Class" in *Moral Man and Immoral Society* (New York: Scribner's, 1960; originally published in 1932): "[The proletarian]— does not differ from the privileged classes in attempting this universalisation of his particular values. . . . [Yet] the fact that the equalitarian ideal does not spring from pure ethical imagination, but is the result of the peculiar circumstances of proletarian life, does not detract from its validity as the ultimate social ideal" (pp. 153, 160).

37. Jackson, *Straight from the Heart*, 307.

38. Barry Commoner, "The Case for Jackson," *Village Voice*, April 3, 1984.

39. Jackson, *Straight from the Heart*, 131.

40. King, *Where Do We Go From Here?* 157.

41. Jackson, *Straight from the Heart*, ix.

42. See my analysis of his 1984 campaign, "Jesse Jackson's Presidential Campaign: A Religious Assessment," *Soundings* (Fall-Winter 1987): 379-405.

Part III

TENSIONS OF DIFFERENCE:
VOTING AND GROUP BEHAVIOR

In politics Americans express their religious beliefs primarily through voting and interest group activity. Kenneth D. Wald analyzes the voting behavior of Americans from a religious standpoint and lays the groundwork for a new theoretical approach. Allen D. Hertzke looks into religious interest groups and how they fit into American democracy. Thomas J. O'Hara examines thirty-one Catholic lobbying groups and finds a microcosmic version of American diversity.

9. ASSESSING THE RELIGIOUS FACTOR IN ELECTORAL BEHAVIOR

Kenneth D. Wald

The image of elections as "the democratic expression of class struggle" has been effectively undermined by revisionist accounts of American political development. To historians of nineteenth and early twentieth century America, "past electoral behavior makes most sense when seen as the effect of cultural issues playing on the ethnoreligious group identities of the mass electorate."[1] Even though the disputes responsible for generating religion-based political conflict had largely receded from living memory by the mid-twentieth century, the pioneering scientific analysts of elections documented impressive residues of religious polarization in postwar voting patterns. The remarkable staying power of religious differences in other national electorates prompted one leading scholar to conclude that "religious differentiation intrudes on partisan political alignments in [an] unexpectedly powerful degree wherever it conceivably can."[2]

The most recent research, casting considerable doubt on the long-range survival of religious cleavages in American political behavior, suggests that the era of "confessional" politics may have passed. Though acknowledging the paramount historical importance of religion, political scientists contend that religion has lost influence as a predictor of candidate choice in presidential elections, a correlate of partisan loyalties, and a source of public attitudes on policy issues.[3] As additional evidence for the "secularization" of American political conflict, scholars can point to the growing attitudinal convergence on policy issues with moral implications and the limited impact of such issues, particularly abortion, on candidate choice in national elections.[4] Even as religious themes have gained renewed prominence in recent presidential elections, behavioral research suggests a continuing decline in the level of religious differences at the polls, denominational convergence in partisan loyalties, and a general tendency for voters to choose candidates on the basis of perceived managerial competence rather than positions on "morality" issues.[5] Summarizing these findings, the authors of a widely used textbook on American political behavior have concluded that "voting patterns of American religious groups usually are not particularly distinctive" and become so only under unusual circumstances.[6] Though predictions are seldom articulated, many researchers appear to believe that religion has only a small role to play in the politics of the future.

The apparent discovery of diminished religious influence on the vote is compatible with a widely accepted model of social development that predicts declining significance for religious identity and religiously inspired political conflict. According to the classical modernization perspective, the hold of traditional religious values is challenged by industrialization, mass education, technological sophistication, population mobility, rapid urbanization, and the proliferation of complex forms of social organization. These developments undercut religion by rendering its theological claims less plausible and by restricting its moral impact to the realm of privately held values and orientations. Under the impact of modernity, it is commonly hypothesized, "the salience of cultural similarity as a social bond should give way to political alliances between individuals of similar market position."[7] To judge by recent voting studies, that process is well underway in the electoral realm.

The image of a secularized political system, largely cleansed of "confessional" voting patterns, seems wildly inconsistent with the palpable evidence of religious impact documented by the other contributors to this volume. If religion has been consigned to political obsolescence in contemporary America, it is hard to understand, for example, how ministers could become credible presidential candidates, why religion-based issues rank so high on the national agenda, or what accounts for the respectful hearing granted to religious organizations in public policy debates. Surely there is some fire behind all that smoke! Indeed, it is the argument of this chapter that the apparent secularization of American electoral behavior is less the product of social change than a function of the way scholars have attempted to assess religious influences on the vote. Specifically, in writing off religion as a politically salient factor, scholars have overlooked three important factors that may shape the contemporary interaction between religious commitment and political behavior: (1) the fragmented condition of American religion, (2) the variability of individual religious commitment, and (3) the nature of candidate mobilization efforts.

Because these factors may have disguised the magnitude of confessional patterns in recent American voting and led to premature conclusions about a desacralized political system, this chapter is devoted principally to establishing their existence and political relevance. The chapter concludes with evidence that the linkage between religion and

American electoral politics persists in a more complex form than recent research has allowed. The major implication is that future investigations of the relationship between religion and politics must be sensitive to new trends and mechanisms lest they prematurely discard one important explanatory variable in American political life.

The Nature of Religious Affiliation

Rejecting the assumption of a linear decline in religious attachment, most students of contemporary American religion suggest that modernizing forces have altered the form of religious commitment rather than extinguished it altogether. The principal changes in American religious affiliation have derived from an intensification of individualist tendencies.[8] Always a strong theme in American religious life, individualism became even more important as an outgrowth of rapid social change in the 1950s and 1960s. The literature identifies two important modes of religious adaptation to modernity that can be traced to the growth of a more personal style of religious expression: differentiation and voluntarism. As used in the following discussion, *differentiation* refers to the fragmentation of large religious bodies and *voluntarism* refers to the evolution of religious identity from an ascriptive trait, conferred at birth, to a matter of choice and discretionary involvement. Both trends may have affected the manner in which religious commitment influences political decisions.

Differentiation has produced a complex pattern of religious affiliation in the United States, registering most keenly within the numerically dominant Protestant community. At the very least, American Protestantism is now bifurcated between an "evangelical" perspective and the "mainline" outlook. The two sides in what Martin Marty aptly labeled the two-party system of American Protestantism differ greatly over questions of religious authority and practice, with the evangelicals maintaining a revivalistic tradition and the mainline denominations proving more receptive to modern reformulations of Christian doctrine.[9] To some extent a regional phenomenon, the gulf between the two forms of Protestantism encompasses such fundamental issues as the meaning of Christian dogma, church polity, style of worship, the source of religious authority, and the social role of the church. Even this broad distinction does not do justice to the full extent of differentiation within contemporary American Protestantism. The evangelical community harbors a disparate array of fundamentalist, charismatic, and reformed traditions. Researchers have similarly argued that the mainline label is no more than a weak common denominator loosely covering the historic "liberal" churches ascendant at the time of the American founding and the "moderate" churches that date from the nineteenth century. Yet another line of distinction within Protestantism must be drawn on the basis of race. Predominantly black churches combine the theological affinities associated with evangelicalism and the progressive social role championed by mainline Protestantism. The creative synthesis has produced a distinctive black religious style standing apart, theologically and organizationally, from predominantly white American Protestantism.

The same tensions have marked other religious communities in the United States. Although broadly accepted by the majority of Roman Catholics in America, the liturgical reforms adopted since the Second Vatican Council polarized traditionalists and modernists. The conflicting perspectives now extend to fundamental debate about the contemporary meaning of Catholic doctrine. Some Catholics also responded to the growing interest in charismatic religion by adopting a more emotive style of worship quite at odds with the dignified and somber nature of the traditional mass. The immigration of Hispanic and Asian Catholics to the United States introduced a new ethnic division to what has always been a heterogeneous American Catholic community. In Judaism, the lines of division between the Reform, Conservative, and Orthodox communities also appear to have strengthened despite predictions that such differences would become less relevant with the passage of time. The unity of the American religious landscape has been further fractured by the durability and growth of Christian denominations outside the Protestant and Catholic world—for example, Mormons, Christian Scientists, Jehovah's Witnesses, and the Unification Church—and by the appearance, particularly in urban areas, of both Middle Eastern and Asian faiths. A discussion of fragmentation would be incomplete if it did not also acknowledge the growth of a secular stratum outside the embrace of any organized religious community. Taken together, these trends render hopelessly inadequate the traditional portrait of American religious identity encapsulated in Will Herberg's trinity of Protestant, Catholic, Jew.[10]

The pluralistic religious universe in America, reinforced by the progress of differentiation, has been further magnified by another trend—a pervasive privatization of religious faith. The result has been a system of voluntary affiliation that leaves individuals free to choose both *whether* and *how* to associate with the various religious communities. As a consequence, the intensity of religious affiliation varies greatly among individuals, and denominations exhibit diverse degrees of solidarity. For those members whose attachment is nominal, the church may constitute merely one of many voluntary associations making a claim upon the individual's time, attention, resources, and perspective. In a phrase that has gained widespread acceptability, such a loosely attached individual may only "happen to be" a member of a particular religious tradition and is unlikely to behave like fellow congregants outside the confines of the local church. At the other pole of commitment, the congregant may choose to be immersed in a highly articulated church-based subculture that encompasses school, work place, social relations, and recreational activity. By virtue of such encapsulation, the religious community may monopolize the individual's access to information and restrict the flow of external behavioral cues.

The effectiveness with which religious norms are transmitted and maintained would seem to depend upon the congregant's standing on this continuum of social integration. As deepening involvement with the religious organization increases exposure to formal agencies of religious socialization and enhances the probability of social interaction with fellow church members, "the degree to which an individual participates in a religious group would be expected to be related to the degree to which he subscribes to the values and norms of the group." [11] Correspondingly, the more concentrated the exposure to group-based socialization and social interaction, the greater the likelihood of group influence upon attitudes and behavior in external settings.

The Political Relevance of Religious Change

Religious change becomes important to political scientists when it alters or affects the characteristic expression of religious cleavage in politics.[12] The trends of differentiation and voluntarism should command attention precisely for that reason. The failure to take adequate account of these tendencies may explain why the scholarly studies cited earlier in this chapter routinely—and in my view, wrongly—suggest the decline or extinction of religious influence in American voting behavior.

If there once was a time when "Protestant versus others" accurately described the prevailing religious cleavage in American electoral politics, such a simple distinction no longer does justice to the extent of religious fragmentation within the American electorate. The search for religious differences in politics must be sensitive to the possibility that new lines of politically relevant conflict have replaced the traditional duality between Protestants and all other religious communities. By and large, political scientists have paid scant attention to that possibility, and it is still common to observe electoral analyses that simply apportion voters between the Protestant camp and a heterogeneous alternative that comprises Catholics, Jews, adherents of nontraditional faiths, and the irreligious.

Such a strategy flies in the face of evidence, collected primarily by sociologists, showing that political differences now run between denominations or respect even finer distinctions within religious communities.[13] Similarly, the significant population share outside churches or traditional American faiths also seems to maintain a distinctive political identity.[14] The subtlety of religious differences in politics—indeed, the political relevance of religious differences altogether—is likely to be lost when submerged by simple dichotomies between Protestants and "others." Fidelity to the fragmented condition of American religion requires apportioning respondents among multiple religious categories that correspond to the new theological and organizational strains within broad religious traditions.

Voluntarism takes on political relevance by influencing the level of individual conformity to group political tendencies. The success of religious groups in transmitting behavioral norms, political or otherwise, depends largely upon the congregants' level of involvement with the religious community.[15] For churches, just as for other secondary associations, the more concentrated the exposure to group-based socialization and social interaction, the greater the likelihood of group influence upon attitudes and behavior in external settings. Though that insight has seldom been incorporated in voting models, there is no good reason to think that political norms and tendencies would be exceptions. On that logic, differential exposure to a religious community should correlate with the degree of fidelity to the dominant political tendency of the religious community.

Both local studies and national survey data indicate a tie between strength of religious affiliation and individual compliance with group political norms. The complexity of such patterns was captured by Lenski's conclusion that churchgoing accentuated Republican propensities among white Protestants in Detroit and that social interaction with fellow Protestants had the same effect on working-class members of Protestant congregations. For Catholics, communal attachment encouraged Democratic loyalty but church attendance diminished it.[16] The early national election studies revealed that churchgoing Protestants voted Republican by higher margins than "nominal" Protestants and, conversely, that Catholics and Jews who strongly identified with their respective religious group voted more heavily Democratic than weakly identified members of the faith.[17] In the highly charged atmosphere of the 1960 presidential election, the most observant members of the Protestant community were more willing than their less observant coreligionists to cross party lines when their party nominated a Catholic presidential candidate.[18] The advent of Ronald Reagan appears to have intensified political cleavages between the observant and less observant members of the major religious communities.[19]

If, as these studies suggest, partisan traditions are strengthened by exposure to the socialization processes and social interaction that occur within the religious community, then simply lumping coreligionists together under a common label will disguise the full extent of religious influences on the vote. Rather, the analyst must differentiate members of a common faith by their level of involvement in church life and receptivity to church influence. Religiously distinctive voting patterns may be evinced in varying degrees depending upon the level of integration in church life.

In addition to differentiation and voluntarism, there is yet a third factor—mobilization—that may affect the relationship between religious affiliation and political behavior. Social cleavages normally become politicized only by the determined efforts of elites to forge an identity between members of the social group and a political party.[20] In societies with a modicum of religious tolerance, the activation of political tendencies among religious groups thus depends upon the mobilizing efforts of political and religious elites. The mechanisms of mobilization are not yet fully understood but may include pledges by candidates to incorporate the policy preferences of the group in the party platform, to seek out members of the group for public office, and, more generally, efforts to portray the party as the natural political expression of the group's religious values. Such efforts are likely to pay dividends if religious leaders confer legitimacy upon them by stressing an affinity between candidate, party, and group.

What are the implications of this view? Because linkages between religious groups and political parties are conditional, depending upon circumstances such as candidates and issues, the connections are subject to short-term change and should be treated as variable rather than constant. Of course, the scope of variation is constrained by historical traditions that may freeze cleavage patterns into persistent alignments. Nevertheless, the recent dealigning tendencies in the American electorate have imparted a fluidity capable of loosening the ties between parties and social groups such as religious communities. In an analysis of religious-political linkages over a string of national elections, Paul Lopatto demonstrated how the strength of religious influence varied from one election to the next, presumably as a function of the candidates' appeal to religious blocs.[21] Some Democratic presidential candidates—John F. Kennedy, George McGovern, Jimmy Carter— appear to have elicited very strong reactions from religious groups that together composed the core voting strength of the party. Kennedy strengthened the Democratic propensities of Catholics and Jews, important elements of the party's constituency, but diminished the traditional loyalties of white southern Protestants, who had also been an important component of Democratic electoral strength. McGovern's candidacy in 1972, which became associated in the public mind with libertarian policies toward controversial forms of personal conduct, drove away the more religiously observant among all the major religious groups normally associated with the Democratic coalition. When Carter first ran for president in 1976, his Southern Baptist background appears to have drawn a sizable number of white southern Protestants back into the Democratic camp but inspired less enthusiasm among Jewish and Catholic Democrats. That voters picked up such cues may have owed much to the efforts of religious leaders in alerting congregants to the implications of candidate qualities and issue positions.

These variations across campaigns attest to the conditional nature of religious-political linkages. The analyst who is not sensitive to the operation of candidate appeals and the mobilizing efforts of religious and political leaders can easily mistake short-term fluctuation for long-term decline. Religious cleavages, like other social divisions, will become more or less relevant politically as circumstances vary. The earlier discussion in this chapter admonished scholars to consider the political implications of religious change. The importance of mobilization makes it equally necessary that analysts pay attention to the religious implications of political change. Like differentiation and voluntarism, mobilization patterns may disrupt traditional forms of religious-political alignment without diminishing the overall political significance of religious cleavages.

Religion in Electoral Behavior: A Case Study

To illustrate the consequences of the analytic strategy suggested above, I will demonstrate how recognition of differentiation, voluntarism, and candidate mobilization might alter understanding of religious cleavage in the 1980 presidential election. Despite its temporal distance, the 1980 campaign presents an excellent case study because it has often been cited to illustrate the shift away from confessional politics. Despite a high level of activity by religious leaders throughout the 1980 campaign, religious differences in voting are widely reported to have declined from previous levels, with the Protestant-Catholic gap narrowing appreciably, Jewish voters moving considerably closer to the national partisan pattern, and evangelical Protestants—even after prodigious mobilization efforts—diverging little from voters outside their religious tradition.[22] If religion exerted so little effect in an election marked by strenuous appeals for confessional voting, then the case for secularization appears strong. By the same token, if the magnitude of religious influence has been underestimated because of the inappropriate application of obsolescent research strategies, that would raise doubts about the validity of the secularization hypothesis.

Because of its detailed information about religious attitudes and behavior, the General Social Survey (GSS) is the best data source available to support the type of analysis called for above. The GSS is a large, full-probability sample of the noninstitutionalized adult population conducted by the National Opinion Research Center. The 1983 and 1984 waves were combined to yield approximately 1,300 respondents who reported casting a vote for president in 1980 and who otherwise answered all relevant questions about religious background and involvement.[23] The task of the analysis will be to distinguish between those who voted for Ronald Reagan and those who voted either for Jimmy Carter or John Anderson.

To take account of differentiation, voters will be apportioned among five religious groups—Jews, Catholics, nonaffiliates, mainline Protestants, and evangelical Protestants.[24] While finer distinctions are possible, this scheme respects differences among non-Protestants and separates Protestants by their major internal division. The task of distinguishing between the two types of Protestants is exceptionally complicated because surveys are blunt instruments to measure divisions on issues such as "the sinful nature of man; the infinite but personal nature of God (a theistic conception); the role of Christ as savior through his life, death, and resurrection; the centrality of the Bible for its revealed truths about the faith and as the authoritative guide for daily life; and a concern for sharing the essentials of the faith with others, i.e., evangelism." [25] Even though conflict over these doctrines corresponds imperfectly to denominational lines, sometimes splitting confessions and congregations down the middle, researchers commonly rely on denominational identity as a surrogate for commitment to either the evangelical or mainline perspective. Following that strategy, respondents were assigned to the mainline category if the denomination belonged to the National Council of Churches and to the evangelical group if the church was affiliated with the National Association of Evangelicals.[26] The twenty groups in the mainline category included such traditional and high-status denominations as Episcopalian, Congregationalist, Disciples of Christ, Unitarian, Quaker, United Church of Christ, and selected branches of Methodists, Lutherans, Presbyterians, and Baptists. The major groups in the evangelical classification were Assembly of God, Church of Christ, Church of God, and the theologically conservative wings of Baptists, Methodists, Lutherans, and Presbyterians. These large denominations were supplemented by a number of smaller churches, sects, and splinter groups that are preponderantly evangelical in theological orientation. Despite the admitted crudeness of this scheme, ancillary data confirm that the partition corresponds to genuine theological differences.[27]

To measure the concept of voluntarism, we created a measure of "religious integration" from items indicating frequency and intensity of respondents' encounters with their religious community. The integration index was based on subjective strength of attachment to current denomination, frequency of worship, frequency of prayer, childhood affiliation with current denomination, parents' frequency of church attendance, and membership in church-affiliated organizations.[28] The resulting measure is intended to represent depth of religious commitment, a function of both current religious involvement and childhood socialization to denominational norms. Individual scores for the religiously affiliated ranged from a minimum of 1 to a maximum of 17, and the currently unaffiliated were assigned a value of 0 on the integration measure. The members of each religious group were subdivided into categories of low, medium, and high integration levels based on integration scores for the entire sample. This procedure thus produced a total of thirteen groups for analysis—three subsets of Catholics, Jews, mainline Protestants, and evangelical Protestants and the remaining group of the nonaffiliated.

We cannot directly measure candidate mobilization efforts but must instead attempt to discern the impact of such activity on the various religious communities. During the 1980 presidential campaign, the Republicans undertook a concerted effort to detach Catholics, Jews, and evangelical Protestants from their traditional roles in the Democratic coalition.[29] The Reagan campaign hoped to capitalize on Jewish doubts about President Carter's fidelity to the interests of Israel, positive Catholic reactions to Republican calls for abortion restriction and tuition tax credits, and the attractiveness to evangelicals of candidate Reagan's embrace of moral conservatism on a host of issues. This Republican effort to raid Democratic religious groups, vocally supported by some religious leaders, should have worked to greatest effect among the most strongly affiliated members of the target religious communities. By virtue of their intensive involvement with the group, the strongly affiliated were most likely to encounter the party-switching cues from clergymen and from their fellow church members. Even without such cues, the deeply involved were probably more likely to recognize the salience of the issues raised by the Republican campaign and to perceive that Reagan was closer than Carter to the position preferred by most members of the denomination. These factors suggest that defection from the group partisan tradition in 1980 would be most probable for the voters who were most deeply integrated with their religious denomination.

The research strategy thus involves a search for interaction between specific religious communities and candidate appeals. To recapitulate, the measure of religious affiliation recognizes the displacement of a Catholic-Protestant dichotomy by a broader division between five religious communities (including the unaffiliated). Assuming that the impact of religion varies with level of integration, respondents are further subdivided by degree of religious involvement. To exhibit sensitivity to the particular mobilization patterns in 1980, we will pay particular attention to the behavior of three historically Democratic religious communities targeted for mobilization by the Republican campaign.

Results of Analysis

The analysis in Table 9-1 reveals the role of religion in voting in the 1980 presidential election. It is based on an ordinary least squares regression equation that attempts to predict whether respondents voted for or against Reagan. To control other factors possibly associated with presidential voting and religious commitment, the analysis included control variables representing socioeconomic attainment (education, occupational prestige, and family income), region of residence, and gender. Because these variables are intended merely to check for the spurious influence of religion, we will limit comment to noting that the results are consistent with previous research in revealing a Republican advantage associated with education, income, nonsouthern residence, and male gender.

The coefficients associated with the religious categories must be interpreted as the difference in the probability of a vote for Ronald Reagan relative to the nonaffiliated and with all other social traits held constant. Perhaps the most striking conclusion is the variation in political behavior from the traditional Protestant versus others framework. Among the "others," candidate choice differed depending upon whether the respondent was nonreligious, Catholic, or Jewish. Judging by the negative signs, the latter two groups were considerably less likely to support Reagan than the baseline category of the religiously uninvolved. The "Protestant" coalition appeared equally heterogeneous in its political tendencies. In particular, while members of the mainline denominations retained a historic tie to Republicanism that set them apart from the nonreligious, most of the evangelicals were not significantly different in candidate choice from the comparison group. If the two wings had been combined as is customary in electoral analysis, the distinctiveness of the mainline Protestants would have been diminished by the inclusion of the substantially less pro-Republican evangelicals. Analysis that makes use of the traditional duality between Protestants and other religious communities does indeed seem likely to understate the significance of religious cleavage.

Table 9-1   Presidential Vote in 1980 by Major Religious Categories
($N = 1252$)

Variable	Coefficient
Unaffiliated	1.56
Jewish	
Low integration	−.17
Medium integration	−.31*
High integration	.23
Roman Catholic	
Low integration	−.06
Medium integration	−.14*
High integration	−.02
Evangelical Protestant	
Low integration	.07
Medium integration	.08
High integration	.17*
Mainline Protestant	
Low integration	.14*
Medium integration	.21**
High integration	.19*
Control variables	
Education	.01**
Income	.02**
Occupational prestige	.00
Region (1 = South)	−.07*
Gender (1 = female)	−.05

Note: The value for the unaffiliated represents the preference of nonreligious voters between Carter and Anderson (1) or Reagan (2). A value of 1.5 would indicate an even split between the two choices. Subsequent entries represent the difference in preference between the identified group and the unaffiliated with controls for relevant social variables. Thus, moderately integrated Jews would average 1.25 when compared with comparable nonaffiliates, indicating that the former were significantly less inclined to support Ronald Reagan in 1980.

*p < .05
**p < .01

The results also confirm the need to measure intensity of religious commitment. There were sharp differences in political behavior among adherents of some faiths when they were subdivided by level of social integration. The most pro-Democratic constituency within the Jewish community consisted of voters who were moderately attached to Judaism. Likewise, Roman Catholics who ranked on the middle range of the integration continuum were the most supportive of the Democratic candidate in 1980. Among the evangelicals, the highly integrated showed a pronounced tendency to deviate from group tradition by supporting the Republican nominee. The mainline Protestants do not appear to have voted according to level of integration but rather exhibited a fairly uniform Republican preference.

These patterns become explicable in light of what was said earlier about the need to consider the nature of mobilization efforts in 1980. Had the candidates appealed to religious groups in a manner that reinforced traditional group patterns of partisanship, it would have been reasonable to expect linear relationships between religious involvement and Democratic support for Catholic, Jewish, and evangelical Protestant voters. However, the possibility of Reagan's encroachment upon the highly integrated voters in those three religious communities sets up the possibility of nonlinear patterns. For Catholics and Jews, the most likely pattern would be a curvilinear relationship with low fidelity to the Democratic candidate among the least integrated, who exhibit the social traits associated with Republicanism, and defection among the highly integrated due to the appeals of the Republican nominee. That leaves the moderately involved as the group exhibiting loyalty to the traditional partisan norm. As the class milieu of many evangelicals is normally conducive to Democratic loyalty, we expect only those who receive clear religious cues to defect from traditional loyalty. Indeed, the responsiveness of evangelical Protestants to Republican mobilization efforts does vary as a linear function of religious integration. Once again, these findings suggest that religious cleavages in the electorate may be masked when analysts ignore differential exposure to denominational norms.

This interpretation hinges upon the assumption that the Republican nominee capitalized on short-term concerns to move highly integrated Jews, Catholics, and evangelical Protestants out of their normally pro-Democratic position. There is supportive evidence for this supposition in the form of questions that inquired about the salience of various issues to survey respondents. Though the item only approximates concern for Israel and the number of cases is pitifully small, the most highly integrated Jewish respondents gave Israel the maximum possible rating of 5.0 on a scale designed to assess approval of that nation. This average was approximately half a scale point more than the mean for the two other groups of Jewish respondents. The questions on abortion provide firmer support for attributing the defection of highly integrated Catholics to that issue. There was a significant difference in abortion attitudes between the moderately integrated and highly integrated Catholics. Whether asked about the importance of the issue, the firmness of their beliefs, or their personal concern about abortion policy, the most highly committed were more likely to attribute the greatest possible salience to the issue. The same pattern was discovered when the most observant evangelicals were compared to their less observant coreligionists on questions assessing moral traditionalism. These findings cannot prove that Republican mobilization efforts were responsible for partisan defection, let alone that these issues influenced candidate choice, but they are consistent with the argument that the most highly integrated voters exhibited political volatility when short-term forces conflicted with group norms.

Conclusion

The results of even this cursory analysis pose some challenge to the notion that modernization inevitably entails the secularization of political conflict. Students of political behavior need to recognize the capacity of religion to adjust and adapt to the conditions of modernity and how such adaptation alters the relationship between religion and politics. Because of the new complexity in religious alignments, it is no longer enough to compare Protestants with all others or even to contrast several religious communities—although that is a major improvement over the traditional duality. The differences *between* religious groups are overlaid by differences *within* groups according to level of involvement. The decline of traditional partisan loyalties has further complicated analysis by producing volatile new patterns of affiliation between candidates and religious constituencies.

On the evidence presented here, one promising avenue for further exploration is to consider the mechanisms that promote responsiveness to denominational political tendencies. We have inferred but not established the existence of denominational socializing processes, social interaction, and elite mobilization as agents promoting political uniformity in religious communities.[30] Similarly, it was assumed that a particular set of religious attitudes, behavior, and experience could signify the degree to which individuals absorb and act upon political cues emanating from religious communities. Subsequent research needs to establish whether such indicators have common meaning across religious communities or vary from one faith to another. These are the kinds of issues requiring exploration if the growing religious motif in American politics is to be better understood and appreciated.

Notes

1. Melvyn Hammarberg, *The Indiana Voter: The Historical Dynamics of Party Allegiance during the 1870s* (Chicago: University of Chicago Press, 1977), 9-10.

2. Philip E. Converse, "Some Priority Variables in Comparative Electoral Research," in *Electoral Behavior: A Comparative Handbook*, ed. Richard Rose (New York: Free Press, 1974), 734.

3. Paul R. Abramson, John H. Aldrich, and David W. Rohde, *Change and Continuity in the 1980 Elections* (Washington, D.C.: CQ Press, 1982), 111-115; Robert Axelrod, "Communication," *American Political Science Review* 76 (June 1982): 393-396; Richard E. Dawson, *Public Opinion and Contemporary Disarray* (New York: Harper & Row, 1973), 132-134; Evelyn Deborah Jay, "Religious Commitment: Its Origins and Its Consequences for Social Conservatism and Political Action" (Ph.D. diss., University of California at Berkeley, 1981), 312-335; William S. Maddox, "Changing Electoral Coalitions from 1952-1976," *Social Science Quarterly* 60 (September 1979): 309-313.

4. Donald Granberg and James Burlison, "The Abortion Issue in the 1980 Elections," *Family Planning Perspectives* 15 (September-October 1983): 231-238; Carol Mueller, "In Search of a Constituency for the New Religious Right," *Public Opinion Quarterly* 47 (Summer 1983): 213-229; Tom W. Smith, "General Liberalism and Social Change in Post-World War II America: A Summary of Trends," *Social Indicators Research* 10 (1981): 1-28; Michael W. Traugott and Maris A. Vinovskis, "Abortion and the 1978 Congressional Elections," *Family Planning Perspectives* 12 (September-October 1980): 238-246; Maris A. Vinovskis, "Abortion and the Presidential Election of 1976: A Multivariate Analysis of Voting Behavior," *Michigan Law Review* 77 (August 1979): 1750-1771.

5. Stephen D. Johnson and Joseph B. Tamney, "The Christian Right and the 1980 Presidential Election," *Journal for the Scientific Study of Religion* 2 (June 1982): 123-131; Jerome M. Himmelstein and James A. McRae, Jr., "Social Conservatism, New Republicanism and the 1980 Election," *Public Opinion Quarterly* 48 (Fall 1984): 592-605; Everett C. Ladd, "The Brittle Mandate: Electoral Dealignment and the 1980 Presidential Election," *Political Science Quarterly* 96 (Spring 1981): 12-13; Jerry Perkins, Donald Fairchild, and Murray Havens, "The Effects of Evangelicalism on Southern Black and White Political Attitudes and Behavior," in *Religion and Politics in the South: Mass and Elite Perspectives*, ed. Tod A. Baker, Robert B. Steed, and Lawrence W. Moreland (New York: Praeger, 1983), 57-83.

6. William H. Flanigan and Nancy H. Zingale, *Political Behavior of the American Electorate* (Boston: Allyn and Bacon, 1983), 79.

7. Michael Hechter, *Internal Colonialism* (Berkeley: University of California Press, 1975), 16.

8. Wade C. Roof and William McKinney, *American Mainline Religion: Its Changing Shape and Future* (New Brunswick, N.J.: Rutgers University Press, 1987). For a comprehensive discussion of the effects of modernity on religion as a political force, see Kenneth D. Wald, "Social Change and Political Response: The Silent Religious Cleavage in North American Politics," in *Politics and Religion since 1945*, ed. George Moyser (London: Croom Helm, forthcoming).

9. Martin E. Marty, *Righteous Empire: The Protestant Experience in America* (New York: Harper & Row, 1970).

10. Will Herberg, *Protestant, Catholic, Jew* (Garden City, N.Y.: Doubleday-Anchor, 1960).

11. Benton Johnson and Richard H. White, "Protestantism, Political Preference and the Nature of Religious Influence: Comment on Anderson's Paper," *Review of Religious Research* 9 (Fall 1967): 33.

12. Kenneth D. Wald, *Crosses on the Ballot: Patterns of English Voter Alignment since 1885* (Princeton: Princeton University Press, 1983), chap. 8.

13. Kathleen Murphy Beatty and Oliver Walter, "Religious Preference and Practice: Reevaluating Their Impact on Political Tolerance," *Public Opinion Quarterly* 48 (Spring 1984): 318-329; Steven M. Cohen and Robert E. Kapsis, "Religion, Ethnicity and Party Affiliation in the United States: Evidence from Pooled Election Surveys, 1968-1972," *Social Forces* 56 (December 1977): 637-653; David Knoke, "Religious Involvement and Political Behavior: A Log-Linear Analysis of White Americans, 1952-1968," *Sociological Quarterly* 15 (Winter 1974): 51-65; David Knoke, "Religion, Stratification and Politics: America in the 1960s," *American Journal of Political Science* 18 (May 1974): 331-345.

14. Kenneth D. Wald, *Religion and Politics in the United States* (New York: St. Martin's Press, 1987), chap. 4.

15. Charles H. Anderson, "Religious Communality and Party Preference," in *Research in Religious Behavior*, ed. Benjamin Beit-Hallahmi (Monterey, Calif.: Brooks-Cole, 1973), 336-352; J. M. Bochel and D. T. Denver, "Religion and Voting: A Critical Review and a New Analysis," *Political Studies* 18 (June 1970): 205-219; Johnson and White, "Protestantism," 28-35; Larry R. Petersen and K. Peter Takayama, "Religious Commitment and Conservatism: Toward Understanding an Elusive Relationship," *Sociological Analysis* 45 (Winter 1984): 355-371; Rodney Stark, "Religion and Conformity: Reaffirming a *Sociology* of Religion," *Sociological Analysis* 45 (Winter 1984): 274-282; Richard H. White, "Toward a Theory of Religious Influence," *Pacific Sociological Review* 11 (Spring 1968): 23-28.

16. Gerhard Lenski, *The Religious Factor* (Garden City, N.Y.: Doubleday-Anchor, 1963).

17. Angus Campbell, Philip E. Converse, Warren E. Miller, and Donald Stokes, *The American Voter* (New York: Wiley, 1960), 309-310; Morris Janowitz and Dwaine Marvick, *Competitive Pressure and Democratic Consent* (Ann Arbor: Institute of Public Administration, University of Michigan, 1956), 27.

18. Philip E. Converse, "Religion and Politics: The 1960 Election," in *Elections and the Political Order*, ed. Angus Campbell, Philip E. Converse, Warren E. Miller, and Donald Stokes (New York: Wiley, 1966), 119.

19. John R. Petrocik and Frederick T. Steeper, "The Political Landscape in 1988," *Public Opinion* 10 (September-October 1987): 41-44.

20. Alan Zuckerman, "Political Cleavage: A Conceptual and Theoretical Analysis," *British Journal of Political Science* 5 (April 1975): 231-248; Shimson Zelniker and Michael Kahan, "Religion and Nascent Cleavages: The Case of Israel's National Religious Party," *Comparative Politics* 9 (October 1976): 21-48.

21. Paul Lopatto, *Religion and the Presidential Election* (New York: Praeger, 1985), 63-67.

22. Abramson, Aldrich, and Rohde, *Change and Continuity*, 113; Alan M. Fisher, "Jewish Political Shift? Erosion, Yes; Conversion, No," in *Party Coalitions in the 1980s*, ed. Seymour Martin Lipset (San Francisco: Institute for Contemporary Studies, 1981), 327-340; Seymour Martin Lipset and Earl Raab, "The Election and the Evangelicals," *Commentary* 71 (March 1981): 25-31; Martin P. Wattenberg and Arthur H. Miller, "Decay in Regional Party Coalitions, 1952-1980," in *Party Coalitions*, 341-367.

23. Only the 1983 and 1984 waves included both a question about recalled presidential vote in 1980 and the complete religious information necessary to measure the level of respondent involvement with a religious community. Despite the possibility of a

bandwagon effect in memories about the 1980 presidential vote, the respondents do not appear to have distorted their recollections to favor the incumbent at the time the survey was administered.

24. Because of their virtual unanimity on behalf of the Democratic candidate, black voters have been excluded from the analysis.

25. Lyman A. Kellstedt and Corwin E. Smidt, "The Impact of Religion on Politics: Some Prior Questions of Conceptualization and Measurement" (Paper presented to the annual meeting of the American Political Science Association, New Orleans, August 1985), 4.

26. The 1983 survey did not code Methodists, Baptists, and Presbyterians by specific organizational affiliation. Because regional differences within those traditions tend to correspond to the evangelical—mainline divide, members of the three groups were subdivided on the basis of region. Those who lived in the South as children were assigned to the evangelical camp and nonsoutherners were assigned to the mainline category.

27. The 1984 GSS included questions about Bible interpretation and relationship with God. The respondents classified as evangelicals were significantly more likely than Protestants in the mainline category to endorse a literal interpretation of the Bible and to report that they felt "extremely close" to the deity. These differences are consistent with the portrayal of evangelicals as distinctly committed to biblical inerrancy and to an intimate, personal embrace of God.

28. For the four groups of affiliates, the integration variable was calculated as a simple additive measure with points received for activities or dispositions likely to encourage and/or reflect involvement in the group. It was created by adding points for childhood membership in the current denomination (1 point), frequency of church attendance by respondent, father, and mother (0 through 3 points), intensity of identification with the current denomination (1 through 3 points), membership in a church-affiliated organization (1 point), and reported frequency of prayer (0 through 3 points). The values can be examined by consulting James A. Davis and Tom W. Smith, *General Social Surveys, 1972-1984* (Chicago: National Opinion Research Center).

29. See Elizabeth Drew, *Portrait of an Election* (New York: Simon & Schuster, 1981).

30. The attitudinal effect of the local congregation has been explored in Kenneth D. Wald, Dennis E. Owen, and Samuel S. Hill, Jr., "Churches as Political Communities," *American Political Science Review,* 82 (June 1988): 531-548.

10. THE ROLE OF RELIGIOUS LOBBIES

Allen D. Hertzke

From the abolitionist movement of the nineteenth century, to the crusade against alcohol, to the more recent civil rights struggle, religion-based movements in America have attempted to influence public policy often with dramatic results. What is striking about the contemporary era, however, is the extent to which religious engagement, across the theological and ideological spectrum, is institutionalized into national lobbying organizations. In 1950 there were only sixteen major religious lobbies in Washington representing fairly narrow concerns. By 1985 there were at least eighty and the list is growing. Drawn by the same imperatives that brought hundreds of groups to the nation's capital in the "advocacy explosion," religious lobbies now roughly mirror the pluralism of faith and practice in America.[1]

Their political agenda has broadened as well. Religious groups, not surprisingly, are deeply involved (on all sides) in such highly charged issues as abortion, school prayer, the Equal Rights Amendment, and aid to parochial schools. But they will also be found embroiled in battles over a host of social welfare, military, and foreign policy issues.

This institutionalized activism is a potentially far reaching development, for both religion and American politics. But while a number of scholars have explored facets of this trend, no one has examined systematically the collective and interactive role of contemporary religious groups in the national pressure system.[2] Yet it is the very nature of the pressure system, as described by interest group scholars, that makes the religious contribution potentially significant.

This study seeks to address this gap by examining the representational role of national religious lobbies. It is based upon wide-ranging interviews with the Washington leaders of thirty national religious groups, including representatives of Roman Catholic, "mainline" Protestant, "peace" Protestant, Jewish, and Christian evangelical and fundamentalist constituencies. Interviews with a comparable sample of key Washington elites, including members of Congress and their staffs, White House officials, and political party leaders, are used to corroborate statements made by the religious leaders. Finally, the study draws upon the 1984 American National Election Study to evaluate the match between lobby policy and member views.

Religious Lobbies and the Elite Pressure System

The problem of representation, as Cigler and Loomis observe, is the central issue in scholarly treatment of the "pressure system" in Washington. It is a theme that stretches half a century, from the devastating analysis of the politics of tariffs in the 1930s, to contemporary treatments of political action committees in the 1980s. E. E. Schattschneider, for example, argued that whereas mass-based political parties have the incentive to reach out and mobilize those weaker, less articulate, less wealthy, and otherwise hard to organize citizens, interest groups are by nature elite in membership. Even unions and farm groups, he observed, represented the most well heeled of the working classes.[3] The poor, for a variety of reasons, are the least represented by interest groups, a theme echoed by Bachrach and Baratz. Mancur Olson, of course, provided the economic rationale for the failure of those with a shared interest to organize a group to represent them, challenging a major component of Truman's more benign explanation of groups in the American polity.[4] The logic of collective action, Olson observed, ensures that the interest group universe will be skewed in favor of those groups that represent few members, can compel membership, or offer some selective benefit to members only. Later research on organizational maintenance refined, but did not refute Olson's basic insight—that some interests are more easily mobilized than others. Central to the critique of interest groups was a concern with the inordinate power of narrow economic interests, which meant, in Schattschneider's celebrated phrase, that "in the pluralist heaven the choir sings with an upper class accent."[5] Even when business interests are viewed as occasionally checked by countervailing power, few dispute the prevailing elite bias in Washington lobbying.[6]

Recent developments have heightened concern over the nature of the pressure system. While social, technological, and political trends have favored the proliferation of interest groups in the last two decades, political parties have declined, weakened by diminishing public support and reforms that have reduced the electoral influence of party leaders.[7] This broad trend, coupled with related developments in Congress that dispersed power and undermined party leadership and cohesion, has enhanced the influence of interest groups. The rise of political action committees (PACs), technological innovations in information processing, and the decline of parties have created a context in which interest groups are more important in politics than at any other time, leading scholars to question anew their role in the American polity. Summarizing the changes in the American political system over the past two decades, Jeffrey Berry concludes:

> Even with the increase in citizen groups, the universe of lobbying organizations favors business, labor, and the professions, at the expense of the poor, minorities, and diffuse, hard-to-organize constituencies. . . . Thus both the decline of parties and the proliferation of interest groups have worked to the advantage of those already well represented in the political process.[8]

The politicization of churches and the mobilization of self-consciously religious people intersect this picture in a number of intriguing ways. Indeed, it is the very nature of the pressure system that makes religious lobbying of potential import. First, of all the reasons for violating economic self-interest, in light of the Olsonian dilemma, the religious motivation is one of the most compelling. The religious message, at least in its Christian form, is a suprarational, paradoxical call for transcendence over one's narrow selfish interest. Christians are called, as Jesus says, to "lose their lives" to gain the kingdom. Thus, religious motivation potentially undercuts the Olsonian dilemma of economic rationality and the attendant "free rider" problems of collective action. Giving money to a church or to a direct-mail religious group is not just a form of advocacy or self-interest; rather, it is a modest way of giving oneself, of losing one's (selfish) life to save it. Indeed, Olson's rational economic actor looks remarkably like the person on the negative side of Jesus' dictum, the one who seeks to gain life, who seeks economic self-interest, and hence, cannot gain the kingdom.

At the operational level it appears that this message has not lost its modest salience. Religious scholars have documented the seemingly paradoxical fact that it is often members of less elite churches who contribute the greatest share of their incomes to their local parish; having less to lose in this world, they have the most to gain in the kingdom.[9] Olson alludes to the complex nature of religious motivation when he observes: "In philanthropic and religious lobbies the relationships between the purposes and interests of the individual member, and the purposes and interests of the organization may be so rich and obscure that a theory of the sort developed here cannot provide much insight."[10] This is not to suggest that religious interest groups can avoid completely the problems of institutional maintenance that other groups face, but it suggests that they may call upon a level of sustained commitment that other groups cannot approach.

A second intriguing feature of religious interest groups is the breadth of their work. Religious groups, defying easy categorization, operate simultaneously as institutions with economic interests, as ideological advocates, and as public interest lobbies. Indeed, the religious leaders interviewed for this study do not see themselves as representing narrow interests, but instead consciously attempt to advance their competing visions of the public good. Moreover, most Jewish and Christian lobbies, across the ideological spectrum, see their roles as explicitly representing Olson's hard-to-organize citizens, and they argue that lobbying on behalf of institutional self-interest is merely a means to serve better the "voiceless" in society. To be sure, they disagree profoundly about what those citizens need or want. But one could make a case that all are partially correct: that poor and working class citizens do in fact want economic security along with a share of the pie (as liberals argue), but simultaneously feel threatened by cultural change and the undermining of traditional values—and want to see family life strengthened and their religious faith taken seriously (as conservatives argue).

The nature of the religious constituency is also unique among interest groups. Not only do the majority of citizens claim religious affiliation, but, contrary to Schattschneider's contention, the lower classes dominate church attendance, which led Paul Weber to conclude that "identifiable religious societies are important for interest group theory partially because they are by far the largest non-elite group in the nation." [11] Churches and synagogues indeed present a powerful contrast to the image of America as a "mass society" of atomized individuals physically unconnected with each other. In any given week over 40 percent of all Americans attend church, and nearly 60 percent can be described as regular churchgoers.[12] Organized religion is thus the premier voluntary association in the country, an association particularly important to those historically excluded from participation elsewhere. For example, when survey respondents are asked how important religion is to them on a scale of 1 to 10, American blacks surpass all other subgroups with an average response over 9.[13]

The significance of this peculiar American attachment to religion has escaped most interest group scholars, but with the increasing politicization of churches and religious people, it emerges as an important point of departure. Effective religious mobilization, in short, could enhance the articulation of diverse, nonelite interests in the American political system. To evaluate this proposition it is necessary to assess the nature and effectiveness of the activities of religious groups, and then to test whether those activities correspond to member concerns or broader public opinion.

The Impact of Religious Lobbying

National religious leaders operate much as other lobbyists do. They propose bills and amendments, testify before congressional committees, track legislation, provide information on the impacts of public policies, and bring pressure by mobilizing their constituencies in congressional districts and states. But their effectiveness, by their own admission and the analysis of other elites, is sporadic and issue-specific. Thus to understand the actual impact of religious lobbying one must look beyond the spectacular and public—whether the militant rhetoric of the fundamentalist right or the "leftist" pronouncements of the National Council of Churches—to the strategic level, where religious values meet the hard, seductive reality of practical politics. What emerges is a pattern of issue-specific influence based upon tactical decisions, constituent support, and fortuitous circumstances.

There is considerable ideological diversity and texture among the religious lobbyists, but for our purposes here it is useful to highlight the two ideological poles. Anchored in the United Methodist Building is the left-leaning "peace and justice" cluster, comprising the liberal mainline Protestants (Methodists, Presbyterians, Lutherans, Episcopalians, the United Church of Christ), the peace churches (Mennonites, Friends, Brethren), the black churches, and some Catholic groups (Network, Maryknoll). Often associated with this cluster are the Jewish groups (although tensions with liberal Protestants over U.S. aid to Israel are straining relations). At the other end of the spectrum are those emphasizing traditional values—Christian fundamentalists (Moral Majority, Christian Voice, Concerned Women for America), some evangelical groups, and Catholic anti-abortion lobbies. Between the poles are those groups, such as the U.S. Catholic Conference and Evangelicals for Social Action, that combine the anti-abortion lobbying of the right with support for the economic and foreign policy goals of the left.

Christian fundamentalists have been most effective in shaping the congressional agenda on issues that resonate with the cultural conservatism of their constituents, such as support for school prayer and opposition to abortion and pornography. Most of this influence comes from the ability to mobilize their sympathizers to flood Washington with letters and calls. The most dramatic example of this was the 1984 school prayer mobilization, which by all accounts produced an unprecedented constituent response.[14] Noted one unsympathetic Republican senatorial aide: "They play hard ball. Compared to the whole universe of lobbies out there, they are tough. On school prayer they had mass rallies on the Capitol, and generated an incredible amount of phone calls and mail." While the school prayer amendment ultimately failed, this mobilization set the stage for the successful passage of the Equal Access Act (PL 98-377), which partially addressed concerns of evangelicals and fundamentalists about faith and secular schools. On other issues New Right leaders are learning to combine outside pressure with classic insider strategies to capitalize on the multiple veto points in the decentralized Congress. Thus they have used killer amendments and delaying strategies to block public funding for abortions and the reintroduction of the Equal Rights Amendment.

When Christian Right leaders have moved beyond social issues to a conservative military and economic agenda, they have been far less successful, in part because they have not been able to generate the same intensity of member responses, but also because they find it strategic to concentrate on issues that are "hot buttons" for fund raising. Supply-side economics and "opposition to Communism in South Africa" have not, as yet, proven salient to their constituents. One congressional source summarized it this way: "The fundamentalists are mobilizing large numbers. But most of the fundamentalist churches cater to working-class, blue collar people. . . . Some tilt to the Democratic party on income distribution issues. They are pretty united on abortion, but it is harder to galvanize on other issues."

For the "peace and justice" cluster the picture is similarly mixed. While these groups have been less successful at mobilization than the fundamentalists, they have access to information gained through church networks and institutions that makes up for this deficiency. The mainline churches run a multitude of domestic social service agencies, soup kitchens, and food pantries, and are also connected to international relief agencies, development programs, and members scattered across the globe. On the basis of these networks, church lobbyists routinely testify on the Hill about the effects of domestic and foreign policies, and key congressional committees find this information useful in countering statements made by the administration. But long-term credibility on the Hill is intimately linked to the ability of national groups to galvanize their members in congressional districts. One member of Congress stated flatly that he does not listen to the national groups. "You ought to be lobbying your own members in my district," he advised one group, a sentiment echoed frequently. While liberal church lobbies take positions on scores of issues, ranging from labor legislation to the environment, it appears that only on hunger and peace has the liberal community collectively generated respectable constituent pressure on members of Congress.[15] The hunger issue seems to provide an unambiguous and ideologically neutral way to appeal to the Christian charity of members in pews. The main locus for mobilization on hunger issues has been Bread for the World (BFW), which calls itself a "Christian Citizens Lobby." The brainchild of Arthur Simon, brother of Illinois senator Paul Simon, BFW conducts research on complex domestic and foreign policies that influence food availability for the world's poor, and mobilizes letter campaigns from members and offerings from covenant churches. The hunger focus has a greater bipartisan flavor than much of the liberal agenda, and some congressional Republicans take seriously its grass-roots appeal. Said one Republican aide, "I can tell you when a Bread for the World alert went out in Connecticut. They have the ability to generate [constituent pressure]."

Liberal groups, collectively, have also successfully mobilized constituents on peace issues—especially opposition to nuclear weapons and American involvement in Central America. The Christian peace network is orchestrated by the pacifist denominations, such as the Quakers and Mennonites, which have sizable lists of mobilizable members, by the mainline Protestant churches, and by Catholic groups such as NETWORK (the "nuns" lobby) and elements of the U.S. Catholic Conference. Sensing support in the pews, many churches have grown increasingly bold in opposing U.S. support for the Nicaraguan contras. The American Lutheran Church (ALC), for example, took the unusual step of mailing hundreds of thousands of bulletin inserts to its churches. The one-page insert concluded with this clear statement of policy: "Official ALC resolutions have called for an end to U.S. military involvement in the region, especially an end to support of the 'contra' forces attacking Nicaragua. The ALC calls for negotiated settlements of the region's conflicts and for justice for its impoverished majority." [16] This statement was distributed in Lutheran churches on April 6, 1986, one week before the House of Representatives was scheduled to vote on contra aid.

Lobby effectiveness is in part a function of strategic focus. Some religious leaders admit they have a hard time making tactical decisions—what to fight, what not to fight. But President Reagan's embrace of the contras, an unpopular policy according to public opinion polls, galvanized the liberal religious community and, in a peculiar twist, focused the religious leaders on a policy they could champion and not be accused of being out of step with members. As Gretchen Eick, a lobbyist for the United Church of Christ, put it: "You have to focus to be effective, and to manage a grass-roots network. We don't spend time on all issues. We think we can win on aid to the contras, so there are lots of things we don't concentrate on." Religious groups organized demonstrations in Washington against contra aid, initiated letter-writing campaigns, and sponsored congressional visitations and testimony by clerical leaders returning from the region with fresh reports of alleged contra atrocities.

Church groups constituted the strongest lobby against the president's aid package, in part because foreign policy issues lack the kind of natural constituencies we see with most domestic concerns.[17] Indeed, so important were the religious groups that the House Democratic leadership, at the direction of Speaker Thomas P. (Tip) O'Neill, Jr., D-Mass., took special measures to communicate with them about strategies, timing, and wavering members.[18] The congressional rebuke to the president, as reflected in the Boland restrictions, is testament to the growing importance of this religiously mobilized constituency, which played a part in the still unfolding drama.

To summarize, while liberal and conservative religious communities do clash with each other, there is a degree of specialization that arises out of strategic considerations and constituency support; each cluster, in effect, has its own sphere of influence. Thus, assessments of religious political activism that exclude this strategic realm miss an important aspect of representation in the pressure system, as the discussion below amplifies.

Oligarchic Leadership and Representation

History is filled with examples of disparities between leaders and members of organizations. Indeed, much of the treatment of single interest groups has centered on the oligarchical nature of leadership, which, of course, Michels took to be the universal trait of organization.[19] Evidence suggests this oligarchic tendency operates for religious groups too, as leaders often take positions at variance with their members.[20] This study departs from previous works in evaluating religious elites in light of *strategic* choices they make. In this context we find that "representative" lobbying is generally more effective than "oligarchic" lobbying, and smart leaders pick their targets accordingly. Thus the religious groups, by virtue of their pluralism, contact with citizens, and issue specialization, provide countervailing power in the pressure system.

Breakdowns by religious preference in the 1984 American National Election study highlight this tendency. The Christian Right's sphere of influence, for example, is on such social issues as abortion, pornography, and school prayer. And contrary to assertions that the Moral Majority represents only a small minority of Americans, evidence suggests that on cultural issues fundamentalist groups do articulate broad public sentiment.[21] Fully two-thirds of Americans surveyed support recited prayer in the public schools, a position exclusively advanced by fundamentalist lobbies. Moreover, the denominational breakdown on Table 10-1 reveals the overwhelming sentiment in favor of school prayer among Southern Baptist, born again, and

Table 10-1   Opinion on School Prayer by Religious Affiliation
(Percentage of Respondents)

| | Allow School Prayer | | | |
Affiliation	*Yes*	*No*	*Depends*	*(N)*
Presbyterian	56	37	7	(75)
Lutheran [a]	64	27	9	(92)
Episcopal	61	27	12	(41)
Methodist	71	22	7	(175)
Baptist [b]	78	17	6	(139)
Fundamentalist [c]	83	9	8	(149)
Southern Baptist	85	10	5	(147)
Roman Catholic	64	26	10	(384)
Jewish	14	80	6	(35)
Born Again	83	9	8	(485)
Black [d]	83	11	5	(167)

Source: 1984 American National Election Study.

Note: Some totals do not equal 100 percent due to rounding.

[a] Excludes Missouri Synod Lutherans.
[b] Excludes Southern, Independent, and Free Will Baptists.
[c] The American National Election Study included as "neo-fundamentalists" members of Holiness, Nazarenes, Pentecostal, Assemblies of God, Church of Christ, Missouri Synod Lutheran, and Independent and Free Will Baptist churches. For brevity I refer to them as fundamentalists.
[d] Inclusion of this racial category is explained in the text.

independent fundamentalist constituencies, indicating that New Religious Right leaders acted shrewdly when they made school prayer the centerpiece of their legislative agenda in 1984. Indeed, one can assert that fundamentalist groups forced an issue with broad public support but few institutional backers to the forefront of the congressional agenda. In this case the oligarchic or unrepresentative lobbying was done by the liberal church groups, which universally opposed the president's school prayer amendment (though some supported equal access). Ironically, the sentiment of American blacks, overwhelmingly supportive of school prayer, was represented on this issue by the fundamentalists and not the liberal churches.

On abortion the picture is a bit more complex. Contrary to feminist assertions that the majority of Americans support unconditional choice, the apparent sentiment reflects a deep ambivalence on the issue, particularly when survey respondents are given conditions under which they would permit abortions. While a mere 13 percent of the national sample would bar all abortions, only 36 percent support unconditional choice. The majority would restrict it to such specified circumstances as rape, incest, or perceived necessity. In light of these findings the Moral Majority's strategy of opposing abortion except in the cases of rape, incest, and where the mother's life is at stake, places it in the center of American opinion. Opposition to unconditional choice is not only prevalent among fundamentalists and Baptists, as Table 10-2 indicates, but with broad segments of the churchgoing public as well.

The liberal lobbies enjoy a similar pattern of popular support on targeted issues. On Central America, for example, while 73 percent of the respondents said the Reagan administration wanted more U.S. involvement in Central America, only 25 percent shared this goal, with over 55 percent wanting less involvement. This corroborates other polls that reveal widespread opposition to U.S. support for the Nicaraguan contras. The religious breakdown on this issue, presented on Table 10-3, reveals across the board resistance to increased involvement. Interestingly, the least support for activist policies in the region comes from the fundamentalist group, 63 percent of whom said they wanted less involvement. While this may reflect isolationist sentiment along with opposition to the ideological thrust of the Reagan administration, it does reveal impediments to mobilization that New Right leaders face in supporting the president's initiatives. In contrast, the liberal churches appear to articulate broad opposition to, or anxiety about, U.S. military ventures in the region.

When a broader range of issues is assessed we see a patchwork of varying constituent support, as Table 10-4 indicates. The liberal Protestant groups appear out of step with their own members on school prayer and abortion, but not on support for the environment or opposition to the contras. The fundamentalist groups articulate well

Table 10-2 Opinion on Abortion, by Frequent Attenders for Selected Denominations (Percentage of Respondents)

	Woman's Choice	Conditional or Never	(N)
Presbyterian	41	59	(41)
Episcopal	55	45	(20)
Lutheran	16	84	(73)
Methodist	25	75	(106)
Baptist	20	80	(125)
Southern Baptist	23	77	(110)
Fundamentalist	16	84	(117)
Catholic	26	74	(334)

Source: 1984 American National Election Study.

Table 10-3   Opinion on U.S. Involvement in Central America by
Religious Affiliation (Percentage of Respondents)

	Want More	*Same*	*Want Less*	*(N)*
Presbyterian	23	26	51	(80)
Lutheran	23	19	58	(104)
Episcopal	30	11	59	(47)
Methodist	29	21	50	(175)
Baptist	29	21	49	(133)
Fundamentalist	19	18	63	(134)
Southern Baptist	36	15	49	(131)
Roman Catholic	22	21	56	(447)
Jewish	9	36	56	(45)
Born Again	29	20	51	(387)
Sample	20	25	55	(1,541)

Source: 1984 American National Election Study.

their followers' sentiments on school prayer, abortion, "getting tough
with the Soviet Union," and increasing defense spending. But they
diverge on support for the president's Central American policy and food
stamp cuts. The U.S. Catholic Conference, intriguingly, appears
well supported in both its conservative anti-abortion lobbying and its
liberal economic and military positions, and Jewish groups, among the
most effective, operate with strong member support. Charges that
groups do not represent their constituents are thus partially correct.
However, when strategic specialization and effectiveness are assessed,
the impact is greatest where sentiment is most supportive, a finding that
should help guide inquiry into interest groups generally.

Summary

Religion, at its heart, requires a radical commitment from its
adherents, which explains in part the temptation of some religious
leaders to embody a "prophetic" militancy in their public rhetoric. Yet
the congressional milieu, with its emphasis upon consensus and
strategic compromise, demands that groups articulate their concerns on
its terms. Thus those who criticize political activities of churches, or
fear religious zealots, often miss the actual policy implications of
religious activism. The context of action, as Richard Fenno observes, is
a critical ingredient in political analysis.[22] Thus liberal churches, in the
context of the Reagan era, found themselves lobbying to block
unpopular cuts proposed by the administration for environmental and
social welfare programs, or mobilizing against military expansion in

Table 10-4   Lobby Policy and Lay Member Support by Religious
Lobby and Issue

	Prayer	Abortion	Central America	Russia	Defense Spending	Food Spending	Environmental Spending
Presbyterian	−	−	+	+	0	+	+
Lutheran	−	−	+	0	0	−	+
Episcopal	−	+	+	+	0	+	+
Methodist	−	−	+	−	−	+	+
American Baptist	−	−	+	0	0	+	+
Baptist Joint Committee	−	0	0	0	0	0	0
National Association of Evangelicals	−	+	0	0	0	0	0
Fundamentalists	+	+	−	+	+	−	0
Catholic Conference	0	+	+	0	+	+	+
Jewish Groups	+	+	+	+	0	+	+

Note: Lobby policy is determined by specific strategic actions. Member support is determined by denominational sentiment expressed in the 1984 American National Election Study. Sentiment on abortion is of active church members.

Key: + Apparent member support for lobby policy
− Apparent lack of member support for lobby policy
0 Unclear lobby position or ambiguous lay sentiment

Central America—all activities with reasonable public support. The evangelical and fundamentalist lobbies, in their turn, appear to have articulated broad public anxiety about the drift of cultural change—the abortion culture, family breakdown, the secularization of the schools— in crafting their strategic national initiatives. The impact of religious groups on national representation is thus viewed in a positive light because tactical decisions, specialization, and the imperatives of constituency mobilization overcome, to an extent, the oligarchic effect of leadership. Neither interest group scholars nor those who study religion and politics have emphasized enough this strategic interplay between faith and politics in the American system. Yet this interplay appears to address, in part, concerns expressed about the elite national pressure system.

"We are," as William O. Douglas once observed, "a religious people." What emerges from this analysis of representation and the religious lobbies is the conclusion that, in light of the nature of modern American political institutions, the system may indeed be more representative *because* "we" are religious.

Notes

1. Luke Eugene Ebersole, *Church Lobbying in the Nation's Capital* (New York: Macmillan, 1951); Paul Weber identified 74 groups in 1985, and my study revealed at least a half dozen that were not on his list (see Paul Weber, "The Power and Performance of Religious Interest Groups" [paper presented to the Society for the Scientific Study of Religion, 1982]); on the advocacy explosion, see Jeffrey Berry, *The Interest Group Society* (Boston: Little, Brown, 1984).
2. See Robert Booth Fowler, *Religion and Politics in America* (Metuchen, N.J.: Scarecrow, 1985); A. James Reichley, *Religion in American Public Life* (Washington, D.C.: Brookings Institution, 1985); Kenneth D. Wald, *Religion and Politics in the United States* (New York: St. Martin's Press, 1987); and Paul Weber, "The Power and Performance of Religious Interest Groups."
3. Allan J. Cigler and Burdett A. Loomis, *Interest Group Politics* (Washington, D.C.: CQ Press, 1983), 28; E. E. Schattschneider, *The Semisovereign People* (New York: Holt, Rinehart and Winston, 1960); see also E. E. Schattschneider, *Politics, Pressure and the Tariff* (New York: Farrar and Rinehart, 1942).
4. Peter Bachrach and Morton Baratz, "The Two Faces of Power," *American Political Science Review* 57 (September 1963); Mancur Olson, *The Logic of Collective Action* (Cambridge, Mass.: Harvard University Press, 1965); David Truman, *The Governmental Process* (New York: Knopf, 1951).
5. E. E. Schattschneider, *The Semisovereign People*, 35. On organizational maintenance, see Robert Salisbury, "An Exchange Theory of Interest Groups," *Midwest Journal of Political Science* 13 (February 1969); Salisbury, "Interest Representation: The Dominance of Institutions," *American Political Science Review* 78 (March 1984); Jack Walker, "The Origins and Maintenance of Interest Groups in America," *American Political Science Review* 77 (June 1983); and James Q. Wilson, *Political Organizations* (New York: Basic Books, 1973). For critiques of interest groups, see especially Charles Lindblom, *Politics and Markets* (New York: Basic Books, 1977); Theodore Lowi, *The End of Liberalism* (New York: W. W. Norton, 1979); and Grant McConnell, *Private Power and American Democracy* (New York: Knopf, 1966).
6. See Andrew S. McFarland, "Interest Groups and Theories of Power in America," *British Journal of Political Science* 17 (1987); and Graham Wilson, *Interest Groups in the United States* (Oxford: Clarendon, 1981).
7. Berry, *The Interest Group Society*.
8. Ibid., 66.
9. Jeffrey K. Hadden, *The Gathering Storm in the Churches* (Garden City, N.Y.: Doubleday, 1969).
10. Olson, *Collective Action*, 160.
11. Weber, "The Power and Performance," 10; on affiliation, see George Gallup, Jr., "Religion in America," *Gallup Report*, no. 259 (April 1987); on class, see Wilson, *Political Organizations*, 60.
12. *Gallup Report*, no. 259.
13. *Gallup Report*, no. 236 (May 1985), "Religion in America 50 Years."
14. New phone lines were installed on the Hill to handle the increased volume, and one senator reported over 1,500 calls in one day, virtually all of them urging him to support the school prayer amendment (*Congressional Quarterly Weekly Report*, March 3, 1984).
15. The United Methodist book of resolutions, for example, is a weighty two volumes, and covers virtually all domestic and foreign policies in the nation.

16. "Witnessing for Peace and Justice in Central America," printed by the American Lutheran Church, Division for World Mission and Interchurch Cooperation, Minneapolis, Minnesota.

17. This conclusion is drawn from press reports and interviews with members of Congress, their staffs, and lobbyists.

18. This was confirmed by a Democratic member of Congress who sits on the intelligence committee with oversight over contra policy. Interview, June 1987.

19. Robert Michels, *Political Parties* (New York: Dover, 1953); see also Oliver Garceau, *The Political Life of the American Medical Association* (Cambridge, Mass.: Harvard University Press, 1941); John Colombotos, "Physicians and Medicine: A Before and After Study of the Effect of Legislation on Attitudes," *American Sociological Review* 34 (June 1969); and McConnell, *Private Power and American Democracy.*

20. This theme is echoed in James Adams, *The Growing Church Lobby in Washington* (Grand Rapids, Mich.: Eerdmans, 1970); Jeffrey Hadden, *The Gathering Storm in the Churches;* Alfred O. Hero, Jr., *American Religious Groups View Foreign Policy: Trends in Rank-and-File Opinion, 1937-1969* (Durham, N.C.: Duke University Press, 1970); Harold E. Quinley, *The Prophetic Clergy* (New York: Wiley, 1974); and A. James Reichley, *Religion in American Public Life.*

21. See especially Emmett H. Buell and Lee Sigelman, "An Army That Meets Every Sunday? Popular Support for the Moral Majority in 1980," *Social Science Quarterly* 66 (June 1985); James Guth and John Green, "The Moralizing Minority: Christian Right Support among Political Contributors," *Social Science Quarterly* 68 (September 1987); Clyde Wilcox, "Popular Support for the Moral Majority in 1980: A Second Look," *Social Science Quarterly* 68 (March 1987); and Seymour Martin Lipset, "Beyond 1984: The Anomalies of American Politics," *PS* 19 (Spring 1986).

22. Richard F. Fenno, "Observation, Context, and Sequence in the Study of Politics," *American Political Science Review* 80 (March 1986).

11. THE MULTIFACETED CATHOLIC LOBBY

Thomas J. O'Hara

Although religion has been an important factor in the social and political life of our country from earliest times, the link between religion and politics has until recent years largely been ignored in social science literature. Many of those who have studied the role of religion in politics have focused on the dramatic rise of the Religious Right as an electoral force; conversely, scholars have tended to concentrate on election results as a way of calculating the relative strength of religion in the policy process. And yet there are more components of the political process than electoral politics, and social science analysis should be broadened beyond elections. If religion truly is a policy process variable worthy of investigation, we ought to observe its effect in the increasingly important arena of interest group politics.

The research reported here expands the analysis of religion and politics by focusing on a mainstream religion, Catholicism, and on the role of religion in the policy process by analyzing the formation and activity of Catholic interest groups, in particular those with Washington offices from which to advocate their particular policy positions.

There are few studies of religious interest groups. Luke Ebersole's *Church Lobbying in the Nation's Capital,* published in 1951, was the first systematic study of various religious denominations that had lobbying groups based in Washington. Allen Hertzke's recent work, *Representing God in Washington* (1988), is an important update on the status of religious interest groups in Washington.[1] In the intervening decades between these works, important political changes occurred in the policy process within Washington; these include congressional reforms, the decline of party identification, and the proliferation of interest groups. Thus a reassessment of the role of religion-based interest groups in light of these political changes was much needed.

However, not just the political process but the Catholic Church itself has undergone dramatic changes since 1951, when Ebersole's study was published. At that time, the Catholic Church was known to be highly structured, with a tight hierarchical order controlled by the bishops in this country and ultimately by the pope and the curia in Rome. To understand the Catholic church lobby, all that was really necessary was to examine the lobby organization of the American bishops, the National Catholic Welfare Conference. (In 1967 the name of this group changed to the National Conference of Catholic Bishops/ United States Catholic Conference.) This group could indeed be understood to speak for the Catholic church on public policy issues in the United States.

With the convening of the Second Vatican Council in 1962, the Roman Catholic Church began to change. One of the most significant internal changes was an increased recognition of the role of the laity within the church; the church was more often described as "the people of God." This more inclusive terminology gave new credibility to the role of all people, clerical and lay, within the church. As a consequence of this new theological understanding of the church, the role of nonclerics within the church has been greatly enhanced in the last two decades. No longer is the church structure seen only in terms of priests, bishops, and the pope.

These internal developments have important ramifications for the way in which social scientists examine and observe the church. To continue to examine the church by examining only the activities of bishops is to bias the perspective and ultimately the conclusions of research. And yet, at least when scholars are describing the Catholic presence in the federal policy process, they continue to have a pronounced tendency to look only at the role of the bishops, and their lobby arm, the USCC. They describe the Catholic lobby as if it were a monolith. In fact, such a description is really a distorted view, as some scholars have shown.[2]

This study, by focusing on many Catholic groups, can shed light on the diversity of the Catholic lobby presence and can also expand our understanding of interest groups.

Part of the real value in taking a second and closer look at the Catholic lobby is that we observe behavior that is common to all interest groups. The literature on group formation, group maintenance, and group strategies is relevant for examining the diversity of the Catholic lobby. The pluralism found within the Catholic lobby can be understood in light of David Truman's interest group formation analysis.[3] Groups can form to counterbalance existing groups or to articulate a policy position not voiced by existing groups.

From another direction, Mancur Olson argues that groups do not spontaneously come into existence but rather depend on selective material benefits to induce membership. Robert Salisbury argues that incentives other than selective material benefits also induce group membership. In addition, Jack Walker argues that some interest groups are formed and maintained only because of patrons who help finance their activities.[4] The frameworks developed by these scholars form the basis for the analysis that follows.

Methodology

For this study all Catholic groups that advocated positions on public policy and maintained a Washington office were included. Catholic groups that dealt only with internal church matters or did not maintain a Washington office were excluded. Also, groups had to have a clear Catholic base; a few of the groups have expanded to include non-Catholics, but the essentially Catholic character has been maintained.

The group itself is the unit of analysis; the information that describes each group was obtained by individual interviews with one or more members of that group. The data were collected through semifocused interviews. Both opened-ended and close-ended responses were coded (either by specific response or by key phrase) and tabulated using dBASE III PLUS. Most interviews were conducted with the chief administrative officer of the Washington office of each group. For some of the groups, the public liaison officer acted as the spokesperson. Since the interview covered a variety of topics, for some groups several interviews with persons of different expertise were necessary.

Data and Analysis

Although the literature on the Catholic lobby speaks primarily of the bishops' organization, the USCC, and alludes to a few other groups, there are indeed many more public policy advocacy groups that are primarily Catholic. Besides the USCC, thirty other groups were contacted and studied for this research. These thirty-one groups fall into three broad categories. Eight are clearly institutional, in that they are sponsored by the institutional church; that is to say, the organizational church acted as entrepreneur (in Salisbury's terms) for the formation of these groups or the church acts as financial patron (in Walker's terms) for their maintenance. Eight of the groups are Washington-based offices of religious communities of nuns, priests, or brothers within the church; these groups advocate the policy positions of their membership, but not necessarily the positions of the institutional USCC lobby. Finally, fifteen of these groups have relative autonomy from the organizational church; nine of them were formed by laypersons within the church to voice their concerns on policy issues, sometimes in direct opposition to the policy views of the institutional church as expressed by the USCC.

Diversity of Policy Preferences

Among the many lobbying groups, is there clearly one that speaks most definitively for the Catholic community? Nearly half of the groups surveyed, fifteen of thirty-one, felt that no one interest group represented the policy views of the Catholic community; 38 percent named the USCC; 9 percent named groups other than the USCC as speaking for the Catholic community. Disaggregating further into categories yields interesting but not surprising results. Seventy percent of the institutional groups said that the USCC was clearly the one group that spoke for the Catholic community. Only 50 percent of the religious-community groups felt that the USCC was the most effective representative of the Catholic community. Of the fifteen noninstitutional groups, only three (20 percent) felt that the USCC spoke for the Catholic community on policy issues. Statements such as "The Catholic church is too diverse to be represented by one group," "The USCC represents the bishops but not us," or "The church is a mosaic unable to be captured by any one group" indicate that there is some very strong sentiment among these group representatives that the USCC cannot be looked upon as the totality of the Catholic lobby within the policy process.

Investigation of the issues that are the principal focus of concern for each group further delineates the lobby's diversity. The USCC is unique because its large organization is able to pursue many different agenda items at the same time: in 1987 there were ten major areas of policy concern, ranging from the domestic issues of farm policy and education to the international issues of foreign policy. Many of the other groups act more like single-issue interest groups. Seventeen of the groups are primarily concerned with domestic issues such as health care, education, welfare spending, or issues pertinent to specific social or ethnic groups (native Americans, blacks, or women). Seven of the groups are primarily focused on foreign policy issues such as international development, U.S. policy in Central America, peace and disarmament, and so on. The remaining seven groups work on both domestic and foreign policy issues.

Of course, simply stating that these thirty-one groups have a wide variety of policy concerns does not delineate differences on policy between the institutional USCC and the other groups. Eleven of the thirty-one groups (36 percent) indicated policy differences with the USCC. Some groups objected to the economic pastoral of the bishops for being too socialistic, others for being too moderate. Some groups objected to the peace pastoral of the bishops for being too progressive, others for not being progressive enough. Similarly, on the issue of U.S.

foreign policy in Central America, some groups criticized the bishops for being too sympathetic to the Sandinista government and other groups criticized the bishops for being overly tied to American foreign policy concerns. One group found that the bishops had not worked hard enough for federal aid to parochial schools, claiming that the bishops are too reluctant to align themselves with fundamentalist Christian schools also seeking federal assistance. Other groups claim the bishops have completely ignored the interests of particular groups of people, such as gay Catholics or Catholics concerned with women's reproductive rights. Thus, there are groups within the Catholic community that were organized by people who disagreed with or felt threatened by the policy positions espoused by the USCC. These can be seen in light of Truman's dictum that groups beget countergroups.

Group Formation and Maintenance

Kay Schlozman and others have documented a massive increase in the number of interest groups in the last twenty years.[5] Catholic interest groups have proliferated as well. Nineteen of thirty-one, or 61 percent, of the groups were formed within the last twenty years. The date of formation varies with the category of group. Of the institutionally sponsored or related groups, only one of eight was formed within the last twenty years. Of the groups representing religious communities, six of eight were formed within the last twenty years. Most significantly, twelve of the fifteen noninstitutional groups were formed within the last twenty years.

How a group was formed is relevant to its policy goals. Nine of the thirty-one (27 percent) were founded by nonclerics (that is, not by priests or bishops) within the church. All nine of these groups were from the least institutional category, which means that 60 percent of that category was founded by laypersons. Of all thirty-one groups, nineteen (61 percent) were founded without assistance, monetary or otherwise, of the institutional church. Increasingly, there is evidence that Catholics who have particular policy positions are not willing to have the institutional church speak for them on policy issues. They have been willing to organize without the assistance of the institutional church, and have formed groups through the efforts of individual laypersons rather than clerics. Even among groups founded by clerics and the institutional church, laypersons have had an increasing role. Indeed, a layperson serves as chairperson of the board of directors for nineteen of the thirty-one groups.

Salisbury's concept of an entrepreneur also explains the formation of many of these interest groups. Sixteen of the Catholic groups give clear evidence of the role of an entrepreneur in their formation. For eight of the groups, the institutional church acted as an entrepreneur, providing the crucial organizational and monetary support. It served the church's purposes to have these groups in existence. Yet eight of the remaining twenty-three groups also were founded through an entrepreneur; for at least three of these, the entrepreneur role was played by groups outside the Catholic community, which apparently wanted to have certain issues represented within that community.

Olson argued that selective material benefits are necessary for group formation and ultimately for group maintenance. At least eight of the thirty-one groups concentrate on securing government assistance for their membership in the form of aid to hospitals, schools, social service agencies, and so on. These groups obviously are seeking economic gains from the government, although the benefits would not accrue only to their own membership. But seventeen of the groups see themselves as offering selective material benefits to their membership in terms of consultation, education, workshops, and so on. Salisbury's expansion of benefits to include purposive and solidary benefits clearly helps to explain the formation of religious groups. Twenty-three of thirty-one groups (74 percent) indicated that either solidary or purposive benefits were a major reason for group formation and maintenance; members perceive a benefit either in expressing strongly felt policy positions or in enjoying camaraderie. In either case, purposive or solidary, the Catholic lobby is a clear example of Salisbury's expansion of Olson's theory of group benefits.

Group maintenance is also a monetary proposition. The operating budgets for some of the groups in this study—those in the business of providing direct human services—are in the hundreds of millions of dollars. Other groups in this study have operating budgets of under $100,000, including single-issue advocacy groups that may not be providing any other services. But all of the groups need to solicit money in order to survive. Eighteen of the groups receive most of their money from their membership in the form of dues.

As Walker has indicated, group formation and maintenance may also depend on patrons. There is clear evidence of this in the Catholic lobby: Two of the groups derive over 70 percent of their money from foundations; two receive between 45 and 60 percent of their operating expenses from the government in return for providing social services; three receive over 50 percent of their funding from the institutional church; and five receive over 40 percent of their funding from individual gifts. So whether the patron be the government, foundations, the church itself, or individual giftgivers, there is ample evidence of the importance of the role of patrons in the maintenance of these Catholic groups.

Diversity of Strategy

We can see further diversity in the wide variety of strategies employed in order to influence the policy process. Some of the groups almost exclusively rely on "elite interaction" or "professional lobbying," as described by Robert Salisbury, whereas other groups rely on group mobilization, including political protest.[6] When asked to indicate the two main strategies employed to influence the policy process, representatives of fifteen groups indicated work with congressional staffs as one of them, and respondents from fifteen groups indicated letter writing and calling campaigns directed to members of Congress. Ten groups indicated that providing education on the issues to membership was one of their two principal strategies; seven mentioned direct contact with particular government agencies, bureaus, or departments; seven use political protest; three use litigation as an effective means of influencing policy; and two mentioned cooperation with White House staffers. Groups that employed one method over another often had strong feelings regarding various strategies. One representative of a group that works exclusively with Congress and the agencies said of political protest: "That approach is clearly ineffective. We need to deal in reality and know how and when to compromise." However, a representative of a protest-oriented group criticized church groups that "employ the same old bureaucrats who play the same game over again. They are just cronies with their fellow government bureaucrats."

Conclusion

This study of the Catholic presence in the policy process reveals such diversity that the concept of a monolithic Catholic lobby can no longer be regarded as accurate. Both the proliferation of groups and their increasing diversity mean that the Catholic lobby mirrors interest group behavior in general. In the last several decades interest groups have proliferated for a variety of reasons; for Catholics, significant internal changes within the Catholic church have been an additional incentive to form interest groups. Thus, a monolithic lobby has broken into a diversity of groups and countergroups. That diversity is evident in group formation, maintenance, membership benefits, and lobbying strategies. The study supports the arguments of Truman, Olson, Salisbury, and Walker regarding interest group formation and maintenance. Finally, this study, in continuing the necessary research on the religious lobby as a factor in the policy process, gives further support to the literature documenting the relationship between religion and the political system. Clearly, examination of the diversity of the Catholic lobby presents interesting data both for students of religion and politics and for students of interest group behavior.

Notes

1. Luke Ebersole, *Church Lobbying in the Nation's Capital* (New York: Macmillan, 1951); Allen Hertzke, *Representing God in Washington* (Knoxville: University of Tennessee Press, 1988); see also the intervening work, James Adams, *The Growing Church Lobby in Washington* (Grand Rapids, Mich.: William Eerdmans, 1970).
2. For example, Mary Hanna, *Catholics and American Politics* (Cambridge, Mass.: Harvard University Press, 1979), documents a growing diversity; Frank Sorauf, *The Wall of Separation* (Princeton: Princeton University Press, 1976), 185, notes that the bishops do not represent the entire church.
3. David Truman, *The Governmental Process* (New York: Alfred Knopf, 1971).
4. Mancur Olson, *The Logic of Collective Action* (Cambridge, Mass.: Harvard University Press, 1965); Robert Salisbury, "An Exchange Theory of Interest Groups," *Midwest Journal of Political Science* 13 (February 1969): 1-32; Jack Walker, "The Origins and Maintenance of Interest Groups in America," *American Political Science Review* 77 (June 1983): 390-404.
5. See for example, Kay Schlozman and John Tierney, "More of Same: Washington Pressure Group Activity in a Decade of Change," *Journal of Politics* 45 (May 1983): 351.
6. Robert Salisbury, "Interest Representation: Dominance of Institutions," *American Political Science Review* 78 (March 1984): 64-75.

Part IV

TENSIONS OF CHANGE AND CHALLENGE: EVANGELICAL PROTESTANT POLITICS

So-called evangelicals have been at the point of attack and controversy on issues of religion and politics. Names like Pat Robertson and Jerry Falwell and their organizations and institutions, such as the Christian Broadcasting Network and Moral Majority, reflect the muscle flexing of conservative Protestantism. Just how have they influenced American politics? Corwin Smidt assesses voting behavior among evangelicals in the South, America's "Bible belt." Tod Baker, Laurence Moreland, and Robert Steed examine the relationships between party activists and the New Christian Right in light of religious orientation. James Guth studies the attitudes of Southern Baptist pastors in relation to the New Christian Right.

12. CHANGE AND STABILITY AMONG SOUTHERN EVANGELICALS

Corwin Smidt

Observers of the South have long recognized that religious life there contributes to a regional distinctiveness. Most analysts agree that the character of southern religious life is "of a kind generally called Evangelical Protestantism." And, although conventional wisdom may hold that American society is becoming more homogeneous, geographers of American religion generally agree that regionalism in terms of religion persists in American society.[1] In fact, throughout the twentieth century regional differences in religion have grown stronger; furthermore, the religious commitments of migrants tend to change to reflect the region to which they have moved.[2]

Thus, despite major economic and social changes since the turn of the century and despite a major influx of migrants to the region over the past several decades, the religious distinctiveness of the South may have remained relatively unchanged. Consequently, those who are interested in analyzing the political attitudes and behavior of evangelicals must give particular attention to the South, and those who are interested in the relationship between religion and politics in the South must give particular attention to evangelicals. Likewise, major political changes evident among evangelicals are likely to affect the political character of the South, and partisan attempts to capture southern electoral college votes must also take into account changes taking place among southern evangelical voters.

This paper analyzes the partisan identification and behavior of southern evangelicals in the 1984 presidential election and compares and contrasts such patterns of identification and behavior with those evident among southern evangelicals in the 1980 presidential election. Two general questions will be addressed in this longitudinal analysis: Is there evidence that important changes have taken place among southern evangelicals across the two elections? And, if so, did such changes differ from the patterns of change evident among southern nonevangelicals over the same period of time?

Two factors suggest that the role of southern evangelicals in the

1984 election may be different from that in the 1980 election. First, there were different Democratic candidates; presidential candidate pairings have an important impact upon candidate preference.[3] In 1980, southern evangelicals were confronted with a choice not only between and among several evangelical candidates but also between southern and nonsouthern evangelical candidates. In 1984, however, there was no candidate from the South and only one who seemingly possessed evangelical credentials.

Second, various analysts have suggested that Democratic losses in the 1984 election may indicate that a partisan realignment has occurred within the American electorate.[4] In particular, some have interpreted Democratic losses in the South as reflecting the beginnings of a realignment in partisan identification among southern voters,[5] while others have interpreted the change in the distribution of partisan identification within the South as indicating that such a realignment has already occurred.[6] And, as evangelicals are located disproportionately in the South, evangelicals may very well have contributed to an important shift in partisan loyalties within the region.

Theoretical Framework

It must be recognized at the outset that evangelicalism does not constitute a single, unified phenomenon. It can be very misleading to analyze evangelicalism as a whole, therefore, if only one prominent aspect is taken to be representative of the whole. Yet there are several distinct ways in which evangelicalism, despite its internal diversity, can be viewed as a single phenomenon.[7] One approach is to use the term *evangelical* to refer to some specific form of conceptual unity. This approach may emphasize subscription to certain theological beliefs (for example, beliefs concerning the nature of Jesus Christ and scriptural authority), some manifestation of certain religious characteristics (for example, having had a "born again" experience or attending church on some regular basis), or a combination of the two. When used in this manner, *evangelical* refers primarily to some conceptual entity abstractly identified and unified by the analyst. This approach enables analysts to assess how gradations in subscribing to evangelical beliefs may be associated with the expression of different political attitudes or behavior.

A second approach is to view evangelicalism as a social reality, rather than an abstract category, in that it represents a "dynamic movement, with common heritages, common tendencies, an identity, and an organic character." Different subgroups within contemporary evangelicalism may be somewhat diverse and disconnected; yet such subgroups may have common roots and may have shared substantial historical experiences. These characteristics can, as George Marsden notes, result in certain commonalities (such as views of the Bible, styles of prayer, techniques of evangelicalism, behavioral mores)—despite obvious diversity in many religious particulars among the subgroups. Consequently, evangelicals may have formed a common identity that transcends specific differences in heritages and emphases. Therefore, the analyst can view evangelicalism as a larger social movement or as a distinct socio-religious group.

The choice of the particular approach one uses in understanding evangelicalism has some important implications. To view evangelicals as simply a conceptual unity places greater emphasis upon atomistic conceptions of how evangelicals relate to the world around them and tends to downplay the social context within which their beliefs, experiences, or practices occur. To view evangelicals as an organic unity, however, places at least some emphasis upon the fact that religious beliefs, experiences, and practices tend to be expressed within a larger subculture; the political attitudes and behavior of evangelicals are therefore *not* seen to derive solely from the specific religious beliefs, experiences, or practices they express.

Moreover, it should be noted that according to the latter, "social group," approach a person either is or is not an evangelical; thus, an analysis of where respondents fall along a continuum of evangelical beliefs is not appropriate. In addition, with the social group approach, the mere expression of similar religious beliefs, the profession of similar experiences, or the manifestation of similar religious behavior does not, by definition, require that all such persons be classified together socially; instead, patterns of social interaction and participation within a subcultural context become important. Thus, although the expression of similar religious beliefs, the profession of similar religious experiences, and the manifestation of similar religious behavior may well contribute to a convergence in the political characteristics of white and black evangelicals, the subcultural (racial) context may be of greater influence than their religious commonalities. Consequently, black and white evangelicals may act different politically despite sharing similar religious beliefs and displaying similar religious behavior.

Gerhard Lenski recognized these subcultural differences when he used the term *socio-religious group* to refer to both the communal and the associational aspects of religious groups.[8] Lenski argued that because religion is, in part, a social phenomenon, any analysis of the influence of religion must take into account the subcultural as well as the formal associational values of religious groups. The subculture constitutes the network of primary relationships of such coreligionists, which may overlap with the social relationships evident within the formal religious association (that is, within the local church or denomination) but are never identical with them. As primary groups tend to be rewarding to the extent that the participants share common values, individuals tend to be drawn disproportionately to others who share similar basic values. As a result, primary group membership may cut across various formal religious associations, but the fundamental religious values of such members may still be quite similar. Therefore, once the existence of such religious subcommunities is recognized, a more accurate estimate of the influence of religion upon contemporary life can be formed. It is this framework emphasizing the social group nature of evangelicals that will be employed here.

Operational Definitions

Data were drawn from the 1980 and 1984 presidential election studies conducted by the Center for Political Studies at the University of Michigan (CPS). Three criteria were initially used in classifying respondents as evangelical Christians. First, respondents had to state that religion played an important part in their life. Technically, such a response does not constitute a necessary definitional criterion of an evangelical from a socio-religious group perspective. However, this first question served as a filter in that only those respondents who stated that religion played an important part in their life were subsequently asked whether they had had a "born again" experience. Thus, the second criterion was that respondents had to acknowledge that they had had a "born again" experience. And, finally, respondents had to state that they viewed the Bible as "God's word and all it says is true."

However, because evangelicals were conceptualized as a socio-religious group, two further criteria came into play. First, only Protestants were classified as evangelicals. Roman Catholics who met the three religious criteria were excluded because their heritage is outside the evangelical movement and because their patterns of primary relationships are likely to be a part of another religious subcommunity. Moreover, various scholars have argued, either implicitly or explicitly, that Catholics, by definition, should not be classified as evangelicals.[9]

Second, analysis was restricted to white respondents. Because the religious subcultures of white and black evangelicals are likely to be different, and because evangelicals are viewed in this paper in terms of a socio-religious group, white and black evangelicals need to be separated. Unfortunately, however, the lack of an adequate size for the black evangelical subgroup prevented any meaningful analysis of southern black evangelicals. Consequently, analysis was restricted to a comparison and contrast of white evangelicals and nonevangelicals residing in the South.

Data Analysis

Although the 1980 presidential election did not clearly reveal that a partisan realignment had occurred within the American electorate, various analysts suggested that such a long-awaited realignment either already had transpired or was in progress by the 1984 presidential election. Republican identification grew in 1984; and the margin of self-classified Democrats over self-classified Republicans in 1984 reached its lowest point since 1952.[10] Furthermore, the South, in particular, was seen to be the geographical center of such a realignment in partisan identification.[11]

In order to ascertain whether a realignment in partisan forces was evident among either white southern voters generally or southern white evangelical voters particularly, the partisan self-image and partisan behavior displayed by southern white evangelicals and nonevangelicals across the past two presidential elections were analyzed. As can be seen from Table 12-1, little, if any, change is evident within either category of southern voters. Evangelicals were slightly more likely than nonevangelicals to classify themselves as Democrats in 1980, and the same was true in 1984. Moreover, the percentage of self-classified Democrats among evangelicals and nonevangelicals alike did not change between 1980 and 1984, and the percentage of self-classified Republicans among evangelicals and nonevangelicals grew only modestly. Thus, although there may be some evidence of an increase in Republican self-classification among white southern voters, the data presented in Table 12-1 indicate that white southerners still remain overwhelmingly Democratic in terms of their partisan self-image.

Similar patterns of stability are evident when the focus shifts from partisan self-image to partisanship in voting behavior. The voting patterns evident among evangelicals and nonevangelicals alike did not appear to change from 1980 to 1984. Basically, two out of every three white southerners, evangelical or not, cast a vote for Ronald Reagan in 1980, and the same was true in 1984. Similarly, about three out of every five white southerners cast a vote for the Democratic congressional candidate in 1980, and the same was true in 1984. One could hardly find more stable patterns than those evident in Table 12-1.

Yet, important changes may well be taking place in the partisan orientations of white southerners despite this picture of stability. A respondent's partisan self-image does not necessarily reveal the nature of the respondent's affective feelings toward the two parties. Furthermore, a respondent can possess feelings of affection for a particular party without having incorporated that party into his or her political identity. Previous research has demonstrated that partisan affection and

Table 12-1 Partisan Self-Image and Partisan Behavior among White Evangelicals and Nonevangelicals

	1980		1984	
	Nonevangelical	Evangelical	Nonevangelical	Evangelical
Partisan Self-Image				
Democrat	41.0%	47.7%	41.5%	46.9%
Independent	37.7	33.7	33.4	31.3
Republican	21.3	18.6	25.1	21.9
(N)	(239)	(86)	(287)	(128)
	v = 0.6		v = .05	
Voting Behavior				
President				
Democrat	37.6%	36.2%	33.0%	33.3%
Republican	62.4	63.8	67.0	66.7
(N)	(149)	(69)	(191)	(81)
	phi = .01		phi = .00	
Congress				
Democrat	59.6%	59.0%	55.3%	58.9%
Republican	40.4	41.0	44.7	41.1
(N)	(136)	(61)	(161)	(73)
	phi = .01		phi = .03	

Source: 1980 and 1984 National Election Studies, Center for Political Studies, University of Michigan.

partisan self-image can be differentiated empirically as well as analytically and that partisan affection can be linked to subsequent changes in partisan self-image.[12]

Table 12-2 analyzes the direction of partisan affection evident among evangelicals and nonevangelicals over the past two presidential elections—controlling for the partisan self-image of the respondents. The partisan affection of the respondents was tapped by means of the feeling thermometer questions contained in the CPS surveys. Those respondents who expressed greater affection for the Democratic party than for the Republican party were classified as Democratic in partisan affection, those who expressed equivalent levels of affection for the two parties were classified as neutral in terms of partisan affection, and those who expressed greater levels of affection for the Republican party than for the Democratic party were classified as Republican in terms of partisan affection.

Several different patterns emerge from Table 12-2. First, among self-classified Democrats, it is evident that in 1980 evangelicals held a partisan affection that was more consistent with their partisan self-

Table 12-2 Partisan Affection of White Evangelicals and Nonevangelicals, Controlling for Partisan Self-Image

Partisan Self-Image	Partisan Affection	1980		1984	
		Nonevangelical	Evangelical	Nonevangelical	Evangelical
Democrat	Democrat	66.3%	80.5%	66.1%	61.4%
	Neutral	22.8	17.1	11.9	17.5
	Republican	10.9	2.4	22.0	21.1
	(N)	(92)	(41)	(109)	(57)
			v = .17		v = .08
Independent	Democrat	18.4%	10.7%	17.4%	15.8%
	Neutral	58.6	42.9	27.9	23.7
	Republican	23.0	46.4	54.7	60.5
	(N)	(87)	(28)	(86)	(38)
			v = .22		v = .06
Republican	Democrat	0.0%	12.5%	1.4%	3.8%
	Neutral	21.6	18.8	4.3	3.8
	Republican	78.4	68.8	94.2	92.3
	(N)	(51)	(16)	(69)	(26)
			v = .31*		v = .07

* Chi-square statistically significant at .05 level.

Source: 1980 and 1984 National Election Studies, Center for Political Studies, University of Michigan.

image than did nonevangelicals. Thus, 80.5 percent of those evangelicals who expressed a Democratic partisan self-image expressed Democratic partisan affection, whereas only 66.3 percent of the nonevangelicals did so. A substantial percentage of such self-classified Democrats expressed neutral partisan affection (22.8 percent and 17.1 percent among nonevangelicals and evangelicals, respectively), but only a relatively small percentage of nonevangelical Democrats (10.9 percent) and an even smaller percentage of evangelical Democrats (2.4 percent) expressed a Republican partisan affection.

However, by 1984, the Democratic loyalties of self-classified Democrats were being tested among evangelicals and nonevangelicals alike. Only two out of every three self-classified Democrats among both evangelicals and nonevangelicals expressed a Democratic partisan affection. Moreover, the expression of Republican partisan affections among such self-classified Democrats became much more evident in 1984. One out of every five self-classified Democrats, regardless of religious classification, expressed greater affection for the Republican party than for the Democratic party.

Second, it is evident among self-classified independents (1) that evangelicals have tended to be somewhat more Republican in partisan affection than have nonevangelicals and (2) that since 1980 there has been some movement toward increased Republican partisan affection among both evangelicals and nonevangelicals.

By 1984, the partisan affection among self-classified independents was overwhelmingly Republican. The majority of both nonevangelical and evangelical independents expressed a Republican partisan affection (54.7 percent and 60.5 percent, respectively), but less than one out of every five self-classified independents expressed a Democratic partisan affection.

Finally, it is evident from Table 12-2 that there was a growth in Republican affection even among self-classified Republicans from 1980 to 1984—and a growth that was most evident among evangelicals who classified themselves as Republicans. In 1980, evangelical Republicans were less likely (68.8 percent) than nonevangelical Republicans (78.1 percent) to express Republican partisan affection. But, by 1984, nonevangelical and evangelical Republicans were almost uniformly Republican in partisan affection (94.2 percent and 92.3 percent, respectively).

Thus, by the close of the 1984 presidential election, self-classified Republicans in the South appeared to be fairly united in partisan affection. On the other hand, self-classified Democrats did not. A sizable percentage of self-classified Democrats (over 20 percent) expressed Republican partisan affections, and a majority of self-classified independents did so. Moreover, the data also suggest that southern evangelicals have moved in a more Republican direction than have southern nonevangelicals. Among those who classified themselves either as Democrats or as Republicans in 1980, evangelicals were more Democratic in their partisan affection than were nonevangelicals. By 1984, however, such evangelicals were no more Democratic in partisan affection than were nonevangelicals.

While analyzing partisan affection in terms of partisan direction provides some hint at the nature of the partisan orientations of the southern electorate, it does not provide any information concerning the pattern of such affections. Given that an individual can develop negative, as well as positive, affection toward each of the two major parties, six different patterns of partisan affection can be differentiated:

1. *Independents:* no affection, positive or negative, toward either party
2. *Simple positive:* positive affection toward one political party, no affection toward the other
3. *Simple negative:* negative affection toward one political party, no affection toward the other
4. *Amplified positive:* positive affection toward both political parties
5. *Amplified negative:* negative affection toward both political parties
6. *Polarized:* positive affection toward one political party, negative affection toward the other

However, previous research has demonstrated that only a small percentage of the electorate (less than 3 percent) generally falls within the simple negative and amplified negative categories, and the same was true in both 1980 and 1984.[13] Consequently, those respondents who exhibited such negative patterns of partisan affection were dropped from the subsequent analysis.

Table 12-3 analyzes the resultant patterns of partisan affections among southern white evangelicals and nonevangelicals. Several additional observations can be made from the table. First, it is apparent that there was an increase in polarized patterns of partisan affection among both evangelicals and nonevangelicals between 1980 and 1984. For example, less than 20 percent of southern evangelicals expressed polarized patterns of affection in 1980, but that percentage more than doubled by 1984 (46.7 percent); whereas approximately 28 percent of the nonevangelicals in 1980 expressed polarized patterns of affection, approximately 49 percent did so by 1984. This increase in polarized patterns appears to be part of a monotonic increase in such patterns

Table 12-3   Pattern of Partisan Affection among White
Evangelicals and Nonevangelicals

Pattern of Partisan Affection	1980		1984	
	Nonevangelical	Evangelical	Nonevangelical	Evangelical
Polarized Democrat	14.9%	9.5%	18.7%	20.0%
Simple Democrat	12.7	14.9	9.4	8.6
Amplified Democrat	12.7	27.1	7.2	9.5
Neutral	22.1	16.2	6.8	7.6
Amplified Republican	11.6	12.2	13.2	10.5
Simple Republican	12.7	10.8	15.7	17.1
Polarized Republican	13.3	9.5	28.9	26.7
(N)	(181)	(69)	(235)	(105)
		v = .19		v = .06

Source: 1980 and 1984 National Election Studies, Center for Political Studies, University of Michigan.

across all presidential elections since 1972.[14] Nevertheless, the increase between 1980 and 1984 represents a dramatic jump.

Second, although the data in Table 12-1 suggested that there was no substantial change in the partisan self-image of evangelicals in the South between 1980 and 1984, considerable change is evident when patterns of partisan affection are analyzed. For example, while only 32.5 percent of southern evangelicals expressed Republican patterns of partisan affection in 1980, 54.3 percent did so in 1984. Conversely, while a majority of southern evangelicals expressed a Democratic affection in 1980 (51.5 percent), only 38.1 percent did so four years later. Furthermore, a plurality of southern evangelicals could be classified as Amplified Democrats (27.1 percent) in 1980, whereas only four years later a plurality of southern evangelicals were Polarized Republicans (26.7 percent). Thus, not only the direction but also the nature of partisan affection changed among southern evangelicals. In particular, the proportion of southern evangelicals viewing the Democratic party negatively nearly tripled: from 9.5 percent Polarized Republican in 1980 to 26.7 percent in 1984.

Conclusions

The analysis of this paper suggests, first, that the partisan self-image and partisan behavior of white southern evangelicals over the past two presidential elections have not differed significantly from those evident among white southern nonevangelicals. This relative similarity in partisanship between southern evangelicals and nonevangelicals, however, stands in contrast to the significant political differences evident between evangelicals and nonevangelicals outside the South.[15] Why is it, then, that political differences between evangelicals and nonevangelicals should be less pronounced in the South than outside the South? Perhaps such regional differences are due to a greater cultural homogeneity within the South, in which evangelicals are heavily concentrated and in which evangelicalism has so heavily permeated cultural life; evangelicals outside the South have been less dominant in numbers and influence and, therefore, are more likely to perceive themselves as a beleaguered minority estranged from the culture within which they find themselves.

Second, it would appear that there is some analytical utility in differentiating between partisan self-image and partisan affection. In terms of partisan self-image, the data suggest that southern evangelicals and nonevangelicals alike continued to be heavily Democratic in orientation during the first part of the 1980s. Yet it was also evident from the data that many white southerners expressed a partisan affection in direct opposition to their partisan self-image.

Third, it would appear that, despite certain outward appearances of stability, some important changes in partisan orientation were evident among white southerners from 1980 to 1984. While the distribution of partisan self-image among white southerners was relatively stable between 1980 and 1984, there was a marked increase in the percentage of respondents expressing Republican partisan affection over the same period, which was evident among both evangelical and nonevangelical respondents regardless of their particular partisan self-identification.

Fourth, the data suggest that the partisan affections of white southerners are becoming more polarized. At best, only slightly more than one-quarter of white southerners could be classified as polarized partisans in 1980, but nearly one-half of both evangelicals and nonevangelicals could be so classified in 1984. Previous research has revealed that respondents who exhibit polarized patterns of partisan affection tend to be the most politicized and partisan in their electoral behavior: they are not only the most likely to turn out to vote, but they are also the most likely to vote for their party's presidential nominee, the most likely to vote a straight party ticket, and the least likely to swing their vote across presidential elections.[16] Thus, this increase in polarized patterns of partisan affection suggests that a psychological foundation for true two-party competition may be in the process of being established within the South.

Finally, the data suggest that the most fundamental change in the partisan affections of southerners has occurred among evangelicals. In

1980, a majority of southern evangelicals could be classified as Democrats in affection (either Polarized, Amplified, or Simple Democrats). However, four years later, a majority of southern evangelicals expressed some pattern of Republican partisan affection. Consequently, not only was the percentage of evangelicals expressing a Republican partisan affection greater than the percentage of such evangelicals expressing a Republican self-image, but by 1984 a *majority* of evangelicals were more Republican than Democratic in affection. Perhaps even more important, evangelicals changed in their perceptions of the Democratic party: the most marked change in evangelical patterns of partisan affection between 1980 and 1984 was the coupling of a rise in positive perceptions of the Republican party with a rise in negative perceptions of the Democratic party. Thus, whereas evangelicals were largely Democratic in their partisan affection in 1980, they were much more positively Republican and negatively Democratic in 1984. And, as changes in partisan affections can be linked to subsequent changes in partisan self-image,[17] these changes in partisan affections among southern evangelicals may well herald a forthcoming change in the Democratic partisan self-image that has traditionally been evident within their ranks.

Notes

1. Samuel S. Hill, "The Shape and Shapes of Popular Southern Piety," in *Varieties of Southern Evangelicalism*, ed. David Harrell (Macon, Ga.: Mercer University Press, 1981): 89-114; Samuel S. Hill, "Religion and Region in America," *Annals* 480 (July 1985): 132-141.
2. Roger Stump, "Regional Divergence in Religious Affiliation in the United States," *Sociological Analysis* 45 (Winter 1984): 283-299; Roger Stump, "Regional Migration and Religious Commitment in the United States," *Journal for the Scientific Study of Religion* 23 (September 1984): 294-303.
3. Paul Lopatto, *Religion and the Presidential Election* (New York: Praeger, 1985), chap. 4.
4. See, for example, Benjamin Ginsberg and Martin Shefter, "A Critical Realignment? The New Politics, the Reconstructed Right, and the Election of 1984," in *The Election of 1984*, ed. Michael Nelson (Washington, D.C.: CQ Press, 1985), 1-25; and Wilson Cary McWilliams, "The Meaning of the Election," in *The Election of 1984: Reports and Interpretations*, ed. Marlene Pomper (Chatham, N.J.: Chatham House, 1985), 157-183.
5. McWilliams, "The Meaning of the Election," 174.
6. See, for example, Raymond Wolfinger and Michael Hagen, "Republican Prospects: Southern Comfort," *Public Opinion* 8 (October-November 1985): 8-13.
7. George Marsden, "Introduction," in *Evangelicalism and Modern America*, ed. George Marsden (Grand Rapids, Mich.: Eerdmans, 1984), vii-xix.
8. Gerhard Lenski, *The Religious Factor* (New York: Doubleday, 1963).

9. See, for example, Robert Webber, *Common Roots* (Grand Rapids, Mich.: Eerdmans, 1978); and James D. Hunter, *American Evangelicalism: Conservative Religion and the Quandary of Modernity* (New Brunswick, N.J.: Rutgers University Press, 1983), 139-140.
10. Martin Wattenberg, "The Hollow Realignment: Partisan Change in a Candidate-Centered Era," *Public Opinion Quarterly* 51 (Spring 1987): 58-74.
11. See, for example, McWilliams, "The Meaning of the Election," and Wolfinger and Hagen, "Republican Prospects."
12. Corwin Smidt, "Partisan Affections and Change in Partisan Self-Images," *American Politics Quarterly* 12 (July 1984): 267-283.
13. Corwin Smidt, "Changing Patterns of Partisan Affection in the South: 1972-1980" (Paper presented at The Citadel Symposium on Southern Politics, Charleston, S.C., March, 1984).
14. Ibid.
15. Corwin Smidt, "Evangelicals and the 1984 Election: Continuity or Change?" *American Politics Quarterly* 15 (October 1987): 419-444.
16. Corwin Smidt, "Partisan Affections, Partisan Self-Images, and Electoral Behavior in the South" (Paper presented at the annual meeting of the Southern Political Science Association, Gatlinberg, Tenn., November 1979); and Smidt, "Changing Patterns of Partisan Affection."
17. Smidt, "Evangelicals and the 1984 Election."

13. PARTY ACTIVISTS AND THE NEW RELIGIOUS RIGHT*

Tod A. Baker, Laurence W. Moreland, and Robert P. Steed

During the 1980s, the emergence of the Religious Right as a force in American politics has been a matter of considerable interest to members of the academic community.[1] Religious Right leaders have tended to take a conservative stance on most issues, although one, Jerry Falwell, has attempted to broaden the appeal of the movement by renaming his Moral Majority organization the Liberty Federation. The Religious Right has tended to place great emphasis on social issues such as the Equal Rights Amendment, school prayer, abortion, and homosexuality and has tended to draw its adherents from the ranks of fundamentalist and evangelical Protestants. Thus, by focusing attention on an emergent set of social issues and by appealing to people not previously characterized by a high rate of political participation,[2] the Religious Right has the potential of bringing about fairly substantial changes in the composition of party coalitions in the United States as well as of creating new cleavages both within and between the parties.

This chapter assesses the impact of the Religious Right on the two major parties by an examination of delegates who attended state party conventions in twelve states in 1984—South Carolina, Mississippi, Louisiana, North Carolina, Texas, Arkansas, Oklahoma, Indiana, North Dakota, Maine, Connecticut, and Utah. With the exception of Louisiana, in which no Republican convention was held, the data include both Democratic and Republican delegates in each state. The percentage of delegates surveyed varied among the twelve states, from 18 percent for Maine Democrats to 75 percent for South Carolina Republicans; a total of 11,888 respondents were in the study. Only twenty-nine of the black respondents in the study were Republican, and only about one hundred of the black Democratic delegates were outside the South; thus, any discussion of black delegates applies mainly to Democratic delegates in the South.

* The financial assistance of The Citadel Development Foundation is gratefully acknowledged.

Four topics are covered: (1) bases of support for the Religious Right; (2) the effect of orientation toward the Religious Right on delegates' attachment to their political parties and preferences for presidential candidate; (3) the effect of orientation toward the Religious Right on issue differences among delegates; and (4) the possible effects of the Religious Right as a bridge over which activists move between the parties.

Bases of Support for the Religious Right

Since the emergence of the Religious Right has been described as the political mobilization of evangelical Protestants, it seems more than reasonable to assume that members and sympathizers of Religious Right organizations tend to be drawn from the ranks of evangelical Protestants.[3] We attempt to determine the effects of evangelical beliefs on attitude toward the Religious Right in terms of three variables: evangelical versus nonevangelical denomination, the existence or non-existence of a born again experience, and literal or nonliteral belief in the Bible.[4] In addition, the effect of a fourth religious variable, frequency of church attendance, is examined.

Table 13-1 indicates that the attitudes of respondents toward the Religious Right were affected by evangelical beliefs, although a substantial number of the evangelicals were opponents of Religious Right groups. Thus, 40 percent of respondents who were members of an evangelical denomination, were members or sympathizers of the Religious Right, compared with 24 percent of those who were not affiliated with an evangelical church. A similar pattern exists for a born again experience and literal belief in the Bible. With regard to the former, 48 percent of those who indicated that they had been born again were members or sympathizers, compared with only 18 percent of those who had not undergone a born again experience. Conversely, 33 percent of the born agains were opponents compared with 60 percent of those who did not consider themselves born again. With regard to view toward the Bible, 45 percent of those with a literal belief were members or sympathizers, compared with only 17 percent of those whose belief was not literal; 28 percent of those with a literal belief in the Bible were opponents of the Religious Right, compared with 64 percent of those with a nonliteral belief.

An analysis of the relationship between frequency of church attendance and attitude toward the Religious Right indicates that frequency of church attendance is associated with a favorable attitude, suggesting that religious networks are important in developing attitudes favorable to the issue positions of the Religious Right (see Table 13-2).[5] Thus, 39 percent of those who attended church every week were

Table 13-1 Influences on Orientation toward the Religious Right

Orientation toward the Religious Right	Evangelical Denomination		Born Again Experience		Literal Belief in Bible	
	Yes	No	Yes	No	Yes	No
Member	8%	2%	9%	1%	8%	1%
Sympathizer	32	22	39	17	37	16
Undecided	23	23	19	22	27	19
Opponent	37	53	33	60	28	64
(N)	(2,742)	(5,691)	(2,722)	(5,664)	(3,312)	(5,655)

members or sympathizers, compared with 7 percent of those who did not attend church. At the opposite pole, 36 percent of those who attended church every week were opponents, compared with 83 percent of those who did not attend church.

Perhaps the relationship between religious beliefs, experiences, and behaviors, on the one hand, and attitude toward the Religious Right, on the other, can be seen with somewhat greater clarity by combining the four religious items into a three-point religiosity index.[6] The principal finding revealed by this analysis is that a higher degree of religiosity does indeed tend to result in a more supportive attitude toward the Religious Right (see Table 13-3). Whereas only 17 percent of those who ranked low on religiosity were members or supporters of the Religious Right, 54 percent of those who ranked high fit in these categories. However, a second finding of some significance is that 46

Table 13-2 Frequency of Church Attendance and Orientation toward the Religious Right

Orientation toward the Religious Right	Frequency of Church Attendance				
	Every Week	Almost Every Week	Once or Twice a Month	Few Times a Year	Never
Member	6%	2%	1%	1%	0%
Sympathizer	33	24	18	15	7
Undecided	25	25	24	23	11
Opponent	36	50	57	61	83
(N)	(4,584)	(1,806)	(1,060)	(2,167)	(944)

Table 13-3   Religiosity and Orientation toward the Religious Right

Orientation toward the Religious Right	Religiosity		
	Low	Medium	High
Member	1%	2%	11%
Sympathizer	16	26	43
Undecided	22	29	21
Opponent	61	43	25
(N)	(3,976)	(1,544)	(2,085)

percent of the respondents who ranked high on religiosity fit in the undecided and opponent categories. This suggests that evangelicalism is not monolithic; that is, although evangelicalism is a conservative creed, not all politically active evangelicals are attracted to a politically conservative, religion-based movement.[7]

Three other variables were analyzed as bases of support for the Religious Right; party identification, race, and region. Party identification as a basis of support rests on the assumption that regardless of religious beliefs, experiences, and behaviors, Republicans are more likely than Democrats to exhibit a favorable attitude toward the Religious Right. The findings tend to bear this assumption out. Although for both Republicans and Democrats the percentage of respondents with a favorable attitude toward the Religious Right increased as the level of religiosity increased, at each level of religiosity Republicans tended to have a considerably more favorable attitude than Democrats (see Table 13-4). This effect seemed to be more pronounced for sympathizers since

Table 13-4   Party Identification and Orientation toward the Religious Right, Controlling for Religiosity

Orientation toward the Religious Right	Religiosity					
	Low		Medium		High	
	Dem.	Rep.	Dem.	Rep.	Dem.	Rep.
Member	0%	1%	1%	4%	3%	18%
Sympathizer	4	31	9	47	19	63
Undecided	16	28	28	29	33	11
Opponent	80	40	62	20	45	8
(N)	(2,139)	(1,834)	(847)	(696)	(978)	(1,105)

at each level of religiosity a substantial percentage of Republican respondents placed themselves in the sympathizer category. Although it may be risky to speculate that the Republican party is itself a network that draws party activists into support for the Religious Right, the data do rather strongly suggest that the Republican party does provide the Religious Right with a relatively responsive, supportive environment. Thus, it may be that the Republican party is the natural home of the Religious Right.

Race was selected as a basis of support on the assumption that the liberalism of blacks would tend to make the Religious Right unattractive to them. With regard to this assumption, the findings are not at all clear (see Table 13-5). Only 13 percent of the blacks were members or sympathizers of Religious Right organizations, compared with 28 percent of the whites; this suggests that although there was support for the Religious Right among black respondents, whites constituted a considerably more important base; on the other hand, there was no black-white difference in the percentage of members and very little in the percentage of opponents. There were differences in the other two categories, with a lower percentage of blacks classifying themselves as sympathizers and a higher percentage as undecided. Thus, blacks to a considerably greater degree than whites find themselves on the fence. Although there is no reason why the distribution of black opinion should change, the data do suggest that blacks may be poised between taking a position similar to whites and shifting to a strong opposition stance.

Region was selected as a basis of support on the assumption that since southerners are more likely to embrace evangelicalism, they should also be more likely to become members or sympathizers of the Religious Right.[8] For the set of states in our study, this assumption was not borne out (see Table 13-5). Regional differences tended to be slight; as a result, the hypothesis of the South as a peculiarly fertile ground for the Religious Right was rejected, at least among party activists.

Attachment to Political Parties and Candidates

Since the Religious Right is a conservative movement and the Democratic party is the more liberal, Democratic delegates who were members or sympathizers of Religious Right groups should exhibit less attachment to their party and its presidential candidate than would be the case for Democrats who were undecided or opponents. Since the Republican party is more conservative, this relationship was not expected to hold for Republican delegates. We tested this hypothesis by addressing delegates' strength of party identification at both the national and state levels, by measuring delegates' ideological proximity to political parties and presidential candidates, by examining delegates'

Table 13-5   The Effects of Race and Region on Orientation toward
the Religious Right

Orientation toward the Religious Right	Race		Region	
	White	*Black*	*South*	*Nonsouth*
Member	3%	3%	4%	3%
Sympathizer	25	10	26	22
Undecided	22	35	21	25
Opponent	49	52	48	51
(N)	(9,667)	(898)	(4,603)	(6,238)

attitudes toward party supporters who voted a split ticket, and by
examining the defection rate of delegates in the 1980 presidential
election contest.

Table 13-6 supports the hypothesis for white Democrats and
Republicans but not for black Democrats. In terms of national party
identification, white Democratic members and sympathizers were much
less likely than opponents to classify themselves as strong Democrats,
and, indeed, 19 percent did not even consider themselves Democrats.
On the other hand, as expected, orientation toward the Religious Right
tended not to have an effect on Republicans' strength of party
identification. What is unexpected is that orientation toward the
Religious Right also tended to have no effect on black Democrats'
strength of party identification; 80 percent of the members and
sympathizers, 77 percent of the undecided, and 79 percent of the
opponents considered themselves strong Democrats. Also, no black
Democrats classified themselves as independent or Republican.

The findings with regard to strength of party identification at the
state level tend to be in line with findings at the national level.
Although white Democrats were more likely to consider themselves
strong Democrats at the state level, their strength of party identification
was affected by attitude toward the Religious Right. Black Democrats
and Republicans again exhibited uniformly strong party identification.

The findings dealing with delegates' ideological proximity to
parties and presidential candidates are similar to those discussed above
(see Table 13-7). White Democratic members and sympathizers again
emerged as relatively disaffected. These delegates were farther from
Mondale, the national Democratic party, and the state Democratic
party than those in the undecided and opponent categories and were
closer to Reagan, the national Republican party, and the state
Republican party. Indeed, white Democratic members and sympathiz-

Table 13-6 Orientation toward the Religious Right and Party Identification

Party Identification	Democrats — White M/S	White U	White O	Black M/S	Black U	Black O	Republicans M	S	U	O
National										
Strong Democrat	46%	64%	74%	80%	77%	79%	—	—	—	—
Weak Democrat	23	20	14	16	20	15	—	—	—	—
Independent Democrat	13	9	10	4	2	6	—	—	—	—
Independent	10	4	2	—	1	—	—	1%	1%	1%
Independent Republican	7	1	—	—	—	—	9%	5	4	6
Weak Republican	1	—	—	—	—	—	8	6	11	14
Strong Republican	1	1	—	—	—	—	84	89	84	78
(N)	(374)	(834)	(3,356)	(95)	(291)	(446)	(279)	(2,968)	(1,226)	(1,287)
State										
Strong Democrat	61	75	80	81	81	83	—	—	—	—
Weak Democrat	21	15	11	13	16	10	—	—	—	—
Independent Democrat	10	7	8	6	2	7	—	—	—	—
Independent	5	2	1	—	1	—	—	1	1	1
Independent Republican	2	1	—	—	—	—	10	6	5	6
Weak Republican	1	—	—	—	—	—	8	9	14	14
Strong Republican	1	—	—	—	—	—	81	85	80	79
(N)	(375)	(834)	(3,361)	(95)	(291)	(448)	(280)	(2,069)	(1,234)	(1,283)

Note: M = member; S = sympathizer; U = undecided; O = opponent.

[a] Since there are so few Democrats who are members of religious right organizations, members and sympathizers have been placed in a single category.

Table 13-7   Orientation toward the Religious Right and Mean
Ideological Proximity to Political Parties and
Presidential Candidates

	Democrats [a]						Republicans			
	White			Black						
	M/S	U	O	M/S	U	O	M	S	U	O
Reagan	1.9	2.5	3.8	3.5	3.7	4.3	0.6	0.5	0.6	0.9
Mondale	2.4	1.7	1.1	1.2	1.1	1.0	5.1	4.7	4.0	3.7
National Democratic Party	2.2	1.5	1.1	1.0	1.2	1.3	5.0	4.4	3.9	3.5
State Democratic Party	1.7	1.3	1.4	1.2	1.5	1.9	4.4	3.8	3.4	3.0
National Republican Party	1.8	2.3	3.3	3.4	3.7	4.0	1.1	0.8	0.8	0.8
State Republican Party	2.0	2.5	3.6	3.4	3.7	4.2	0.9	0.6	0.7	0.8

Note: The ideological proximity of each group was calculated by taking the mean of the absolute value of the respondents' ideology minus the respondents' perception of the ideology of the candidate or party.

[a] See footnote to Table 13-6.

ers were closer to Reagan than to Mondale and closer to the national Republican party than to the national Democratic one. It is only at the state level that these delegates felt closer to their party, and this by not very much.

Orientation toward the Religious Right tended to have little effect on the ideological proximity of black Democrats and Republicans to their respective presidential candidates and parties. It did, however, affect proximity to the opposite party and presidential candidate. Black Democratic members and sympathizers were closer to Reagan, the national Republican party, and the state Republican party than was the case for black undecideds and opponents, although relative to white Democrats in the same categories, they tended to be remote. Republican members and sympathizers were farther from Mondale, the national Democratic party, and the state Democratic party than those in the undecided and opponent categories.

Third, in terms of attitude toward party supporters voting a split ticket, orientation toward the religious right affected the viewpoint of both black and white Democrats, although whites were more likely to consider ticket splitting permissible (see Table 13-8). For Republicans, the relationship was, if anything, in the opposite direction. While 54 percent of the members, 53 percent of the sympathizers, and 54 percent of the undecided felt that a split ticket was acceptable, 63 percent of the opponents felt this way.

Table 13-8 Orientation toward the Religious Right and Attitude toward Voting a Split Ticket

| Attitude toward Voting a Split Ticket | Democrats[a] | | | | | | Republicans | | | |
| | White | | | Black | | | | | | |
	M/S	U	O	M/S	U	O	M	S	U	O
Yes	65%	47%	51%	38%	25%	29%	54%	53%	54%	63%
No	28	39	40	51	59	65	35	37	34	28
Don't Know	7	14	9	12	16	7	10	9	12	9
(N)	(377)	(828)	(3,322)	(93)	(286)	(439)	(275)	(2,044)	(1,204)	(1,280)

[a] See footnote to Table 13-6.

Table 13-9 Orientation toward the Religious Right and Defection Rate in the 1980 Presidential Election

| Presidential Vote in 1980 | Democrats[a] | | | | | | Republicans | | | |
| | White | | | Black | | | | | | |
	M/S	U	O	M/S	U	O	M	S	U	O
Carter	61%	73%	79%	98%	94%	96%	2%	1%	1%	2%
Reagan	33	19	6	—	1	0	97	97	97	92
Anderson	4	3	10	—	1	2	—	—	1	5
Other	2	2	3	1	—	—	—	1	—	1
Did Not Vote	1	3	3	1	3	1	1	1	1	1
(N)	(374)	(834)	(3,398)	(96)	(294)	(454)	(283)	(2,090)	(1,255)	(1,304)

[a] See footnote to Table 13-6.

Finally, an examination of the relationship between orientation toward the Religious Right and the 1980 presidential vote reveals that white Democrats were much more likely to defect, with members and sympathizers exhibiting the highest defection rate and opponents the lowest (see Table 13-9). Also, among white Democrats the pattern of defection differed between members and sympathizers on the one hand and opponents on the other. Members and sympathizers were much more likely than opponents to defect to Reagan, whereas opponents were more likely to vote for Anderson.

The Religious Right and Party Cleavage

Delegates were asked to indicate their positions on twenty-one issues—two minority rights, four moral, six economic, five defense, three energy and environmental control, and one handgun control (Table 13-10). Discriminant analysis was employed in an effort to determine the manner in which these twenty-one issues discriminated among the ten groups of delegates. This analysis reveals two substantively significant discriminant functions; the first has a canonical correlation of .831 and accounts for 80 percent of the variance, and the second, with a canonical correlation of .529, explains 14 percent of the variance.

The first function can be thought of as lying on a general liberalism-conservatism dimension since issues from the defense, minority rights, economic, and energy and environment issue areas are dominant on it (see Table 13-11). The second function is much more specialized, consisting almost exclusively of issues in the moral realm.

On the first function, party identification is the principal cleavage; the six Democratic groups are the six most liberal and the four Republican groups the four most conservative (see Table 13-12). Within each party, however, orientation toward the Religious Right does tend to rank-order delegates; among Republicans, for example, the order of increasing conservatism goes from opponents, to undecided, to sympathizers, to members. A similar pattern exists for white Democrats and black Democrats, with white Democratic members and sympathizers being the only Democratic group to the right of the overall mean. Finally, on the first function race seems to be consequential since blacks constitute three of the four most liberal groups.

On the second function, among whites, orientation toward the Religious Right is the principal cleavage. The three most liberal groups, all to the left of the overall mean, are Republican opponents, white Democratic opponents, and Republican undecideds. Of the four other white groups, the two Democratic groups are farther to the right than the Republicans. Race is also an important cleavage on the second

Table 13-10   Issues Presented to Respondents

Economic Issues

A government-sponsored national health insurance program

Across-the-board cuts in spending to balance the federal budget

An across-the-board tax increase to reduce the federal budget deficit

A public works program to reduce unemployment even if it increases inflation

A broad-based tax to increase funding for public education

Steps should be taken to reduce the number of people getting food stamps

Military Issues

Continued increase in defense spending even while cutting the federal budget

Increasing America's military presence in the Middle East

Increasing America's military presence in Latin America

More intensive negotiation with the Soviet Union on arms control

A nuclear freeze agreed to by the United States and the Soviet Union

Environmental Issues

More rapid development of nuclear power

Government action to increase energy sources even though it might decrease protection
   for the environment

Government regulation of business to protect the environment is excessive

Minority Rights Issues

The Equal Rights Amendment to the Constitution

Affirmative action programs to increase minority representation in jobs and higher
   education

Moral Issues

A constitutional amendment to prohibit abortions except when the mother's life is
   endangered

The use of marijuana is morally wrong

Homosexual behavior is morally wrong

A constitutional amendment to permit prayers and Bible reading in the public schools

Other Issues

Stricter legislation to control handguns

---

function. The three black groups who tended to be the most liberal on the first function are the most conservative on the second. Although on the second function blacks are rank-ordered from least conservative to most conservative on the basis of orientation toward the Religious Right, the least conservative black group is considerably to the right of the most conservative white group.

Table 13-11   Pooled Within-Groups Correlations
between the Discriminating Variables and the
Discriminant Functions

Variables [a]	*Function 1*	*Function 2*
Increase Defense Spending	.69834	−.05567
Equal Rights Amendment	.63508	−.24414
Increase Military in Latin America	.51641	.07901
National Health Insurance	.51601	−.29809
Affirmative Action	.47005	−.44079
Nuclear Power	.45336	−.03012
Public Works Programs	.45198	−.18501
Business/Environment	.42327	.14880
Tax for Public Education	.37105	−.15894
Regulation of Handguns	.34950	.00485
Increase Energy Resources	.25403	.10046
School Prayer Amendment	.46141	.61286
Amendment to Prohibit Abortion	.33148	.54976
Reduce Food Stamps	.43198	−.03646
Nuclear Freeze	.38948	.00798
Homosexual Behavior Is Wrong	.39823	.39368
Cut Spending to Balance Budget	.34115	−.02434
Marijuana Is Wrong	.33229	.33817
Increase Military in Middle East	.35639	−.08400
Tax Increase to Reduce Deficit	.23637	.11151
Negotiation on Arms Control	.13439	.15124

[a] For the wording on the issues, see Table 13-10.

The Religious Right and Realignment

Given that the Republican party is undoubtedly a much more compatible environment for the Religious Right than the Democratic party, given that white Democratic members and sympathizers tend to exhibit a relatively low attachment to their party, and given that on the two discriminant functions the group means for these Democrats are relatively conservative, it seems plausible that many of these Democrats would give at least strong consideration to shifting their allegiance to the Republican party. If this formulation is correct, the Religious Right can be thought of as a bridge across which Democratic activists are moving into the ranks of the Republican party. Although this notion is intriguing, a rather fundamental problem is that among Republicans who are party switchers it is impossible to disentangle those who switched prior to becoming members or sympathizers of the Religious Right from those who switched subsequent to becoming members or

Table 13-12   Discriminant Functions Evaluated at Group Means

Groups	Group Means	
	Function 1	*Function 2*
White Dem. Member/Sympathizer [a]	0.21705	0.60844
White Dem. Undecided [a]	−0.31619	0.63980
White Dem. Opponent [a]	−1.62797	−0.34558
Black Dem. Member/Sympathizer [a]	−1.21071	2.34822
Black Dem. Undecided [a]	−1.27763	2.33534
Black Dem. Opponent [a]	−1.90840	1.15617
White Rep. Member	2.45635	0.50901
White Rep. Sympathizer	1.89774	0.09219
White Rep. Undecided	1.13744	−0.00962
White Rep. Opponent	0.71294	−0.77232

[a] See footnote in Table 13-6.

sympathizers. Thus, the data on the effects of attitude toward the Religious Right on party switching are, at best, suggestive.

With this caveat out of the way, it does appear that for Republicans orientation toward the Religious Right may affect the decision to switch parties (see Table 13-13). Thus, 34 percent of the members, 27 percent of the sympathizers, 20 percent of the undecideds, and 22 percent of the opponents were party switchers. It may well be that the Religious Right is, if not a four-lane span between the parties, at least a footbridge.

Conclusions

Quite obviously, orientation toward the Religious Right has the greatest impact on white Democrats. To a considerable degree, the strength of party attachment among white Democratic members and sympathizers is so slight that, at least at the national level, many of them can be thought of as Democrats in name only. Furthermore, their rather conservative stance on the two discriminant functions indicates that they constitute a conservative faction in a generally liberal party.

The evidence suggests that over the long run these disaffected Democrats will tend to disappear. To begin with, as pointed out in the first section, Republicans tend to be more favorably inclined toward the Religious Right than Democrats. Hence, as whites who are members or sympathizers of Religious Right groups become politically active, they should have a greater tendency to affiliate with the Republicans. Second, the data suggest that the Religious Right may lie between the two parties, thereby facilitating the movement of Democrats into the

Table 13-13   Orientation toward the Religious Right and the
Decision of Democrats to Switch Parties

Party Switcher	Orientation toward the Religious Right			
	Member	*Sympathizer*	*Undecided*	*Opponent*
Yes	34%	27%	20%	22%
No	66	73	80	78
(N)	(284)	(2,111)	(1,270)	(1,320)

Republican party. When death and retirement from politics are
factored in, it may not be unreasonable to suggest that among white
Democrats the influence of the Religious Right is waning. In the short
run, of course, white Democratic members and sympathizers tend to
function as a conservative brake on the Democratic party.

The situation with regard to black Democrats appears to be quite
different. Although orientation toward the Religious Right has some
weakening effect on the party attachment of members and sympathizers, it is so slight that there seems to be little danger that black
supporters of the Religious Right will shift to the Republican party.
Second, although the positions of black groups on the two functions
were rank-ordered by orientation toward the Religious Right, race
appears to be much more important in determining the placement of
blacks. On the first function three of the four most liberal groups are
black; on the second, the three most conservative are black. Orientation
toward the Religious Right is thus important in moderating or
accelerating black tendencies. On the first function, a favorable attitude
toward the Religious Right moderates black liberalism, whereas on the
second it strengthens or makes more extreme blacks' conservative or
moral viewpoint.

For Republicans, a favorable attitude toward the Religious Right
has little or no effect on attachment to the Republican party but, in terms
of ideological proximity, it does tend to increase the distance from the
Democratic party. Thus, if supporters of the Religious Right move into
the Republican party, interparty differences should increase. Likewise, in
terms of issue positions, a favorable attitude toward the Religious Right
tends to pull the Republican party to the right. On the first function Republican members take the most conservative position whereas on the
second they take the most conservative Republican position.

Finally, it should be pointed out that with regard to moral issues,
the Religious Right could create a relatively deep cleavage within each

party. Assuming that moral issues become relatively highly salient, the cleavage within the Democratic party would align white members, sympathizers, undecideds, and blacks against white opponents. Within the Republican party members and sympathizers would be aligned against the undecideds and opponents. There is, of course, no guarantee that this will occur; indeed, it probably will not. But it does suggest that politics could take a rather bizarre turn.

Notes

1. See David G. Bromley and Anson D. Shupe, eds., *New Christian Politics* (Macon, Ga.: Mercer University Press, 1984); James L. Guth, "The Politics of the Evangelical Right: An Interpretative Essay" (Paper presented at the annual meeting of the American Political Science Association, New York City, August 1981); Stephen D. Johnson and Joseph B. Tammey, "The Christian Right and the 1980 Presidential Election," *Journal for the Scientific Study of Religion* (21): 123-131; Lyman A. Kellstedt, "The Falwell Platform: An Analysis of its Causes and Consequences" (Paper presented at the annual meeting of the Society for the Scientific Study of Religion, Savannah, Ga., October 1985); and Robert C. Liebman and Robert Wuthnow, eds., *The New Christian Right* (New York: Aldine, 1984).
2. See Kellstedt, "The Falwell Platform"; and H. Paul Chalfant, Robert E. Beckley, and C. Eddie Palmer, *Religion in Contemporary Society*, 2d ed. (Palo Alto, Calif.: Mayfield, 1987), 248.
3. Kenneth D. Wald, *Religion and Politics in the United States* (New York: St. Martin's Press, 1987), chap. 7.
4. Although some students (for example, Wald, *Religion and Politics*, 248) place blacks outside the evangelical movement, this study includes blacks. See William H. Bentley, "Bible Believers in the Black Community," in *The Evangelicals: What They Believe, Who They Are, Where They Are Changing*, ed. David F. Wells and John D. Wordbridge (Nashville: Abingdon Press, 1975), 108-121.
5. For a discussion on the importance of frequency of church attendance in forming attitudes on abortion and the Equal Rights Amendment, see Jerome Himmelstein, "The Social Bases of Antifeminism: Religious Networks and Culture," *Journal for the Scientific Study of Religion* 25 (March 1986): 1-15.
6. Each item was coded zero or one, yielding a five-point index ranging from zero, religious on none of the variables, to four, religious on each. This was collapsed into a three-point index by recording zero and one as low, two as medium, and three or four as high.
7. See Anson Shupe and William A. Stacey, *Born Again Politics and the Moral Majority: What Social Surveys Really Show* (New York: Edwin Mellin, 1982).
8. For discussions of the strength of evangelicalism in the South, see Lyman A. Kellstedt, "Evangelical Religion and Support for Falwell Policy Positions: An Examination of Regional Variation" (Paper prepared for The Citadel Symposium on Southern Politics, Charleston, S.C., March 1986); and Robert P. Steed, Laurence W. Moreland, and Tod A. Baker, "Religion and Party Activists: Fundamentalism and Politics in Regional Perspective," in *Religion and Politics in the South*, ed. Tod A. Baker, Robert P. Steed, and Laurence W. Moreland (New York: Praeger, 1983), 105-132.

14. SOUTHERN BAPTISTS AND THE NEW RIGHT*

James L. Guth

After neglecting the field of religion and politics for decades, social scientists have moved in with a vengeance, especially with studies of the New Christian Right. Taken together, these studies have begun to afford us a better understanding of the upsurge of conservative religious activism. Yet despite the universally recognized importance of the local church and its pastor for political mobilization, there are remarkably few studies of clerical politics on the Right: a few local surveys of ministers' reaction to the Moral Majority and of the political ideas of conservative clergy. But none has matched Harold Quinley's 1974 study of liberal "New Breed" clerics.[1]

If clerical activism is an important vehicle for Christian Right mobilization, this should be apparent within the Southern Baptist Convention (SBC), the nation's largest Protestant denomination, with more than 14 million members. Southern Baptists include many lay persons and clergy friendly to the Right; furthermore, the laity supports political activity by clergy. In one study, 61 percent of Baptists said ministers should "play a very active role," the most in any denomination.[2] This chapter provides an overview of political activism among Southern Baptist ministers in 1980 and 1984, based on mail surveys taken just after the presidential elections.[3]

We hope to answer several questions: (1) Has the Christian Right made progress in "recruiting" the SBC's clergy? Among which groups? (2) What issues do ministers care about? Has the Christian Right fostered all-round conservative ideologues? Or do ministers specialize on certain issues? (3) What are Baptist ministers' attitudes toward political participation? Did these change from 1980 to 1984? (4) How active are ministers? Has the Christian Right involvement of 1980 been sustained

* An earlier version of this article was presented at the annual meeting of the Society for the Scientific Study of Religion, Savannah, Georgia, October 25-27, 1985. The author wishes to acknowledge the financial support of the Furman University Research and Professional Growth Committee and the American Political Science Association, as well as the diligent assistance of Dana Research Fellow Alicia Lehnes.

177

or increased? (5) Is there an ideological bias to participation? That is, do activists accurately reflect the opinions of the clergy as a whole? (6) What are the prospects for ministerial activism in 1988 and beyond?

The Growth of the Moral Majority in the SBC

Since 1979 the SBC's militant fundamentalist faction has gained control of elective offices and begun to take over the denominational bureaucracy.[4] Has this internal power shift been accompanied by a parallel surge of "external" activism? To answer this question we asked ministers their opinion of the most visible Christian Right organization, the Moral Majority (now Liberty Federation). In fact, the Moral Majority grew markedly during these four years. From a slight disadvantage vis-à-vis its foes in 1980 (46 percent to 47 percent), the Moral Majority grew to include 61 percent of SBC ministers by 1984. Although actual membership advanced only from 3 percent to 5 percent, the ranks of sympathizers went up from 43 percent to 56 percent. Opponents were reduced to barely a third (34 percent) of the clergy. Whatever its fortunes in the electorate, the Right prospered among Baptist pastors.[5]

Where did this growth occur? As Table 14-1 shows, almost every theological, political, and demographic group gave the Moral Majority greater backing in 1984. The Christian Right's largest advances came among those already favorably disposed: fundamentalists, Republicans, and political conservatives. Big gains occurred among ministers with modest educations, but the Moral Majority also made substantial inroads among the seminary-educated. Even the "liberal" SBC seminaries, such as Southern and Southeastern, witnessed many pro-Right defections among graduates.

Other data also demonstrate pervasive Christian Right gains. Ministers from all regions became more supportive, including the "liberal" South Atlantic region, in 1980 the bulwark of opposition. By 1984 ministers of all ages were equally rightist, whereas in 1980 the younger were stronger adherents. Although pastors from white-collar backgrounds were still less friendly toward the Christian Right, by 1984 many had joined scions of blue-collar and farm homes in the Right camp. Ministers in smaller, working-class or lower-middle-class churches also moved right. Thus, many traditionalist ministers, who opposed the Moral Majority in 1980 because of its activism, not its ideology, apparently decided in favor of politics.

Issue Agendas: Morality Specialists or Complete Activists?

Scholars continually debate the expansiveness of the Christian Right agenda. The movement's leaders emphasize social traditionalism,

Table 14-1 Moral Majority Gains, 1980 to 1984
(Percent Members and Sympathizers)

	1980	1984	Gain/ Loss		1980	1984	Gain/ Loss
Theological ID				*Father's Job*			
Fundamentalist	68%	89%	+21%	Professional	43%	57%	+14%
Conservative	50	70	+20	Business	54	58	+4
Moderate	16	18	+2	Clerical	39	59	+20
Liberal	0	0	—	Skilled Labor	56	65	+9
				Unskilled			
Party ID				Labor	49	71	+21
Republican	64	80	+16	Farmer	50	67	+16
Independent	51	62	+11				
Democrat	41	41	—	*Region*			
				Northern	52	61	+9
Ideology				Deep South	56	74	+18
Conservative	60	76	+16	S. Atlantic	31	55	+24
Moderate	23	24	+1	Southwest	60	66	+6
Liberal	17	11	−6	West	55	64	+9
Secular Education				*Age*			
Grade School	30	100	+70	To 29	57	65	+8
High School	54	76	+22	30 to 39	52	65	+13
Some College	62	77	+15	40 to 49	50	63	+13
College				50 to 59	44	69	+25
Graduate	45	57	+12	60 and over	47	59	+12
Postgraduate							
Work	50	63	+13	*Size of Church*			
				Under 200	50	70	+20
Seminary				200 to 299	46	65	+19
None	56	81	+25	300 to 499	57	60	+3
Bible College	60	78	+18	500 to 999	43	60	+17
Some Seminary	51	73	+22	1000 and over	43	54	+11
Seminary							
Graduate	50	57	+7	*Class of Church*			
Postgraduate				Working	58	71	+13
Work	35	52	+17	Mixed	52	64	+12
				Lower-middle	32	65	+33
Seminary Attended				Upper-middle	41	47	+6
Southern	22	35	+13				
Southeastern	30	53	+23				
Midwestern	46	55	+9				
Southwestern	53	61	+8				
New Orleans	55	74	+19				
Golden Gate	67	56	−11				
Fundamentalist	69	88	+19				

Note: The total *N* for the 1980 study was 460 (63 percent response rate); that for the 1984 study was 901 (55 percent response). Analysis by regional distribution, age, education, size of church, and several other variables indicates that the samples are virtually identical in sociodemographic characteristics.

economic libertarianism, and militant anticommunism in almost equal
doses, but many observers doubt that grass-roots activists reflect the
same balance. The Moral Majority's constituency differs from other
voters primarily by virtue of special concern for social issues, such as
abortion, prayer in schools, the Equal Rights Amendment, and
homosexuality, with defense spending and Soviet policy thrown in.[6]
Still, we might expect ministers to have a fuller agenda, given the
greater linkage ("attitudinal constraint") between their theological,
social, and political orientations.

What political issues do ministers care about? In the 1984 survey
we approached this issue in two ways. First, we used a Gallup question
asking ministers to name the "two or three" most important problems
facing the United States. Baptist ministers have a distinctive agenda, as
Table 14-2 suggests. Although most voters—and most political activists—name economic issues as most important, ministers give a
plurality to a combination of "spiritual" and social issues, with
economics getting only a third of the votes. Foreign policy is less salient,
and few ministers think of political process issues.[7] But agendas differ
by attitude toward the Moral Majority: members stress spiritual and
social problems; sympathizers share these concerns but also worry
about economics; and opponents see economic and foreign policy as
priorities. In many ways, then, the Christian Right and its foes perceive
very different political worlds.

The second agenda measure is tied more closely to actual political
involvement. After a questionnaire section that inventoried ministers'
political activities, we asked how often their political activity, taken as a
whole, addressed a variety of current issues (Table 14-2). Clearly,
Baptist preachers still concentrate on classic "sin" issues, with a recent
infusion of "social" questions. Only hunger and poverty do not fit either
category, but both are addressed primarily in charitable, not political,
terms. Their salience no doubt reflects the African famine and
denomination-wide world hunger emphasis in 1983 and 1984. Other
economic and foreign policy issues attract little ministerial interest, at
least in terms of time and energy expended. Not surprisingly, Moral
Majority activists and opponents tend to focus on different issues: the
former concentrate on Israel, homosexuality, school prayer, and pornography, while the latter show more concern for hunger and poverty,
economic issues, environmental concerns, and civil rights. Note, of
course, that the "liberal" advantage comes primarily on issues that elicit
little clerical interest.

The Christian Right's effective appeal, then, is limited primarily
to traditional "Baptist" issues. Although ministers may well have
conservative views on economics and foreign policy, here they are only

Table 14-2 Issue Agendas of Southern Baptist Ministers, 1984

	All	Member	Sympathizer	Opponent
QUESTION: "What are the two or three biggest problems facing the United States today?" (Percent first response in category):				
Spiritual	29	46	33	21
Social	20	25	23	15
Political Process	3	2	3	3
Foreign Policy	16	16	11	25
Economic	32	11	31	35
QUESTION: "If you have made your views known in any of the ways listed above, how often have you addressed the following issues?" (Percent "Very Often" or "Often")				
Family problems	91	100	90	91
Alcohol and drugs	87	94	89	82
Pornography	74	98	81	58
Hunger and poverty	73	66	68	83
Abortion	67	96	77	44
Gambling laws	55	74	58	45
School prayer	51	78	57	36
Gay rights	47	73	58	26
Civil rights	38	49	34	44
Israel and Mideast	30	58	34	18
Women's issues	28	46	28	26
National defense	27	48	25	26
Economic issues	24	20	22	27
Environment	18	12	15	24
Federal budget	15	20	15	14
Latin America	6	8	6	6

marginally involved. Insofar as the Christian Right movement has intensified and rationalized Baptist ministers' traditional concerns, it has been successful, but only a few ministers have embraced the full ideological agenda advanced by Christian Right leaders. For the most part, Moral Majority adherents have their own narrow and distinctive agenda, which sets them apart not only from their ministerial opponents but from other political activists and the mass public as well.

Participatory Attitudes

Whatever their agenda, between 1980 and 1984 pastors became even more sympathetic toward political participation. The proportion claiming that their "political attitudes" encouraged activism rose from

55 percent to 67 percent, while those saying that their "theological attitudes" stimulated participation grew from 63 percent to 73 percent. And pastors hoping to become "more involved" increased from 25 percent to 31 percent, with only 3 percent wanting to be less active. Pastors also felt quite efficacious: although a small majority agreed that it is sometimes "difficult for clergymen to know the proper political channels to use," over 89 percent concurred that "ministers have great potential to influence the political and social beliefs of their congregations." Apparently preachers don't read social science studies on the limits of clerical influence!

If ministers are sympathetic toward clerical participation, what do they see as appropriate activities? In 1980 Baptist ministers' support for many forms of activism compared quite well with that of 1960s "New Breed" liberal activists.[8] As Table 14-3 indicates, these positive attitudes survived (and in some cases grew) into 1984. And, as in 1980, the Moral Majority was more approving of clerical activism than its foes. Some small changes took place between 1980 and 1984. Moral Majority members were a little more supportive of controversial acts, such as endorsing candidates, engaging in protest or civil disobedience, and forming study groups. Sympathizers' views were remarkably stable. Even opponents were more willing to endorse political preaching, protest and civil disobedience, forming study groups, and joining political organizations.

What factors influence approval of clerical activism? Using a simple additive index of overall approval, we found that the correlates of approval were quite similar in 1980 and 1984, with few exceptions. In 1980, moderate or liberal theology was associated with approval of activism, but in 1984 the correlation disappeared. Also, in 1980 Reagan voters and the Moral Majority were most approving, but by 1984 presidential choice was not a factor (82 percent of the ministers voted for Reagan) and the influence of Moral Majority orientation was somewhat reduced. Socio-demographic factors were also quite similar—and strong—in both years, with youth, urban upbringing, and higher education (both secular and seminary) associated with participatory attitudes. Leadership of large, middle-class churches was also a positive predictor (data not shown). That all these traits are increasingly common among Baptist ministers suggests that Moral Majority political activism may not have peaked.

Do these findings reflect changes in traditional evangelical doctrine on social reform or, for that matter, on the church's role in politics? Until the late 1970s, at least, social scientists assumed that the individualistic, salvationist and otherworldly preoccupations of fundamentalist and evangelical clergymen precluded "this-worldly" politics.

Table 14-3 Approval of Activism, 1980 and 1984

Percent Approving Pastors Who:	All		Members		Sympathizers		Opponents	
	1980	1984	1980	1984	1980	1984	1980	1984
Urge congregation to vote	97	98	100	99	98	99	98	98
Take public stand on issue	90	91	100	96	96	95	86	86
Preach political sermon	70	75	86	79	78	79	66	73
Take pulpit stand on issue	69	68	93	83	80	73	60	59
Take public stand/candidate	65	66	79	87	73	73	57	55
Form study group in church	57	60	50	63	59	56	57	68
Form political action group	45	45	58	53	51	44	45	47
Run for public office	40	40	43	40	41	47	40	44
Join national political organizations	31	40	57	63	40	43	27	35
Participate in protest march	21	27	21	35	21	26	21	30
Take part/civil disobedience	9	12	7	15	6	10	10	16
Endorse candidate from pulpit	—	11	—	31	—	13	—	5

Harold Quinley could predict confidently that "despite the well-known and well-exposed problems of liberal religion, the political future is likely to be influenced more by liberal clergymen than by conservatives." [9] Of course, the conservative onslaught of the 1980s has partially disproved Quinley. The question remains, however, as to whether these new Protestant politicos have forged a rationale for politics comparable to that of clerical liberals in the 1960s. Indeed, a "theology of political activism" may be crucial for the Christian Right's survival.

Have the old evangelical verities changed? It seems not. Whatever their new fondness for clerical activism, Baptist pastors cling to an individualistic, salvationist perspective—at least in theory. Asked if they agreed that "if enough men were brought to Christ, social ills would take care of themselves," only a third expressed any reservation or disagreement (Table 14-4). And Moral Majority members overwhelmingly endorse this view, with sympathizers barely less adamant. Indeed, the clergymen most likely to retain this salvationist notion are fundamentalists, older ministers, those in small, working-class churches, poorly educated or trained in a fundamentalist school, Republicans,

Table 14-4   Attitudes of Clergy toward Politics and the Church

Percent Agreeing:	All	Members	Sympathizers	Opponents
"If enough men were brought to Christ, social ills would take care of themselves."	66	77	75	49
"The church should put less emphasis on individual sanctification and more on transforming the social order in accordance with Christ's teaching."	14	11	12	17
"Clergymen of different faiths need to cooperate more in politics, even if they can't agree in theology."	55	68	59	47

and political conservatives—the core of the Christian Right. But even half of the Moral Majority's opponents accept the easy equation between salvation and social betterment.

Nor do clergy reveal any fundamental reorientation in their view of the church. Asked if "the church should put less emphasis on individual sanctification and more on transforming the social order in conformity with Christ's teaching," only a few ministers in any camp agree with such a shift. Thus, although the visible and constant politicking in some Baptist churches suggests that resources are, in fact, being diverted from "evangelism," there is little theological recognition of this change.

There is sign of movement on one traditional fundamentalist tenet, however. Most fundamentalists have historically argued for separation among clergy (and laity) of different faiths. Although some still cooperate politically only with those of like faith, others (such as Jerry Falwell) argue that theology is irrelevant to the pursuit of public morality. The Moral Majority stresses that adherents come from many different religious—and nonreligious—traditions.

Although the SBC was never run by separatist fundamentalists, denominational chauvinism had similar isolating effects, precluding cooperation with other Protestants—and even some other Baptists. But Falwell's claim that "morality unites" has found a receptive audience. Most Moral Majority members and a solid bloc of sympathizers agree that "clergymen of different faiths need to cooperate more in politics, even if they can't agree in theology" (Table 14-4). And, as a cross-check reveals, these are the very ministers most preoccupied with spiritual and social issues.

Morality is the key to understanding the dichotomy between an individualistic, salvation-oriented theology and the obvious clerical flirtation with politics. Baptist ministers avoid any conflict by denying that they are politically involved. The many write-in comments that "fighting abortion is not politics" or that "school prayer is not a political issue" confirm this hypothesis. Indeed—almost by definition—moral issues cannot be political, regardless of the influence techniques used. And, as long as issues are cast in traditional moral terms, church activism is theologically justified as a mere adjunct to individual sanctification. Indeed, as Robert Wuthnow has argued, the political revival of American evangelicalism came about not so much through theological reformulations as through the "reconstruction of morality to include more public and institutional meanings." [10] Thus, even greater political activism among conservative clergy may not be as unthinkable as social scientists have often assumed, looking only at the incompatibility of fundamentalist theology and this-worldly reform.

Participation in 1980 and 1984

Given favorable clerical attitudes toward politics, has participation itself increased? Unfortunately, this is more difficult to test, as the 1980 and 1984 surveys were not identical. In 1980 ministers were asked whether they had "ever made their views known" in a variety of ways, while in 1984 they were asked if they had "made their views known" in these same ways "in 1984," "only in the past," or "never." Still, with appropriate caution, we can combine the first two 1984 responses to get figures comparable to those from 1980. As Table 14-5 indicates, SBC clergy as a group have become more active: by 1984, more ministers had engaged—at least once—in virtually every activity than had in 1980. Part of that increase reflects replacement of older, inactive ministers by new, politically aggressive pastors, but every age group has become more active.

When we consider activism in 1984 alone, two conclusions quickly emerge. First, the participation record (Table 14-6) is, by any standard, quite impressive. Whether considering activities special to clergy (pulpit statements on issues) or those available to all citizens (contributing money, sending letters to the editor, writing public officials), these pastors were very active. Second, the Moral Majority has the edge in all kinds of activism, with the biggest gaps on frequency of pulpit stands on issues, public stands on candidates, joining national political organizations, and endorsing candidates from the pulpit.

The summary index clearly shows the hyperactivity of Moral

Table 14-5   Activities of Clergy, 1980 and 1984

Percent Having "Ever":	1980	1984	Gain
Touched on controversial issue in sermon	85	90	+5
Taken public stand on controversial issue	85	89	+4
Signed or circulated a petition	69	87	+18
Written a letter to a public official	69	73	+4
Taken pulpit stand on controversial issue	59	70	+11
Taken public stand on candidate for office	53	63	+10
Given money to a candidate, party or PAC	—	43	—
Written letter to editor	34	43	+9
Organized social or political action group	14	22	+8
Organized social or political study group	13	19	+6
Joined a national political organization	11	20	+9
Run for public office	5	5	—
Endorsed a candidate from the pulpit	4	11	+7
Engaged in protest demonstration	4	7	+3
Engaged in civil disobedience	2	3	+1

Majority members, the more restrained activism of sympathizers, and the silence of opponents. Besides Moral Majority sentiments, political involvement is influenced most by predictable factors: higher educational levels and placement in large, middle-class churches. Here, again, long-term trends presage more, not less, clerical involvement.

The Policy Bias of Activism

Scholars have often considered the problems for democracy created by the varying preferences of "political activists" and the mass public. For example, party leaders are often more liberal or conservative than rank-and-file party identifiers and, even taken together, quite unrepresentative of national opinion. Closer to present concerns, in mainline Protestant churches, leaders and activists are disproportionately liberal, even compared to other clergy.[11]

Are the new SBC politicos representative of their colleagues? Or is there a conservative bias to their politics? SBC ministers are a pretty conservative lot, especially on the very social issues they care about: the Equal Rights Amendment, abortion, and gay rights (Table 14-7). But they also have conservative views on devolving federal programs to business, gun control, school prayer, and identifying Christianity with free enterprise. They are more moderate, however, on social welfare programs—vital to their blue-collar constituents—and on questions evoking historic Baptist views on church and state, such as tuition tax

Table 14-6 Activities of Clergy, 1984

Percent Having:	All	Members	Sympathizers	Opponents
Touched on controversial issue in sermon	69	82	70	65
Taken public stand on controversial issue	63	80	65	57
Taken pulpit stand on controversial issue	49	84	51	39
Taken public stand on candidate for office	42	76	47	28
Signed or circulated a petition	38	64	39	31
Written a letter to a public official	35	50	35	31
Given money to a candidate, party or PAC	21	50	20	17
Written letter to editor	13	16	12	14
Joined a national political organization	9	42	9	4
Organized social or political action group	8	18	6	8
Endorsed a candidate from the pulpit	6	22	7	2
Organized social or political study group	5	8	3	9
Engaged in protest demonstration	2	8	3	1
Run for public office	1	0	1	0
Engaged in civil disobedience	1	0	1	1
Participation Index				
None or one	23	6	21	29
Two or three activities	28	6	28	33
Four or five activities	27	22	30	23
Six or more activities	22	66	21	15

credits. They also strongly favor SALT talks and are skeptical of added defense spending. As we might expect, the gap between Moral Majority forces and their opponents is quite wide, especially on abortion, school prayer, defense spending, and tuition tax credits—the core of the Christian Right agenda.

Are clerical activists a microcosm of the SBC clergy? We considered this question in two ways. First, we looked at ministers who engaged in six or more political activities in 1984 (22 percent of the sample). These "hyperactive" pastors were almost invariably more conservative than the sample as a whole. The overrepresentation was often largest on divisive issues: on social welfare, support for friendly

Table 14-7 Opinions of Southern Baptist Clergy

Percent "Conservative" on Issue	All	Members	Sympathizers	Opponents	"Bias" among: Hyperactive	Issue active
Equal Rights Amendment	79	92	88	63	+1	−4
Abortion amendment	76	94	88	51	+1	+10
Gay rights	70	85	80	51	+7	+9
Give government programs to business	67	87	77	47	+8	−5
Stop gun control	64	85	72	48	+2	n.a.
Pass school prayer amendment	54	76	69	25	+6	+16
Christianity = free enterprise	51	79	59	34	0	n.a.
Need more defense spending	48	85	59	24	+9	+10
Oppose affirmative action	48	70	53	37	0	−6
Don't need more social welfare	47	62	52	25	+9	−6
Inflation worse than unemployment	39	45	42	33	+3	−10
Support friendly dictators	38	40	40	33	+11	n.a.
Pass tuition tax credits	36	57	46	16	+9	n.a.
SALT talks not a priority	27	55	33	12	+8	+2
Jobs more important than environment	27	45	30	19	+12	−9

Note: A plus (+) sign indicates added "conservative" advantage on that issue. A minus (−) indicates "liberal" advantage among activists. "N.a." means no matchup was possible on issue.

dictators, defense spending, tuition tax credits, SALT talks, and devolving federal programs to private enterprise.

A second, and arguably more relevant, perspective results from analyzing those who addressed a specific issue "very often" or "often." Here the conservative advantage is either enhanced (on conservative issues), or eliminated (on liberal issues). Conservative margins are substantial on school prayer, abortion, defense spending, and gay rights. "Issue-activists" were disproportionately liberal on unemployment, the environment, affirmative action, and social welfare. Once again, it should be noted, the liberal edge came where the fewest ministers were involved. Thus, conservative views are somewhat overrepresented among activists, even within this very conservative denomination.

Conclusion

The Christian Right has clearly made major inroads into the SBC's clergy. Between 1980 and 1984 the number of ministers joining or sympathizing with the movement dramatically increased, favorable attitudes toward political activism flourished, activism itself grew, and conservative activists seized both the agenda and the initiative. These trends will probably not be reversed in 1988; indeed, they reflect the impact of education and affluence among clergy and, perhaps, the start of a major political realignment, not only among SBC clergy, but within their southern congregations as well.[12] In fact, fundamentalist control of SBC bureaucracies may provide critical institutional encouragement for expanded conservative activism.

Still, the Christian Right's clout should not be overstated. Only the small coterie of members and a few sympathizers, not the entire clergy, adhere to the full Moral Majority agenda. Indeed, to some, concerns of Southern Baptist pastors have changed distressingly little since the 1880s.[13] And, despite their social traditionalism, Baptist ministers are still divided on economic and foreign policy—and on some issues a liberal remnant outperforms the Moral Majority. Nor do they show much interest in a Christian Right presidential candidacy from among their own: in a 1986 survey, fewer than 10 percent indicated support for Pat Robertson's budding presidential campaign, although the number grew somewhat as the 1988 primaries began.[14] Nevertheless, the Christian Right has achieved much success in a long-term effort: to infiltrate and mobilize a major Protestant denomination.

Notes

1. The classic study of mainline "liberal" ministers is Harold Quinley, *The Prophetic Clergy* (New York: Wiley, 1974); for one of the few surveys targeting evangelicals,

see Stuart Rothenberg and Frank Newport, *The Evangelical Voter: Religion and Politics in America* (Washington, D.C.: Institute for Government and Politics, 1984); for local studies of ministerial reaction to the Moral Majority, see Robert Zwier, *Born-Again Politics* (Downer's Grove, Ill.: Inter-Varsity Press, 1982), as well as Anson Shupe and William A. Stacey, *Born Again Politics and the Moral Majority: What Social Surveys Really Show* (New York: Edwin Mellen, 1982); see also Kathleen Beatty and Oliver Walter, "Fundamentalists, Evangelicals, and Politics," *American Politics Quarterly* 16 (January 1988): 43-59.

2. Rothenberg and Newport, *The Evangelical Voter,* 124.

3. For details on the 1980 and 1984 surveys, see James L. Guth, "The Southern Baptist Clergy: Vanguard of the Christian Right?" in *The New Christian Right,* ed. Robert C. Liebman and Robert Wuthnow (New York: Aldine, 1984), 118-130; and James L. Guth, "Political Converts: Partisan Realignment among Southern Baptist Ministers," *Election Politics* 3 (Winter 1985-86): 2-6.

4. A good popular account of the fundamentalist movement in the SBC is Nancy Ammerman, "The New South and the New Baptists," *The Christian Century,* May 14, 1986, 486-488.

5. Lee Sigelman, Clyde Wilcox, and Emmett Buell, Jr., "An Unchanging Minority: Popular Support for the Moral Majority, 1980 and 1984," *Social Science Quarterly* 68 (December 1987): 876-888.

6. For similarities in Christian Right and New Right ideologies, see Jerome Himmelstein, "The New Right," in *The New Christian Right,* 13-30. For an empirical study of evangelicals' political attitudes, see Corwin Smidt, "Evangelicals and the 1984 Election: Continuity or Change?" *American Politics Quarterly* 15 (October 1987): 419-444.

7. For the agenda of political activists, see John Green and James Guth, "Big Bucks and Petty Cash: Party and Interest Group Activists in American Politics," in *Interest Group Politics,* 2d ed., ed. Allan Cigler and Burdett Loomis (Washington, D.C.: CQ Press, 1986): 91-113.

8. James Guth, "The Politics of Preachers: Southern Baptist Ministers and Christian Right Activism," in *New Christian Politics,* ed. David G. Bromley and Anson D. Shupe, (Macon, Ga.: Mercer University Press, 1984): 239-249.

9. Quinley, *The Prophetic Clergy,* 20.

10. Robert Wuthnow, "The Political Rebirth of American Evangelicals," in *The New Christian Right,* 184.

11. A. James Reichley, *Religion in American Public Life* (Washington, D.C.: Brookings Institution, 1985), 269-278.

12. Guth, "Political Converts"; Everett Carl Ladd, "On Mandates, Realignments, and the 1984 Presidential Election," *Political Science Quarterly* 100 (Spring 1985): 1-25.

13. For the historic Baptist preoccupation with "sin" issues, consult Rufus Spain, *At Ease in Zion: A Social History of Southern Baptists, 1865-1900* (Nashville: Vanderbilt University Press, 1961); and James Thompson, *Tried as by Fire: Southern Baptists and the Religious Controversies of the 1920s* (Macon, Ga.: Mercer University Press, 1982).

14. For Southern Baptist ministers' support for Pat Robertson's presidential bid in 1988, see Helen Lee Turner and James L. Guth, "The Politics of Armageddon" (Paper presented at the annual meeting of the Midwest Political Science Association, Chicago, April 14-16, 1988); also, Hal Straus, "Robertson Wins Backing of S.C. Clergy," *Atlanta Journal,* March 1, 1988, 1.

CONTRIBUTORS

Tod A. Baker is professor of political science at The Citadel. In conjunction with Robert P. Steed and Laurence W. Moreland, he is a director of the Symposium of Southern Politics and has edited books on the South, including *Religion and Politics in the South* (1983).

Clarke E. Cochran is professor and chairman of the Department of Political Science at Texas Tech University and chairman of the Religion and Politics Section of the American Political Science Association for 1987-1988. He is the author of *Character, Community, and Politics* (1982) and coauthor of *American Public Policy: An Introduction,* 2d ed. (1986).

Charles W. Dunn is professor and chairman of the Department of Political Science at Clemson University. He is the author of several books, including *American Political Theology* (1984), *Constitutional Democracy in America* (1987), and *American Democracy Debated* (1982).

Robert Booth Fowler is professor of political science at the University of Wisconsin—Madison. He is author of *Religion and Politics in America* (1986) and *Unconventional Partners: Religion and Liberalism in American Culture* (1988).

James L. Guth is professor of political science and chairman of the faculty of Furman University. He is a contributor to *Interest Group Politics* (CQ Press, 1983, 1986) and to various political science journals.

Anne Motley Hallum is assistant professor of political science at Stetson University, where she teaches a course on religion and politics in America. She is currently engaged in research on the impact of mainline religious denominations on American politics.

Mary Hanna is Miles C. Moore Chair of Political Science at Whitman College and author of *Catholics and American Politics* (1979).

Roger D. Hatch is professor and chairman of the Department of Religion at Central Michigan University, where he teaches social ethics. He is author of *Beyond Opportunity: Jesse Jackson's Vision for America* (1988) and coeditor of *Straight from the Heart* (1987), a collection of Jesse Jackson's principal speeches.

Allen D. Hertzke is assistant director of the Carl Albert Congressional Research and Studies Center at the University of Oklahoma, where he is assistant professor of political science. He is author of *Representing God in Washington: The Role of Religious Lobbies in the American Polity* (1988).

Laurence W. Moreland is professor of political science at The Citadel. In conjunction with Tod A. Baker and Robert P. Steed, he is a director of the Symposium of Southern Politics and has edited books on the South, including *Religion and Politics in the South* (1983).

Thomas J. O'Hara is assistant professor of government at King's College. He received his doctorate from American University, where he taught religion and public policy.

A. James Reichley is senior fellow in the Governmental Studies Program at the Brookings Institution. He served on the White House staff of President Gerald R. Ford and is a former political editor of *Fortune* magazine. He is author of *Religion in American Public Life* (1985) and editor and contributor to *Elections American Style* (1985).

Neal Riemer is Andrew V. Stout Professor of Political Philosophy at Drew University. He is author of *James Madison: Creating the American Constitution* (Congressional Quarterly, 1986), *The Future of the Democratic Revolution: Toward a More Prophetic Politics* (1984), and *Political Science: An Introduction to Politics* (1983).

Corwin Smidt is professor of political science at Calvin College and is director of the Calvin College Conference on Religion and Politics.

Robert P. Steed is professor of political science at The Citadel. In conjunction with Tod A. Baker and Laurence W. Moreland, he is a director of the Symposium of Southern Politics and has edited books on the South, including *Religion and Politics in the South* (1983).

Kenneth D. Wald is professor of political science at the University of Florida and author of *Religion and Politics in the United States* (1986).

Paul J. Weber is Distinguished Teaching Professor of Political Science and chairman of the Department of Political Science at the University of Louisiana. He is coauthor of *Private Churches and Public Money* (1982).